DATE DUE

KNOCKOFF

'A Criminal Empire'

With the astonishing growth in counterfeit goods and fake medicines being traded illegally, the international community can no longer tolerate the export of economic misery and even death around the world. Customs have already taken the first serious steps to secure and facilitate legitimate trade. We are determined to deal a damaging blow to the counterfeit market and will pursue and engage these sinister criminals across the globe. The counterfeit trade is now regarded as **the** crime of the 21st century, and Tim Phillips' book provides us with a deeper insight into this knockoff economy which he so aptly calls 'a criminal empire of huge proportions'.

Michael Danet, Secretary General, World Customs Organization

KNOCKOFF
THE DEADLY TRADE IN COUNTERFEIT GOODS

The true story of the world's fastest growing crime wave

Tim Phillips

KOGAN
PAGE

London and Sterling, VA

First published in Great Britain and the United States in 2005 by Kogan Page Limited

120 Pentonville Road
London N1 9JN
United Kingdom
www.kogan-page.co.uk

22883 Quicksilver Drive
Sterling VA 20166–2012
USA

ISBN 0 7494 4379 0

British Library Cataloguing-in-Publication Data

A CIP record for this book is available from the British Library.

Library of Congress Cataloging-in-Publication Data

Phillips, Tim, 1967–
  Knockoff: the deadly trade in counterfeit goods / Tim Phillips.
   p. cm.
  Includes bibliographical references and index.
  ISBN 0-7494-4379-0
  1. Product counterfeiting. 2. Licensed products. 3. Intellectual property.
4. Trade regulation. I. Title.
HF1040.7.P55 2005
364.1'33—dc22

2005022214

Typeset by Saxon Graphics Ltd, Derby
Printed and bound in Great Britain by Creative Print and Design (Wales), Ebbw Vale

Contents

Acknowledgements   *ix*

Introduction: The knockoff economy   **1**

PART 1:   ANYTHING UNDER THE SUN

1   The second-oldest profession   **7**
Super Cow   8
Lies, damn lies, knockoffs   10
Counterfeit equals theft   11
The little guy loses   12
It's your responsibility   15

2   Brand bandits   **19**
Fake economics   20
Knockoffs can seriously damage your health   21
The ghost shift   25

3   Counterfeit Alley   **31**
Something for the weekend   32
Showdown in Midtown   35
Canal Street   38

4	**Sex and the purse party**	**43**
	The handbag of success	43
	Party bags	48
	Infiltrating the middle classes	50

PART 2:   INSIDE THE KNOCKOFF ECONOMY

5	**Copying is a beautiful thing**	**55**
	Silk Alley	55
	Waking the sleeping cat	57
	The top of the speed	60
	The big country	63
6	**A greater Europe**	**67**
	The Italian job	68
	Making crime pay	70
	The dark side	73
	The Wild East	73
	Crossing borders	77
7	**I thought I had seen everything**	**79**
	It's war	80
	Under the surface	83
8	**Where buyers and sellers meet**	**87**
	The global marketplace	88
	Trust and safety	89
	Anything goes?	92
9	**War and peace**	**95**
	Money talks	96
	Where are the good guys?	97
	Tough Love	100
	Closing the deal	102

PART 3: YOU CAN'T COMPETE WITH FREE

10 Illusions   **109**
The content crisis   110
Pirates ahoy   112
A silent spring in Hanoi   113

11 Lifting the stone   **117**
A hidden problem   118
One in three   121
Organized criminals   123

12 Ordinary criminals   **127**
Snide   128
Global cottage industry   130
The lowest priority   132

13 Turning guns into CD burners   **137**
The Lion Kings   138
Everybody loves a bargain   140
A black hole   143

14 Making a scene   **145**
Behind The Scene   146
From the top   147
Stop, thief   150
It's like an addiction   152

15 From Russia with Windows   **155**
One out of three ain't bad   155
Evolution, not revolution   157
Under the counter   159
Quick! Send for the ferret   162

PART 4:   COUNTERFEIT KILLERS

16 The capital of bogus parts   **169**
   Bogus beware   170
   Blind and toothless?   172
   The $10,000 bolt   174

17 Under the hood   **179**
   A perfect environment   180
   A workshop near you   182

18 Show us the dead bodies   **187**
   Redefining the problem   188
   Tap water doesn't cure cancer   190
   A good-looking tablet   191
   Controlling the supply chain   192
   The 1 per cent solution   195

19 Men in white coats   **201**
   A deal you can refuse   202
   Drug tourism   204
   Someone has to pay   207

20 Dora Akunyili must not die   **209**
   The NAFDAC woman   210
   Cleaning up   212
   Muddying the waters   215

Conclusion: Whack a mole   **219**

Appendix   *223*
Index   *233*

Acknowledgements

To list everyone who helped would take a long and boring chapter. I'm grateful to all the people I have quoted, and some of the organizations whose contribution isn't reflected in the number of mentions they get in the text: the International Trademark Agency, the International Intellectual Property Institute, the International AntiCounterfeiting Coalition, the Association Against Counterfeiting and Piracy and the Anti-Counterfeiting Group were all extremely helpful.

I can't acknowledge some of the people who were most helpful for the same reason of confidentiality that I couldn't use their names in the book. I am grateful to all the people who helped in this way, when there was no benefit to them. I can, however, thank Chris Dickon by name, whose research was invaluable.

Introduction:
The knockoff economy

At the end of 2004, I was finishing up an interview with a senior government employee. 'Have you seen my new watch?' he asked, pulling back the sleeve of his pinstripe suit to show it off. 'It's fake.'

'It's a good one, look at the sweep of the second hand,' said his colleague, admiring what was, admittedly, an extremely convincing counterfeit Rolex, bought for £50 – five times as much as the standard price for a knockoff. We took turns at trying to find the flaws – pulling out the winder to see if the second stopped moving (good), checking to see if the strap was put together using cheap pins or tiny screws (screws), weighing it in our hands (heavy). We had to admit, 50 quid buys a convincing counterfeit of a watch that costs 60 times as much.

He had, he explained, bought it on an official trade mission to Beijing. 'Luckily my meeting finished on time so I had literally 30 minutes to get it before I had to go to the airport. So I went out on the street, down to the area where I remember they were on sale,' he said.

> What happens is, someone comes up to you and asks what you want. This guy is leading me down a narrow street, then an even smaller one, then off to the left and into someone's house, and into a bedroom. And I sat on the bed, and an old woman gets a case out and opens it up, and there's every brand of watch you could want in there, all fake, but, wow, great quality. That's where you get the real stuff, not in the markets.

Anyone who has braved the hutongs of Beijing, a dark zigzag switchback of tiny alleys clogged with bicycles – both hundreds of years old – will know what he went through to get his watch. Inside the maze of streets, some only the width of a single government employee, it's impossible to know where you are. Every turn increases your sense of disorientation and makes you feel more like you have stepped back in time – until you see the shiny metal case on the bed, packed with booty, and you know you are exactly where you want to be.

For a Big Nose[1] civil servant from the suburbs, it's quite a rush.

Fake kudos

In the developed world, most of us at one time have admired a new bag, watch, pen, cigarette lighter or scarf, to be told conspiratorially, 'It's fake.' Often, when we buy knockoffs, we don't even bother to hide it any more: buying a counterfeit and having it admired in a dull meeting wins you kudos. You got a great deal and haggled for the price. You used your know-how and daring to hunt out a bargain. You have inside knowledge. You experienced the feeling of danger and excitement that's missing from today's chain-store, fixed-price retail experience.

Or maybe you're having a go at the global brands who think that £50 is a fair price for your team's shirt every year, and that's £50 you don't have.

Or perhaps it's the closest we will get to having the bag we saw in the newspapers that cost £3,000 – if you can get one, which you can't, because you're not some cosseted movie brat who can skip the waiting list.

On the other hand, knockoff luxuries are, according to the World Customs Organization (WCO), only 4 per cent of the trade in counterfeits today. The next fakes you encounter might be the pills you are about to take for your heart condition, the brake pads the mechanic just fitted to your car, or the engine parts on the aeroplane you will be boarding this afternoon. You won't know about those, but you don't have to go looking for that kind of counterfeit in a dark alley half-way round the world. The global counterfeit economy means that those fakes can find you.

Measuring the amount of counterfeiting there is in the world is impossible, because we only know about the counterfeits that get caught. Much of the best, most sophisticated stuff never gets noticed, because it is much harder for anyone – customs, police or purchasers – to detect and, anyway, customs officers can't open every parcel, van, lorry and container they see. The WCO estimates, based on its seizures, that the trade in fakes is currently worth about $512 billion, or 7 per cent of the world's trade.[2] In 1984, it was $5.5 billion. Other estimates put the size of the knockoff economy at 10 per cent of world trade. Whoever you believe, it's a criminal empire of huge proportions.

If the knockoff economy was a business, it would be the world's biggest, twice the size of Wal-Mart, its nearest competitor.

Counterfeiting is thousands of years old, but conditions have never been better for it. As manufacturing has spread around the world, overseas factories are accustomed to making goods for the developed world, legally or not. The internet has made buying and selling from people we have never met into a matter of clicking on a few web pages. As global trade barriers are lowered, goods reach us by travelling through a confusing spaghetti of intermediaries, often travelling through more than one country on the way. Films, music and computer programmes can travel as a series of bits across the internet to be reassembled at the other end as a perfect copy.

If future historians were to pinpoint the year in which the global counterfeit economy took off, they might pick 2001. It should not be so: in 2001, governments all over the world tightened banking regulations so that it was harder to hide the proceeds of crime following the 11 September terrorist attacks. Customs officers were told to tighten inspection regimes. China, the source of most of the world's counterfeits, joined the World Trade Organization, and so agreed to a stringent set of anti-counterfeiting rules. E-commerce gave us access to retailers everywhere, allowing us to seek out a good price, or bid in an auction.

The opposite has been the case. Tightening banking regulations meant that organized crime had money it needed to invest in business rather than the bank, and the counterfeiting business is perfect: no questions asked, cash based, extremely profitable. The routes by which illegal importers of drugs, arms or humans brought their products from one place to another are the same routes by which counterfeits reach us: the same ships, the same ways to evade customs officers, the same, or better, profit margins. The difference is that the penalties were lower, and customs officers weren't looking for knockoff sports shoes. Since 2001, we have seen a massive shift of business among these gangs into trading knockoffs.

China continues to struggle to rein in its counterfeiters, but the short-term effect of its WTO membership has been to make trade easier, not to cut the volume of knockoffs. It's no accident that the world's largest wholesale trading website, Alibaba.com, is based in China; a quick search on it shows how it is helping counterfeiters reach their customers. Elsewhere on the net, it's easy to find a bargain, and just as easy to find an illegal knockoff, as your spam email demonstrates.

As long as we look the other way, we're accomplices to a criminal network that costs thousands of jobs, retards developing country economies, kills and maims thousands of people a year, breeds corruption and bribery, has become the cash cow that funds serious crime and violence, and one day might even kill you.

Notes

1. A Chinese slang expression for Europeans and Americans.
2. Figures for calendar year 2004.

PART 1

Anything under the sun

1 The second-oldest profession

In a suburb of north-eastern Paris, in a small glass case at the offices of the Union des Fabricants (Association of Manufacturers), there's an object that can claim to be one of history's first knockoffs. It's a stopper for a wine amphora, dated 27 BC, found close to Arles in the south of France.

In 27 BC, Arles was a Roman town, and Romans liked Italian wine. A network of trusted wine merchants filled their amphorae in Italy and shipped them to Arles and other Roman towns along the Via Aurelia, so that the expat Romans didn't have to drink the cheap local plonk.

One day, an illiterate Gaulish wine merchant had an idea. Roman wine was expensive, and French wine was cheap. One amphora looks very much like another. You could tell where the wine came from because the clay stoppers were marked with the name of the merchant. It was a guarantee of quality, and the short cut to a better profit.

If he had the stopper, he reasoned, he could sell cheap wine for a high price to the Romans. But he didn't have the stopper, so he decided to make his own, to look like the stoppers provided by a merchant called Lassisus. This cunning plan, the inspiration of counterfeiters of toothpaste, theme parks, caviar and brake pads – among other things – for the next 2,000 years, had only one flaw. The wine merchant couldn't read or write. Instead of marking the name of Lassisus on the stopper, he notched a series of indecipherable characters. The stopper looks like it has a bird's footprints where the name should be. History doesn't record Roman concern about a knockoff wine problem in the empire of Augustus, so we don't know if he succeeded, but, if consumers then had much in common with consumers today, chances are he would have found at least one customer whose delight at a discount price overruled any suspicion.

Or, perhaps his customers were entertaining friends and, wanting to impress their guests with their generosity and sophistication, bragged about their imported wine and hoped that no one who popped round to try it saw the stopper. Couples might have walked home after the party whispering to each other, 'I'm no expert on Roman viniculture, but didn't that plonk he served taste sort of French to you?'

Super Cow

Today, the wine stopper is one small exhibit among hundreds in three packed rooms at the Union des Fabricants' Museum of Counterfeiting. In the 2,000 years since the Gauls faked the stoppers in amphorae, counterfeiting has been a fact of life. The joke among intellectual property lawyers, who need a laugh at the moment, is that it is the world's second-oldest profession. It's definitely one of the most lucrative as well.

Five days a week, small groups of children wander from glass case to glass case playing an elaborate game of spot-the-difference between real French Hermès scarves and their copies, or real British Lea & Perrins Worcestershire Sauce and a knockoff from Honduras: take a second glance and you realize it is called 'Lee Perkins' and claims to be 'Superior a lo Original'. There are packages of after-shave from Ralph Lauren and Giorgio Armani and their almost identical imitators side by side, counterfeit Citroën and Peugeot car parts that would crumple on impact if they were on a real car driven by real people, but look identical to the eyes of 15,000 school-children a year who see them. Glass cases house faked dictionaries and food blenders and disposable razors and lots and lots of processed cheese. We can comfortably state that the Museum of the Union des Fabricants has one of the finest collections of fake cheese in the world.

Perhaps spurred by the realization that few customers are going to return to a shop to complain that it doesn't taste real, counterfeiters of Laughing Cow cheese from all over the world are immortalized, if not exactly celebrated, in one of the largest cabinets. The distinctive Cow logo is bastardized on the packaging; some of the boxes are almost identical to the real thing, but others are more free-form copies, featuring oddly shaped and oddly coloured cows on the packet that don't inspire much confidence in the filling. The less slavish copies are made in countries where products called 'Gardens Cow', 'The Two Cows', 'Three Cows', 'Wonder Cow' and 'Super Cow' look good enough to buy, if not always to eat.

It's no accident that Paris is home to this eccentric museum. If 2,000 years ago Gaul was home to a wine-counterfeiting scandal that its cunning merchants perpetrated on the Romans, the rest of the world has been having revenge on the French national industries for at least 150 years. The Union dates from 1877, when French pharmaceutical companies banded together to resist widespread knockoffs of their products made by German competitors, starting a trend that persists to this day: when an industry feels threatened by counterfeiters, it immediately forms an association to talk about how it must be stopped. Unlike most of the associations of the last 150 years, though, the Union is much more than a talking shop. Thanks to its pressure, France has some of the toughest anti-counterfeiting laws in the world. If you are a counterfeiter, you might get three years in prison and a fine of 300,000 euro, and, in case you are thinking of wearing your fake Chanel handbag as you sashay past French customs, be aware that France is the only country in the world with a strict no-tolerance policy towards private citizens who buy knockoff luxury goods. If the customs officers feel like it, your bag might end up in a glass case at the museum.

The 450 members of the Union today are no longer just pharmacists: they encompass consumer and luxury goods, software and music, engineering, drugs and everything in between. 'We don't just work for the famous,' says the Union's lawyer, Marine Guillou. 'We have more members who are small companies than big. It's not all bags and T-shirts.'

The museum is evidence that, in our knockoff culture, there's nothing that can be made that's not counterfeited. Its packed rooms, and the working lives of the 30 staff of the Union des Fabricants and the thousands of lawyers, investigators, legislators, police and customs officers whose lives are dedicated to trying to stop counterfeiters, are proof that when there is money to be made by breaking a law then that law is going to be broken. For some of us, counterfeiting is fun. For others, it's a protest against powerful companies. For others, it's an inconvenient fact of life and, for some, it's a death sentence. For Guillou, who gets the call at all hours of the day and night from customs when they need someone to identify suspected contraband that they have impounded, trying to beat the counterfeiters is a job that never ends.

Lies, damn lies, knockoffs

This book is about the attempts that some people make to lie about where a product came from: counterfeits, where the product is made with the specific intention to deceive, are the most obvious manifestation, but they are not the whole story. There is also the category of knockoffs: we buy them knowing they are not real, because of the price, the quality or the place where we get them. What they have in common is that they are both, according to the law in most countries, stealing.

Most countries today have a scheme of laws that allow individuals or companies to profit from ideas or products that they created. When the United States Congress reformed its 160-year-old patent laws in 1952, Congress expressed the opinion that 'anything under the sun made by man' could potentially have its design protected by a patent. If that sounds like a wide definition, it is: it excludes only 'laws of nature, natural phenomena, and abstract ideas'.

Patents are one form of Intellectual Property, or IP. To get a patent, something has to be a new idea, has to have some creative step involved in making it, and it has to be useful in some way; the other major form of IP is copyright, which protects the creations of artists, musicians, people who write books and other creative souls from having their work copied. Patents expire after a set period of time, at which point anyone can copy the idea; because, when you file a patent, you explain what you are patenting in detail, patent law actually helps other companies copy your work once you no longer have the right to protect it. Copyright also expires a number of years after the creator dies; the idea is that copyright can be a financial benefit for his or her immediate descendants, but after that the artistic creation should benefit all of us.

Fundamentally, under our system of laws, intellectual property is just the same as any other property you own. It can represent most of the value of a company: a company's intellectual property includes all its patents, its product designs, the know-how with which it makes those products, its trade secrets, the company name or the design of its logo. For example, Coca-Cola's value isn't about the stocks in its warehouse or the size of its factories or the money in the bank. Its value is bound up in the effectiveness of its logo, which makes us point at a familiar bottle when the label is written in Chinese and say, 'I want that one', and the trust that we have that it won't poison us. It's the value of the secret recipe, which means other cola does not taste the same. These are intangible. You can't hold intellectual property in your hands or lock it in a safe. In 2002 the World Intellectual Property Organization reported that, for the Fortune 500 largest companies, IP represented anything between 45 and 75 per cent of their value.

When you hear stuff like this on the radio, it's the sort of thing that reminds you to retune to another station. So why should you care? Because the price you pay for a product depends on the value of that company's IP. Because the success of the company you work for, and ultimately your job, depends on your employer's ability to protect its IP. And because the people who steal IP by producing knockoffs are some of the most ruthless, most cunning and most dangerous criminals in the world today, as we will see.

Counterfeit equals theft

When we are taught about stealing, we're taught not to steal another kid's lunch money, or chocolate from the local shop. We are rarely taught that creativity and ideas have a value too. When Debbi Mayster visits elementary schools in Fairfax County, Virginia, she asks all the eight-year-olds to paint a picture each, but not to put their name on it, as they usually do. The pictures are stuck to the wall, and then all the kids in turn are allowed to choose the picture they want, write their name on it and claim it as their own. This,

Mayster tells the sniffling children, is what they are doing when they illegally copy a company's software.

This harsh and frankly rather upsetting lesson – which will one day give the psychiatrists of Fairfax County good business – is the latest attempt to convince children that software piracy, perhaps the most widespread example of IP theft in the world, is wrong. Mayster's employer is a not-for-profit organization called the Business Software Alliance, a group that contains just about every software company you have heard of. The BSA members pay a subscription, and the BSA uses the money for what it calls 'promoting a safe and legal digital world'.

In the knockoff culture, upsetting small children is the price that the BSA pays to promote this world. Mayster isn't doing this for fun; it's a way to demonstrate to the children the value of intellectual property. 'We conducted research last year, asking 1,000 eight- to 18-year-olds about piracy,' she says, 'and we found that they generally understood what piracy was. But they still do it.'

Producing knockoffs, counterfeits and pirate copies is easy money. If your company makes a product, a thief can try to steal it from you, or a counterfeiter can make a copy of it, sell it and pocket the money. The first approach is usually quite difficult: you have to break in to somewhere physically, getting past locks, security cameras and guard dogs, you are limited by the amount of product you can find and you have to find someone willing to 'fence' it. When your product is knocked off, counterfeiters have usually never been near your building, they can make as many as they can sell and, if you have been robbed, you might not find out for months, or years, or even at all. By the time you can do something about it, it's often too late.

The little guy loses

Making money from IP isn't as easy at it seems; it's often a dirty business, where might beats right. And it's not just big, rich companies that get knocked off – sometimes they are the aggressors. In the late 1990s, British inventor Mandy Haberman created the Anywayup Cup, a toddlers' drinking cup that wouldn't spill. She was one of the few inventors who actually managed to patent a viable product, and recruited 70 people to manufacture the cup for a large supermarket chain. Then, she spotted a remarkably similar design made by the much larger rival manufacturer Tommy Tippee. 'It was 18 August, 2 o'clock in the afternoon,' she remembers. 'We'd invested everything in it.'

The company that was parroting her design in the UK was owned by a huge multinational. In court it didn't pretend that it hadn't infringed her patent, but it challenged the validity of her patent instead. It took Haberman two years to prove the patent was valid in the UK, which if she had lost 'would have bankrupted my colleagues and I would have lost the shirt off my back', she says. Almost seven years after Haberman first saw the rival cup, she is still fighting to have her patent enforced in other countries. While she seeks to prove it, companies overseas are free to copy her design. 'I was totally naive. As soon as you have something valuable, that's when the problems begin,' she says. 'Only 0.02 per cent of products that are patented ever get to market. If you're looking to make money, you're probably better off playing the lottery. Or becoming an intellectual property lawyer.'

Counterfeiting has about as many definitions as there are specialist lawyers to define it, but there is one central principle at stake: counterfeiting uses someone else's IP for profit. If you accept that IP exists, counterfeiting is stealing. It's that simple.

The fundamental idea of intellectual property, and the brands it has created, isn't to allow chief executives to grow rich on our credit card debt, though for some of us it sometimes seems that way. The original concept, in the words of Thomas Jefferson, who created the first IP laws in the US, is to encourage 'liberal thought'. That is, if you think of a better way to do something, or come up with a product that no one has seen before, or simply design something in a more beautiful or efficient way, you should reap the benefits of your talent.

Used well, intellectual property has been a huge benefit to society. Whether you agree with it or not, the system of IP laws means that inventors have a personal motivation to invent, because when they invent successfully they own the right to make the product and make money from that. The promise that they can make a profit creates an incentive to sell the product in other countries. When the market for the product is exhausted, the employer has an incentive to develop an improved product to protect its position – and the jobs of its employees. When a patent expires (usually after 20 years), other companies can produce low-cost copies of the product to benefit more people.

Originally, brands were simply an easy way to show us who made the product. They have come to symbolize a more abstract idea of quality in our minds – few of us know what patents Nike holds, but many of us associate the product with quality, excitement or sophistication and, given the choice between two similar products, we often pay a little more for one that we think represents those values.

Consumer society is about giving that choice, and treating us as adult enough to make it. The deal we ask of the companies that own the brands is that they deliver what they promise, that your Nike trainers don't fall apart after a week, that your sunglasses protect your eyes, that the brakes on your Ford car have been manufactured to strict safety specifications, and that the antibiotics you are taking have been made with the right amount of active ingredient to heal you.

On our side, we accept that we pay a premium for this. It's a social contract that works most of the time.

It works for us because we don't settle for things that aren't perfect, and there's an incentive for brand owners to improve them. Of course, we are not always told what we are settling for: we don't know exactly what happens in a factory that prepares food. There is nothing on a label that states how much we pay for the patent and how much for the product. Also, it's hard to put the IP in a designer handbag in the same category as the IP in a cancer drug.

It works globally because it doesn't condemn developing economies to become giant sweatshops to make stuff for our use for ever. When countries like India create their own intellectual property, it has value too. An example: if you are a Russian software developer, it's going to be tough to compete with Microsoft, even if Microsoft's software is five times as expensive as yours. But it's impossible to compete with someone who illegally copies the same Microsoft software and sells it for half the price of yours. It's hard to imagine that Japanese cars were once considered to be poor quality: but the technological advancement that the Japanese put in their cars created a market globally, which created an affluent society in Japan, and happy drivers everywhere. When the US – whose car makers had failed to keep up with the pace of change – limited

Japanese car imports between 1981 and 1984, car prices in the US climbed by 41 per cent. One million fewer cars were sold. Japanese workers suffered; the US car business suffered; US consumers suffered.

But perhaps because we are suspicious that brands have become a way to overcharge us, they are under attack: critics argue that we are hoodwinked by advertising into believing that empty brands make us attractive, successful and sexy, that fashion has created peer pressure and kiddie pester power, that boy bands with no talent are packaged by svengalis who know how to manipulate teenagers just to sell overpriced CDs before they go out of fashion, and that drug companies create new drugs that we don't need and then convince us that we do by inventing and naming ailments that the drugs apparently treat.

Not everyone accepts that 'everything under the sun made by man' should be parcelled up and shared out among companies who can sell it back to us for profit; many more of us look at the argument and simply don't care, as long as we can have that darling knockoff bag. This is a book partly about why you should care, and partly about who gets robbed, hurt and killed because you don't.

It's your responsibility

The knockoff culture in which we live isn't just a problem for inventors like Haberman, or organizations like the BSA. It's about our rights and responsibilities as consumers. Just as there's not one type of counterfeiting, there isn't one type of customer. There are several reasons why we might buy a knockoff. We might know it's not genuine, but we don't want anyone else to know. We equate our own worth as people with the status symbols we own. This is why there is a market for fake Rolex watches that cost $1,500 or more – far more than almost any genuine watch (if you don't believe it, visit http://www.replicenter.com, a site dedicated to hooking up sellers and buyers).

We might know the knockoff is fake, and so does everyone else. We might be making a point that we don't care about brands (a not especially convincing one in this case, given the evidence), or we might, if we buy a fake disposable lighter, be saving a few pennies.

We might not know the product is a fake, nor does anyone else. This is why trademarks are useful. What spares do you buy for your car? What prescription drugs are you taking? When a counterfeit label lies to us, it often puts us and the people we care about in danger.

Lastly, we might not know we bought a fake, and embarrassingly everyone else does. You're really hoping you don't fall into this category.

In the developed world, on average we live in the greatest comfort and luxury we have ever seen. The majority of the population can make choices denied to our parents on what we eat, wear or listen to, where we travel and how we get there. At the same time, we are faced with a bewildering variety of brands that would have shocked our parents: our clothes now have labels on the outside. Our sunglasses have the manufacturer's name written on them, and aren't just for keeping the sun out of our eyes. We hear that Coke Is The Real Thing: the hidden message is that The Fake Thing isn't as good.

This wealth of opportunity has created unprecedented levels of debt too. The more we have, the more we are conscious of what we do not have yet. In the US, the average credit card debt is almost $9,000, according to American Consumer Credit Counseling. In the UK it is almost as much at £4,004, according to Datamonitor, and in Europe the levels are smaller but comparable. Whatever wealth we have, it seems, we could use a bit more.

We're also often alienated from the companies that sell to us, and, given a choice between giving up on something we want and buying a counterfeit, the knockoff usually wins. Compare how eager we are to buy knockoffs with the anguish of a sports fan who has no alternative but to pay for the genuine experience. A season ticket to watch Manchester United, if you could get one, would cost between £389.50 and £684.[1] The club didn't play better in 2005 than in 2004, but the club put up prices of its most expensive seats by 24 per cent just the same. But if someone offered fans the chance to watch a knockoff Manchester United for half the price, using poor-quality players pitched against a similarly ersatz Liverpool or Arsenal, there's not a single fan who would take that option, because they care about the authenticity of the experience more than they care about money, even if it means waiting 10 years for a ticket.

On the other hand, there's a thriving market in knockoff Manchester United shirts. Many of us have an emotional need for authenticity in experiences that doesn't compare to our need for authenticity in products. So the same devotion is not often true for our relationship with Hermès, Rolex or Laughing Cow cheese, for example. We buy guilt-free knockoffs.

And a lot of us do buy, knowingly. In January 2005, The Gallup Organization polled 1,304 US adults. When asked whether they had purchased counterfeits in the last year, 13 per cent said they had – and half had purchased two or more types of counterfeit product. More than half of the 13 per cent had bought knockoffs knowingly.

Bizarrely, among the purchasers of knockoffs, 57.7 per cent called for stricter counterfeiting laws, and only 7.7 per cent for less strict laws. That is, they wanted to tighten the laws that they had recently broken. Almost half of the public believed terrorists were involved in selling counterfeits, and 83.4 per cent believed that organized crime certainly was. One in 40 believed knockoffs helped people on low incomes, but one in five believed that they helped criminals or organized crime. Lord, make me chaste – but not yet.

A poll conducted for the British government's Select Committee on Trade and Industry in June 1999 found that 40 per cent of Brits, not noted as natural anarchists or rebels against society, would knowingly buy a counterfeit product.

Few of us, when we buy knockoffs consciously, are doing it for a political purpose. It's hard to imagine anyone mounting the barricades over the right to own Gucci, or blockading Tower Records over the price of the Top 40 CDs, though many of us have grizzled at the prices. But we are increasingly aware that global brands, their strategy dictated by quarterly profits and shareholder value, can exploit the poor and powerless. We're encouraged to buy ethically: don't pollute; buy fair trade (in the UK, for example, fair trade sales are going up by 40 per cent a year[2]); make sure your football boots weren't stitched in sweatshops by child labour.

When you hear about a corporate sweatshop scandal, it's enough to make you want to buy a knockoff, just to teach them all a lesson.

If you do, however, you're blinding yourself to the obvious fact that the knockoffs were made somewhere. The International Labour Organization reports that, of the 246 million child labourers in the world, most work in the 'informal' economy – hidden from regulation by the authorities. In some cases, the informal economy can be a valuable defence against extreme poverty, but counterfeiting is also a valuable part of that economy. If you buy the real product, it might have been made by child labour, or in a sweatshop, but you can do something about it. For example, every legitimate Chinese product has to have the name of the factory and a phone number on it, so the factory can be inspected. If you know that a company exploits its workers, you can refuse to buy its products. If you buy a fake product, there's no inspection of the factories and no way for you to find out what goes on there.

But here's a clue: a manufacturer who knowingly breaks the law to make the product and ship it, perhaps with dangerous design flaws, isn't likely voluntarily to raise working conditions for the staff employed.

Right now, you probably don't care much either way, and the manufacturers of knockoffs rely on that. It's one reason why, in the 21st century, knockoffs are all around us. The effect of globalization in the last five years has been that, if anything under the sun can be patented, then anything under the sun could also be knocked off at a profit. Thanks to our indifference to the consequences, that has already happened.

Notes

1. 2005–06 season.
2. The Fairtrade Foundation, 2005.

2 Brand bandits

'Harry doesn't know how long it will take to wash the sticky cream cake off his face,' begins the latest Harry Potter blockbuster. 'For a civilized young man it is disgusting to have dirt on any part of his body. He lies in the high-quality china bathtub, keeps wiping his face, and thinks about Dali's face, which is as fat as the bottom of Aunt Penny.'

If you're familiar with the Harry Potter novels of JK Rowling, you'll sense already that this novel isn't up to her usual standard, which makes it surprising that she allowed her picture to be used on the cover of 'Harry Potter and Leopard Walk Up to Dragon', published for an enthusiastic public in China in July 2002. That's because she didn't write it. Apparently it's a ripping yarn. Harry gets turned into a fat hairy dwarf, which for those of us who never cared much for the little wizard anyway isn't such a bad result. But the book is a knockoff, written by a Chinese author to cash in on Chinese Pottermania, and published to an enthusiastic reception in Beijing's markets as if it were the real thing.[1]

President Clinton's memoirs were counterfeited in a sneakier way: *My Life* was changed to someone else's life when it was hijacked by counterfeiters in China.[2] In the knockoff copy of the book, Clinton apparently admits that China's inventions 'left us in the dust' and that, when courting Hillary, he impressed her mother with his praise of the Eight Trigrams from *The Book of Changes*. There's also a scene where President Clinton tells Hillary that his nickname is 'Big Watermelon'. I'm sure I'd have remembered that if it had been in the original.

Fake economics

When consumer goods are involved, the economics of manufacturing dictate that, the lower your operating costs are, the more potential profit there is. When counterfeiting was a small-time, local business, it wouldn't have been economic to counterfeit a book, a tube of toothpaste or a tea bag. Now, it is.

The nightmare for brand owners is that, whether they look at China, Russia, Thailand, Brazil, Paraguay, Italy, Ukraine, Nigeria or any other country that's far away from home, it's not a question of whether your product will be faked, but when. Then it's just a question of what they are prepared to do about it. As hard as they struggle, the problem just gets worse; for many companies, the best they can hope for is that the counterfeiters find them enough of a nuisance that they knock off another product instead.

If you thought that counterfeiting represented a few Swiss watches (actually, it is more than a few – around 40 million fake Swiss watches are made every year, compared to 26 million real ones), some bags and baseball caps, and a few films sold on a street corner, you haven't been paying attention. We are being buried in a landslide of sophisticated and convincing fakes. We're on the verge of the big company nightmare: we don't notice the fakes any more. They are a part of everyday life, and for some products have long since lost their ability to shock. But when you grasp the breadth of the knockoff culture, you'll look a little more closely at what's in your shopping basket, your fridge and your medicine cabinet.

Today's consumer goods counterfeiters can be just as sophisticated as the consumer goods suppliers, and sometimes more so. An example: in the late 1980s, Wrigley Chewing Gum Co decided that more Chinese people should chew gum. It built factories and in the early 1990s marketed its gum to a largely mystified Chinese population, who soon decided they liked it. Chewing gum became cool in China, and sales soared. By 2001, AC Nielsen reported that the Chinese were chewing 20 billion sticks of gum a year – 46 per cent of them were made by Wrigley. It was the second-largest market for the company after the US, and was growing by more than 10 per cent a year, even though local chewing gum manufacturers made a cheaper product. In 2001 Wrigley paid 26,000 yuan ($3,100) for a ton of gum-base ingredient, for example. Its counterfeiters used non-food-grade ingredients that cost 6,000 yuan ($720).[3]

They didn't just make counterfeit gum. US Commerce Secretary Don Evans used a speech in September 2003[4] to reveal the Chinese knockoff gum conspiracy, as told to him by Wrigley's investigator: 'Chinese had pirated their products in the city of Guangzhou. The pirates were selling counterfeit gum. They copied the Wrigley truck. They drove Wrigley's distribution routes', he said, 'and when they called on Wrigley's accounts the pirates paid "premiums" to the shop owners for accepting the counterfeit gum. That's a pretty ugly story.'

It's especially ugly for the residents of Guangzhou, who were chewing non-food-grade gum-base as a result. The Wrigley gum story happened a long way from the Western world, but it shows that, if the oldest profession has remained largely unchanged in the last 2,000 years, the second-oldest has undergone a revolution. We're experiencing the results of that revolution in the US and Europe today. If you think that bad chewing gum is the worst knockoff purchase you could make in London, Paris, New York or Los Angeles, you're in for a shock.

Knockoffs can seriously damage your health

At the Counterfeiting Intelligence Bureau (CIB) in an anonymous suburb of east London, senior analyst Stephen Matz shows off the display case that contains some of its prize finds. 'There's very good stuff,' he says. 'We have examples here where even people from the legitimate companies have a tough time telling the real from the fake.' He picks out a bottle of Johnny Walker Black Label, bought in an off-licence in Hackney, less than five miles away. From the outside, it looks perfect. Inside, it's a different story. The whisky contains a large quantity of methyl alcohol. 'Drink that and you get more than a headache,' says Matz. 'You'll wake up in hospital.'

Waking up at all would be a bonus for hundreds of people worldwide who are killed by fake booze. In 2001, vodka containing methyl alcohol killed 60 people in Estonia.[5] In Guangzhou, China, 11 people died in 2004 after buying spirit that turned out to be industrial alcohol mixed with water.[6] In March 2005, at least 21 Turks died after drinking counterfeit raki in bars. Counterfeiters had stolen genuine labels, and applied them to bottles with 200 times the permitted level of methyl alcohol.[7]

Our desire to earn a discount on our addictions gives fakers guaranteed revenue. Take counterfeit cigarettes. At CIB headquarters, Matz picks two boxes of Benson & Hedges cigarettes off the shelf: it's a CIB test for visitors, to see who can tell the difference. It's virtually impossible. 'Most of the time counterfeit cigarettes are only discovered when someone lights up and realizes they don't taste right, and phones the manufacturer,' says Matz. The two packets look identical, but when the fakes were tested they contained five times the carcinogens of the genuine brand.

In the UK alone, 1 million smuggled cigarettes are seized every day, and half of them are counterfeits – that means that about one in 12 cigarettes in the UK is a counterfeit.[8] In the last four years in the UK alone, 9 billion cigarettes have been seized; each year, 1,000 counterfeit cigarettes for every man, woman and child in the UK are imported. Since 2001, 259 smuggling gangs have been investigated by police. A government survey of three areas in inner London in 2004 – Holloway Road, Dalston and Whitechapel – found that every cigarette tested was a fake.[9]

If you're looking for an incentive to give up, consider this: tests on counterfeit cigarettes at St Andrews University in the UK found that they had on average five times as much cadmium as genuine cigarettes, and cadmium causes kidney disease and damages your lungs. There's six times as much lead in them too, which will damage your nervous system. And then there's the elevated level of arsenic, which could cause cancer.[10]

You don't need to be told that smoking could kill you: but if you just bought 200 cigs, no questions asked, from a man in a bar, it probably just got a lot more dangerous.

If you manage to buy genuine cigarettes, you might want to light them, in which case avoid the counterfeit disposable Bic lighters that you often see in markets or being sold on the street. In Brazil, which has an unhappy combination of knockoffs (one in three cigarettes is a counterfeit, and one in two pairs of eyeglasses), smokers and good weather, drivers suffered an unexplained rash of dashboard fires. The problem: some knockoff Bic lighters, left on dashboards, exploded when they got hot. This could also happen if you use one to light a cigarette.

Before you pick up your mobile phone to warn your friends who are lighting their cheap cigarettes with their fake Bic lighter, you might want to check the battery. In October 2004, Kyocera recalled batteries for its KE/KX 400 Series, 3200 Series and Slider Series phones, after dangerous counterfeit mobile phone batteries were found in some models.[11] How dangerous does a mobile phone battery get? The United States Office of Information and Public Affairs gives us a clue in a warning it published in June 2004, recalling 50,000 knockoff LG-branded TM-510 mobile phone batteries sold by Verizon Wireless. 'Some LG-branded TM-510 batteries may be counterfeit and susceptible to overcharging, especially if used with a non-LG charger. LG Infocomm U.S.A. Inc. states that these are counterfeit LG-branded batteries, which do not contain a safety device in the circuitry to prevent overcharging. In turn, the counterfeit batteries can overheat, posing a fire and burn hazard to users.' That's a fire and burn hazard to your ear. There had been 18 separate incidents reported.

It's not only Verizon that suffered. In 2003, Nokia admitted that three exploding handsets – two in the Netherlands and one in Vietnam – were due to counterfeit batteries.[12] It admitted in a statement that it had already destroyed 5 million counterfeit batteries in that year alone.

Is your Coca-Cola the Real Thing? It isn't if you bought it from Vatchagan Petrosian. In 1997, the US government prosecuted him for refilling Coke bottles with his own version of the product. His defence was that he wasn't guilty of counterfeiting, because the packaging was genuine. It's just the stuff he put in it that was faked. The United States District Court for the Central District of California, not surprisingly, ruled against him.

It's enough to make you want to go to bed and pull the covers over your head. Be careful. 'Anyone who has purchased a packet of Durex Fetherlite or Extra Safe condoms should check the packaging,' warned a trading standards spokesman in the UK in April this year. 'If the number on the bottom is VR3073C or E, or 20602503, do not use them.' The Chinese counterfeit condoms, which had a tendency to split or fall off, had been sold to shops across the UK. The failure rate in tests was 2.5 per cent, which isn't a gamble you want to take.[13]

Best have a cup of tea instead. 'We found one Armenian guy in November 2004 who was living in the basement of a house in Moscow,' an undercover investigator told me.

> He hired 15 illegal immigrants from Moldova, and he had a big load of the powder and all the other shit from the floor that gets left over when you make tea bags, and a stock of paper, and he had some labels. He was very clever, this Armenian, and he was using this leftover shit and making two types of tea bag: Lipton's and Brooke Bond. Every day we watch him; every day a truck leaves his house loaded with tea. It costs him nothing.

When you shower or brush your teeth tomorrow morning, imagine what it would be like if you didn't know what was going to come out of the shampoo bottle or toothpaste tube. In 1995, Procter & Gamble placed advertisements in US newspapers warning about counterfeit Head & Shoulders shampoo. 'People who have impaired immune systems, such as chemotherapy or radiation patients and anyone taking immunosuppressant drugs, should be particularly careful,' it said. The warnings came after its sales reps had discovered shampoo on sale in Kroger Co supermarkets around Cincinnati that was faked: it had at most half the level of active ingredients, sometimes none at all, and had dangerous levels of bacteria. The wholesaler had bought the product from a seemingly legitimate importer, all 48,000 cases of it. Two years earlier, Colgate had been the victim when dangerous fake toothpaste showed up in US stores.[14]

The Western economy is riddled with fake consumer goods. 'I spoke at a conference on consumer safety,' says Darren Pogoda, staff attorney at the Washington DC-based International AntiCounterfeiting Coalition, which was set up by consumer goods manufacturers in the 1980s to try to cooperate in stamping out knockoffs. 'One of the gifts they handed out to delegates was a little transistor radio. I opened mine up, and it had counterfeit batteries in it.'

The counterfeit batteries were two of the millions of Duracell knockoffs that you can get in almost any flea market in the world. They are one of the great global brands: cheap batteries with a fraction of the life of the real thing. Counterfeiters drive James Kitts, the chairman and CEO of The Gillette Company, crazy. 'You're dealing with a creature that is so large, potentially so powerful, that no single action can be taken against that creature that results in its death. It takes multiple strikes at different parts of the creature to stop it, and hopefully lead to its demise,' he says. 'Counterfeiting makes a mockery of research and development. It stifles innovation. You can understand why companies may be reluctant to spend millions of dollars on research when the risk is that all of that investment will be threatened by the work of the counterfeiters.'

A study carried out by the University of Leicester in the UK for Gillette[15] calculated that the total market for illicit consumer goods every year was $56 billion. That's just the everyday, low-value stuff.

The ghost shift

There's a trend we can blame for this: globalization. The mush-rooming of the global economy offers opportunities for large brands like Gillette, but arguably even greater opportunities for counterfeiters.

First, it creates a world of international 'superbrands'. It would have been pointless trying to counterfeit Wrigley's gum in China until Wrigley's created a market in China for any type of gum. It's economic to knock off Head & Shoulders or Duracell or Bic because they are products that are understood across the globe, even by people who cannot read. The success of multinational companies at marketing themselves has helped create the problem, because it creates a global market to exploit.

In the last two decades, multinational companies have also used the opportunities offered by developing countries to their advantage. Outsourcing, by which a company based in the US or Europe, where wages and costs are high, can employ a company in India, China, the Philippines, Malaysia, Taiwan or many other loca-tions to manufacture those products cheaply, is a controversial fact of business life. The World Trade Organization reports that in the developed world 70 per cent of employment is in the service industry. Put simply, we don't actually make the products we use any more, because there are people who do it more cheaply. On one hand, outsourcing drives down the prices of consumer goods and gives employment to developing nations. On the other, it has been accused of creating a 'sweatshop economy' that exploits their lack of bargaining power. This can be taken to some odd extremes: in her book *No Logo*, Naomi Klein quotes author Lorraine Dusky worrying about her choice of footwear when watching the 1998 riots in Indonesia on TV: 'Were my Nikes somehow to blame? That bereft young girl might still have a father if Nike had insisted that workers be better paid.'

Nike, The Gap, Gillette and hundreds of other companies outsource their manufacturing using what the business jargon calls 'self-reporting relationships'. This is why intellectual property is vital to them. In the past, IP was usually about stopping anyone from copying your product. Today, it's often about licensing someone to copy it. Some companies – for example, many silicon chip designers – don't make anything except patents to license.

This can, and does, go wrong. The mobile phone batteries in the Kyocera phones, both real and counterfeit, were made by the same company. The real ones were manufactured under licence. The fake ones looked like the real thing, because they were manufactured to a lower standard using the same machines. It was the difference in manufacturing quality that caused the fakes to be dangerous.

So often the difference between real and fake in consumer goods is less about where something was made, but when, how and with whose permission. If you own a factory and you are licensed to make 100,000 mobile phone batteries, it's tempting to make 150,000, using extra materials that you bought for yourself, and hide the extra 50,000 when the inspectors from the company that employs you come to call. If you sell the extra 50,000 out the back door as knockoffs, they can be far more profitable than the genuine articles, because you were using cheaper materials and labour, and you haven't paid your licensing fee.

Outsourced manufacturing is called a 'self-reporting' relationship because the factory declares how many items it made and pays a licensing fee to the company based on that figure. It's as if you got to the front of the supermarket queue and told the cashier what the value of your shopping is. Anyone who has ever been asked 'Did you have anything from the minibar last night?' can see the temptation. Global accountancy firm KPMG reports that the value of the self-reporting economy is about $500 billion – but, when it surveyed 11 companies that used outsourcing as a way of manufacturing products, 70 per cent of the relationships produced reporting errors. In some cases, they were more cock-up than conspiracy, simple accounting errors. In some cases, they were due to fraud: the company simply lied, so it could pay less.

This type of fraud is exotically often named 'ghost shift'. It's the only exotic thing about it: instead of two eight-hour shifts, the factory runs for 24 hours, with an unofficial extra shift using cheap materials, unofficial labour and safety short cuts. '[Manufacturers] can't have a cop in every factory,' says Michael Kessler of New York-based Kessler International, an investigator who represents multinational companies that have been the victims of ghost shift knockoffs.

You might think that outsourcing is evil, exploitative and little more than 21st-century slavery. It might be a reason to buy a knockoff: instead of contributing to licensing payments, your money goes straight to the owner of the factory.

If you think that, you're not thinking straight. Consumer activism has succeeded in highlighting abuses of the system, and driving up wages and working conditions, by embarrassing companies that exploit their workers in the developing world. You're not going to do that by buying knockoffs. The staff of the ghost shift was never legally there – you can't change their working conditions or wages or ensure that children aren't employed, because Nike or Microsoft or Gillette or The Gap don't know the ghosts exist. And if you buy the knockoff, you're lessening the demand for the real product, and it's the demand for the real product that gives the factory, and other factories like it, the contract in the first place.

Even if you don't care about other people on the far side of the world, you should care about your health, and the health of your family. The list of dangerous faked consumer products that inspectors see every year goes on and on. You might not drink raki or smoke cigarettes, and you might think that some mobile phone users deserve exploding handsets, but dangerous infant formula and birth control pills – both of which are real cases – would be a different matter.

If you really want proof that there is nothing you can't counterfeit, have you checked whether the flowers you bought today are genuine? In February 2004, Peter Quinter, partner at the Fort Lauderdale, Florida law firm of Becker & Poliakoff, helped prosecute a case against counterfeiters of Valentine roses from Colombia. You may be surprised to know that roses, like many other flowers, are covered by intellectual property rights if the growers have bred a specific variety. Seventy-one boxes, with 400 roses per box, were intercepted on their way to the Port of Miami. Companies often only notice they are being counterfeited when they suddenly see a surplus of their products on the market, Quinter says. For a product like roses, where a surplus means your stock is literally worthless overnight, it can put a genuine company out of business.

At the Counterfeiting Intelligence Bureau, Matz has seen how wide open the second-oldest profession is: 'If I was going to be criminal, I'd get into counterfeiting,' he says.

Yet to grow, cut and ship roses, to create packaging for shampoo, to manufacture and export millions of items a year, even to lose 300 lorry loads of tea bags a year, needs a sophisticated network of buyers and sellers, shippers who ask no questions and wholesalers who don't look too closely. There's a group of people who have these skills: the world's criminal gangs. We know them as 'organized crime', because the crimes involve more than one person working together. They create the routes to market, the distribution networks, and supply the investment that allows everything under the sun to be counterfeited.

It's all illegal – but it's happening near you, right now. In the developed world's major cities, you might be surprised to learn that counterfeiting is today the dominant business; as Matz predicts, the criminal gangs have moved in, and are squeezing out other trades. It has already happened in the centre of the commercial world: Midtown New York.

Notes

1. *Times*, 4 July 2002.
2. *Harper's Magazine*, 1 November 2004.
3. *China Consumption Times*, 12 June 2001.
4. Speech to The Detroit Economic Club, 15 September 2003.
5. Fighting the fakers, *Engineer*, 26 April 2002.
6. *China Daily*, 21 May 2004.
7. BBC News, 10 March 2005.
8. BBC News, 15 December 2004.

9. Government's fake cigarettes warning, HM Customs press release, 15 December 2004.

10. Research carried out by Dr Ed Stephens, quoted in Government's fake cigarettes warning, HM Customs press release, 15 December 2004.

11. IDG News Service, 28 October 2004.

12. IDG News Service, 14 November 2003.

13. *Guardian*, 18 March 2005.

14. Newsday, 27 August 1995.

15. The illicit market in stolen fast-moving consumer goods: a global impact study, 2004.

3 Counterfeit Alley

A middle-aged woman sits in her SUV, illegally parked on Broadway, in the heart of New York's borough of Manhattan, outside a local deli, from where I'm watching. It's 5 pm on Friday afternoon. Two hours ago, the streets were filled with their normal mix of shoppers, tourists and office workers. Some were browsing, but the shops in this part of town aren't great, so most were on their way to somewhere else.

Suddenly, this area has become a destination, but not for any type of shopper. The woman in her SUV with New Jersey plates isn't unusual: look up and down the streets in a two-block radius, and there are plenty more, often with out-of-town licence plates. All have come to buy from shops that have no shop front, purchasing goods that aren't what they claim to be, from wholesalers whose warehouses are unmarked.

The woman takes out a mobile phone and makes two calls. After the second, she gets out, looks up and down the street. A man approaches, a quick conversation. Two minutes later, two more males, both teenagers wearing bandannas and low-slung jeans, show up, carrying large black plastic bags that bulge with unseen boxes. The bags are loaded into the back of the SUV, squeezed around the baby seat. Five minutes later, the SUV is on its way out of Manhattan.

Something for the weekend

This is just one more purchase on New York's 'Counterfeit Alley', a block of warehouses between 5th and 6th Avenues, cut through by the diagonal of Broadway. Thirty years ago, Counterfeit Alley was the Garment District, and the warehouses were premises for the clothing business. Ten years ago, they were being snapped up by the dot-com crowd, who were looking for cheap, central office space at low prices. Then it was known as 'Silicon Alley'.

Today, the dot-commers having exhausted their funds and left to return to whatever jobs they came from, Silicon Alley's buildings are warehouses once again. Counterfeit Alley is the storehouse for the knockoff trade on the entire US East Coast, and on Friday night and Saturday the district hums with buyers doing business in a lucrative, flourishing and illegal trade.

Walk the streets at this time, and you can hear the deals being made around you. 'Got any now? Will you have them later? How many?' says a middle-aged guy into the public phone on the same corner that the SUV woman has just vacated. Nearby, a woman sits on an unmarked brown packing case. All the boxes being shipped into the doors around her are unmarked – there are three courier delivery vans being unloaded on this block alone, in the middle of rush hour. She's talking on her mobile phone: 'I'll take them, but don't forget I want the boxes this time,' she says.

'It's getting so you can't walk on the sidewalk on a Saturday,' says Andrew Oberfeldt, the boss of private investigator Abacus Security, which operates from an office one block away. He has been chasing counterfeiters in Manhattan for most of his adult life, first in the New York police force, then as a private consultant. His face is familiar. As he approaches, teenage lookouts stationed on the corners glance in his direction. Some of the career knockoff merchants now say hello as he passes. They call him 'boss', and he returns the compliment.

Oberfeldt points out a group of kids, no older than 14, carrying business cards to give to prospective buyers. The cards have a number to call. The kids are paid to identify likely buyers. 'That's their only job. If you are the right kind of customer, they will give you a card. You call, and you can see the stuff that is behind that wall,' he says. 'That wall' is visible on the first floor of a warehouse on

6th Avenue. The steps up to the floor have a retailer's name, but what would be a large product display window at the front shows only the back of a partition wall – and behind the wall are the product samples, hidden from general view.

'Look at that lovely window. Why do you think there's a wall right behind it? If I was running a shop selling handbags, I would want to put them in a lovely window like that,' says Oberfeldt, laughing, pointing out the white van parked outside, ready to be filled with the secret stock. 'If you are running a small shop outside New York, you will want to fill a van like this one when you visit. You can drive in from anywhere. I've seen vans on this street that have driven here from Texas.'

When the spotters have done their job, and the buyers, who are often small retailers from the suburbs or towns, have inspected the samples, the cash changes hands (this is, needless to say, not a business that gives credit or takes cards). Then, the couriers deliver from the location where the stock is kept. On Friday afternoon, they are everywhere, emerging from unmarked doors with black plastic bags slung over their shoulders, delivering the merchandise to the out-of-towners in their vans: shoes, sportswear, handbags, luxury goods, mobile phones; all brand-name, all counterfeits or knockoffs.

It's the same way that drugs are sold on the street – you don't do the deal with the guy who holds the merchandise – but with one essential difference. In New York, there simply is no limit where possession of counterfeit goods becomes possession with the intent to distribute them. You can explain a black plastic bag full of 50 knockoff handbags as being for your 'personal use'.

'If there is no limit at which it becomes a serious crime, is a cop going to get involved, ask questions about what is in the black bag? No way,' Oberfeldt explains. The result is that, while the deal is secret, the couriers take over the streets for the weekend.

In between the unmarked lofts, a few enterprising wholesalers have set up shop. 'See this sign?' says Oberfeldt, pointing at a window alongside some handbags that are faithful copies of Louis Vuitton and Kate Spade designs, but without the brand label. The shop is marked 'Wholesale only'. 'That means that an undercover cop can't just walk in. They can ask to see your tax registration, and if you can't supply it they will kick you out. The stuff in the back is the stuff that they don't want you to see – until they know who you are.'

Bags with no label are known in the business as 'blanks', and are considered safe to put in a shop window, as in New York selling a 'blank' is not illegal. The best merchandise is out back, in more unmarked boxes. It may also be blank at this point, because the wholesalers of Counterfeit Alley have learned another law-bending trick. Buy some blanks in Counterfeit Alley, and shopkeepers offer a set of directions, because they have bags but no labels. Down the street, there's a room where the missing labels are – brands that turn your blanks from quasi-legal items 'inspired by' famous makers into fully fledged counterfeits. The labels were probably imported in a small bag in someone's pocket, someone who didn't have a consignment of blanks. In the room where you are sent, there will be someone whose job it is to apply the labels, but no bags. If the room gets raided, the police find a bunch of labels. It's not a crime, unless the police can put the bags and the labels together in one place.

It's a method learned from armed robbers: if you are going to commit a crime that needs a gun, it's risky to take the gun with you, in case you are stopped and searched. It's riskier still for an accomplice to hang around on the nearest street corner with your gun. The solution: take half a gun each. Neither half is a weapon; you pick up the other half from your accomplice at the last moment, and do whatever you were planning to do with minimum risk.

As darkness falls, the streets are thronging with couriers. You can't walk 10 yards without being thumped in the leg by a black plastic bag full of boxes. On the street, a flea market sells scruffy knockoffs of famous names. According to Oberfeldt, it's a telltale to which companies are using investigators to enforce their rights in Counterfeit Alley and which ones, for whatever reason, prefer to look the other way. If you're going to sell knockoffs on the street, the second question is 'What will sell?' The first is 'What can I sell that won't get confiscated?'

There's another reason that the stalls aren't going to be raided: the stallholders are overwhelmingly over 60 and down on their luck. Again, it's not an accident.

'A lot of the [flea market] permits are given to disabled veterans. Are you going to be the politician that takes a permit from one of these guys? No way. So what the counterfeiters do is go to the disabled shelters, round up a bunch of these guys, get them to apply for a pitch and pay them $50 a day to mind the stall,' says Oberfeldt. 'But are they on a percentage of the profit? No.'

Showdown in Midtown

On 20 December 2004, the huge profits to be made in Counterfeit Alley were there for everyone to see. At 6 pm, police raided just one of the anonymous warehouses in the district: 1158 Broadway. Inside, they found not one Aladdin's cave of counterfeiting, but hundreds, all stored in small, subdivided areas of the space. By dividing the five floors into between 12 and 22 units each, and charging flat rents of around $200 a month for storage, the unit had quickly filled with knockoffs – but the scale of the raid shocked even experienced anti-counterfeiting specialists.

'We closed three city blocks so we could get it all out,' says Heather McDonald, a partner with New York law firm Gibney, Anthony & Flaherty LLP, who represents some of the companies whose products were inside. 'Every single room in this building was filled with merchandise. We had to bag it all, tag it all. Even with every spare police officer in New York working on it, it took three days to do it.'

Thirty-three companies banded together to help offset the cost of the raid. While the NYPD provided the people and a nifty yellow debris chute on the top of the building to drop the bags of merchandise down, much of the resource for the 24-hour-a-day operation came from the companies whose knockoffs were being hauled out of the building. That meant they footed the bill for the nine tractor trailers parked in the middle of Manhattan that were filled with the confiscated products. Someone had to pay for 200,000 clear plastic bags, used to bag up the evidence, and the special sealing tape that the police needed. The joint effort also bought 'a lot of coffee and a fair amount of pizza', McDonald says.

The raid was the most spectacular and effective of a new initiative: The Mayor's Office of Midtown Enforcement. New York might be the hub of the knockoff business in the United States, but it also has a law, dating from 1868, that could allow the authorities to strike at the heart of the problem: Section 715 of the New York State Real Property Actions and Proceedings Law – better known as the 'Bawdy House Act'. It says:

> An owner or tenant... of any premises within two hundred feet from
> other... real property used or occupied in whole or in part as a bawdy
> house... or for any illegal trade, business or manufacture... or any
> duly authorized enforcement agency of the state or of a subdivision
> thereof... may serve personally upon the owner or landlord of the
> premises so used or occupied, or upon his agent, a written notice
> requiring the owner or landlord to make an application for the
> removal of the person so using or occupying the same.

If you are the landlord of the bawdy house (or warehouse full of
knockoffs) and someone makes a complaint, then the Act says that
you're as responsible as the tenant. Over the years it has been used
against pimps, gun-runners, drug dealers and illegal gamblers. Since
1993 it has been turned against counterfeiters and their landlords.

Bob Barchiesi, a tall, imposing former US Secret Service agent
and, as a regional director for the Recording Industry Association of
America, one of the leading figures behind the task force, explains
how the Bawdy House Act changed the way that the NYPD raided
the places where they found counterfeits. 'At first we broke down
doors with battering rams, we made arrests, we confiscated thousands of CDs – and if it was a prize fight we'd have lost in the first
round,' he says. A few days later, the warehouses would fill up with
more product, as soon as it could be shipped in or copied somewhere in the suburbs. The lost stock was, for his enemies, simply the
cost of doing business; in fact, it was about the only significant
overhead they were paying.

There were two problems. The first was that counterfeiting gangs
aren't going to be frightened by a few raids. If one sort of product is
regularly confiscated, they can simply switch to another. The second
was that it was simply impossible to raid all the warehouses all of the
time without swallowing the entire NYPD anti-counterfeiting
budget and taking officers off other duties. The counterfeiters could
simply wait until New York's police ran out of will, or cash, or both.

It was time for a rethink. 'Being New York cops we decided to go
and get a beer. And then we decided, "let's start a task force",'
Barchiesi recalls.

The Midtown task force had simple rules: members paid $3,500 –
for companies accustomed to paying that for a few hours of a law
firm's time to sit and talk about catching counterfeiters, it was a
bargain. The funds were used to pay the cost of transporting and

destroying the goods they confiscated – and, of course, the pizza and coffee. When the kitty ran out, the task force would ask for another $3,500. The more companies that join, the bigger the actions it can take, but the less chance there is of running out of cash. It would target the problem buildings in Midtown, execute a police search warrant, confiscate everything illegal that they found inside and hold the landlords responsible. The police would summon the Department of Buildings, the Fire Department and the Department of Health to inspect the building. If they found violations of the building code, the landlords and tenants would be literally locked out of their own building by a Department of Buildings vacate order. Then the City would sue the building owners and the counterfeiters and, until the case was settled, the police would put a second lock on the door.

Walk down Counterfeit Alley, look closely and you can see doors that are padlocked in this way. They are the distribution hubs that the task force has taken out. Ask the owners of 1147 Broadway (raided on 18 December 2003 and again on 29 January 2004), 1145 Broadway (21 January 2004), 1214 Broadway (11 February) and seven other warehouses. At 1158 Broadway, $12 million of illegal goods were taken out in a single raid. It was, by some distance, the largest seizure of counterfeit in the history of New York, and brought the value of goods seized to $20 million.

Barchiesi likes to quote Edmund Burke: 'When bad men combine, the good must associate, or they will fall one by one' ('Thoughts on the cause of present discontents').

By contrast McDonald enjoys putting the fear into the criminal gangs of Midtown New York for a change. 'When we raided 1158 Broadway, you've never seen it so quiet. There were tumbleweeds blowing down Broadway from 30th to 20th street,' she laughs.

> When they padlock your building and build a wall across your front door, you're not collecting rent, and you can't collect rent until you settle with the City. Suffice it to say; once this happens to a landlord, he makes sure it never happens again. We have landlords now who call us, say 'I think there's a counterfeiter in my building. What should I do?'

Canal Street

To see the real market force that created Counterfeit Alley, you need to walk 15 minutes south, to one of the most lucrative and notorious sources of knockoffs in the world: Canal Street.

'Canal Street is the Disney World version of this trade. The tourists prefer Canal Street. Maybe they don't like it in Counterfeit Alley because there are too many people of colour and it's not glamorous,' says Oberfeldt.

Canal Street isn't exactly a theme park. Cutting through the heart of New York's Chinatown, it is even more populous than Midtown Broadway. Restaurants, bars, tattooists, jewellers and grocers share space with warrens of tiny shops selling watches, luggage, leather goods, sportswear and fashion, the vast majority of it faked, and on sale to a milling crowd of tourists and New Yorkers out for a bargain. The windows are full of poor-quality blanks and tacky watches. To get the good stuff, you have to know where to ask, which a surprising number of shoppers do.

'Is there limitless demand? It certainly seems so,' says Oberfeldt, who knows the area, inside and out. He has been raiding the shops around Canal Street since he was first a street cop. 'I was a policeman for 16 years. I'm used to people doing things that you don't want them to do,' he says, 'but now, can you believe it, there are bus tours through Chinatown where the tour guides point out the best places to get knockoffs.'

If Canal Street is a white-knuckle ride, the thrill is the seediness. 'There's no doubt that customers in Chinatown know they are buying something illegal. They have to go down a corridor and say "Frankie sent me". When you are led off Canal Street, down an alley to a basement lit by generators…', says Oberfeldt, back in his office, sitting in front of the floor plan of a shop that's next on his list for a raid.

> Oh, come on. This isn't a shopping mall. They hide what we're enforcing, and sell what we are not enforcing. So you ask for a handbag from the shop owner, who shows you the picture in a catalogue. A 10-year-old puts your money into his backpack and walks away to a parked car nearby. The door opens, the kid gives the money, gets one bag and runs it back to you.

And that, to Oberfeldt, caught up in a struggle that will surely outlast his career, is a small victory. His clients don't reasonably expect that their goods will disappear from Canal Street – but by taking them off display and by turning a simple one-person retail transaction into a complicated three-person deal, he's making things just a little harder for the counterfeiters. He is driving up their costs, maybe prompting them to stock a different brand of knockoff that won't attract the attention of the investigators, the police and the 20 investigators who sometimes act as secret shoppers on Oberfeldt's staff who stroll through Chinatown making test purchases.

Canal Street won't go legit though, while there are tourists to serve. 'The handbag has a better mark-up than heroin,' Oberfeldt says. Counterfeiting in New York law, it's a C felony. That means no jail time. US law allows prosecutors to make a deal: if you are prepared to plead guilty, you can be offered an incentive, usually a reduced charge, if you cooperate with the investigation and name your accomplices. In the counterfeit business, the prosecutor isn't in a position to make a deal. 'If I catch you as a counterfeiter and I say "Who is your boss?", you will laugh and say to me "Go and get a coffee. I'm calling my lawyer and then I'm walking out of here,"' Oberfeldt says.

The anonymous offices of Abacus Security, the only office I have visited where iron bars stop you from walking out of the elevator until the receptionist has confirmed your identity, are a testament to this reality. It's here that Oberfeldt and his staff plan their strategy using a whiteboard, up to 50 enforcement specialists and a lot of pretzels. Their lives are a continuous series of raids and confiscations around Canal Street, but, without a task force, nine tractor trailers and the vocal backing of Mayor Bloomberg, private investigators are scarcely more than an irritant. It's his job to be a consistent irritant. It's a mistake, he says, to think that any of New York's anti-counterfeit investigators, or even the NYPD, can solve the problem on their own – it's too big and too deeply rooted in the community. 'When people say that all this money goes to terrorism, it does. But it also goes to putting someone in the family through medical school,' he says. To the extended Chinese families who form the ad hoc counterfeiting gangs in Canal Street, the investigators are just business competition.

'This is such an open market that there is no need for the rival gangs to get violent with each other,' he says.

> There are a couple of guys on Canal Street, they wave to me and call me 'boss', I call them 'boss', because we grew up together. Think about it this way: stockbrokers don't hate companies for going up and down in value. If six law enforcement guys hop in a van and set off to go and show the guys in Chinatown who is boss, they will get their asses kicked. It's better to let the counterfeiters have their bragging rights so they can save face when you raid them. They might be mad at us walking in with a seizure order and taking their stuff away, but it is not personal. They are in business, and so are we.

In the last few years, though, Oberfeldt has noticed a disturbing change in Chinatown's knockoff business. His traditional adversaries, immigrants overwhelmingly from Guangdong who were the first residents of the largest Chinese community outside China, have been joined by a new wave of illegal immigrants from the Fukien province, gangs who are not as tolerant of irritants like Abacus taking their stuff. His 'tough but fair' policy doesn't go down as well with counterfeiters who remind him of the Russian mafia he sometimes dealt with as a police officer. 'Firecrackers thrown at me are OK. I can handle that. But you don't need a quarter of a stick of dynamite thrown at you for doing your job,' he says.

> People from countries like Russia taunt the police. They have a lot of people ready to fight, because in their culture that's what you do when the police come after you. So I'm in a raid in the summer of 2004, and for the first time in a long time we found ourselves in one of those old-style brawls with the Fukienese. They started throwing soda cans at us, and then I'm getting a glass window smashed in my face. This brawl goes on into the night. You duck the chair they throw, you get the goods and you're almost out of the door – and someone throws a coffee can full of gunpowder at you.

As long as you're going back to your Manhattan hotel with a fake watch or a knockoff handbag, then guys like Oberfeldt are going to be taking a glass window in the face from time to time. Despite the best efforts of the task force, Counterfeit Alley is the centre of a business that costs US businesses around $20 billion a year in lost sales.[1] Oberfeldt doesn't expect the gangs of Chinatown suddenly to change career, but he's irritated with us, their customers. 'If more people had a realistic view, if more people took responsibility for their actions, we'd be better off,' he shrugs. 'But it's an area of permissiveness in our culture. It is the cheap thrill of getting away with something illegal.'

Note

1. US Department of Commerce estimate.

4 Sex and the purse party

On 5 August 2001, US television comedy *Sex and the City* sent the market for fake Hermès bags soaring. Already in its fourth series, it had become what in the media business argot is called 'appointment viewing' for young, affluent, urban women. That is, they would happily forgo their spinning class or a cosmopolitan in the cocktail bar after work and make a date to see their favourite programme at home on the sofa instead. Despite being shown on minority cable channel HBO, its ratings were up by a third compared to the previous season. More than 6 million viewers every week tuned in. *Sex and the City* was HBO's most valuable show.

That night's episode, called 'Coulda, woulda, shoulda', had two special guest stars: Lucy Liu and a bag. And its long-term effect will be felt long after we have forgotten who Lucy Liu is. The episode helped to kick-start a craze for knockoff bags among the wealthy middle classes of the United States – a craze that, to a lesser extent, we can see across the developed world – that is driving the producers of handbags to distraction.

The handbag of success

The bag that starred in the episode wasn't just any bag. Samantha (the blonde, glamorous PR executive played by Kim Cattrall) wants a Hermès Birkin bag, a big red status symbol. Named after actress

Jane Birkin, it had been introduced in 1984, was handmade in Hermès factories to a strict quota, retailed at the notional price of $6,000, but it had a five-year waiting list – and Samantha was at the bottom of it. When she sees an ordinary citizen carrying a convincing counterfeit Birkin, she's furious, and calls the Hermès shop to drop the name of her latest client in a bid to get to the top of the list:

> Samantha: Hello. Francesca? Samantha Jones. Question. How the fuck long does Lucy Liu have to wait for that Birkin? Well, if they're so hard to get, maybe you can explain why I just saw a fucking nobody in a tracksuit carrying the exact one we want. Lucy Liu is a big, big fucking star and she wants that bag! Is Hermès French for 'We take our good old fucking time'?

The abuse works. The Birkin is delivered – but direct to Lucy Liu, because it is her name that got Samantha to the top of the list. This drives Samantha to wail at Lucy that it is her 'fucking bag'. Samantha gets fired. Lucy keeps the bag. Memo to any of the thousands of women who wanted to be like Samantha: you need a Birkin.

It's not as though the bag needed such prominent product placement: the waiting list for a Birkin has for years been so long that, in many Hermès shops, there's a waiting list for the waiting list. It's a bit simpler for Gwyneth Paltrow, Kate Moss or Lil' Kim – all snapped by paparazzi holding the desirable bag in a way guaranteed to inflame further the desires of those who would barely make the waiting list for the waiting list for the waiting list, if one existed. We can safely assume that – like Lucy Liu – celebrities don't have to wait five years.

Buried in the episode was also the solution to the problem: the ordinary woman in a tracksuit who skipped the list (or list for the list) by buying a counterfeit. Before *Sex and the City*, Hermès Birkin bags were already a fake favourite. Afterwards, the search for a good fake Birkin became a gossip column regular item, and the Birkin knockoff boom is still going on. The Birkin has become a symbol of the unbridgeable gap between 'us', who aspire to own one, and 'them', who actually can. There are even classes of fakes: the true counterfeits, complete with fake logo; the knockoffs, designs 'inspired' by the real bag but missing a couple of essential features; and a host of poor-quality Birkin-lookalike tribute bags.

'I have a contract with one of the best crafters in the world of these fine handmade bags. My bags are NOT mass produced in a Korean factory. These beauties are handmade,' says an advert on http://www.ioffer.com, an auction site where it's not hard to find goods 'inspired by' the genuine article. 'These are worth the price I am selling them for. I am offering these to the women who cannot get on the "waiting list". You always want what you can't have, right? So they tell the ladies they can't have the bag. What does that do? It makes the ladies crave it!'

The Cult of Birkin even made the serious news, if that's the right way to describe Martha Stewart's trial: 'Martha Stewart arrived in federal court on Tuesday to begin her trial,' reported the *Washington Post* on 22 January 2004. 'She was carrying two handbags.'

This might not immediately strike you as the key to Stewart's guilt or innocence – which just goes to show you haven't been watching enough *Sex and the City*.

> One appeared to be the typical working woman's carryall. It was made of dark, sturdy leather... If there was any subliminal message in her bag, it was that Stewart is a working woman, just like so many others. The second bag was a warm shade of brown with a rounded double handle, tiny metal feet, a fold-over top and a beltlike closure that wrapped around its body. It was an Hermès Birkin handbag. And for a certain breed of woman, it is the handbag equivalent of a Rolls-Royce or a dozen illicit Cuban cigars. It is a bag that announces that one has achieved a breathtaking level of success. It can declare its owner's wealth and status from a distance of 50 paces.

Thanks to the researchers at the *Washington Post*, we learn that Stewart has had her Birkin bag for 11 years and, according to one of her legal team, it is 'perfect for files'. But the newspaper doesn't approve:

> Stewart's Birkin was a hand-stitched symbol of the underlying issues – the privileges of success – that have so agitated her detractors. Her advisers have weighed in on a host of issues related to her image, but her choice of handbag was not among them. Yesterday, her second day in court, the Birkin was not on display in front of the cameras. But Stewart had the bag with her and reportedly said that she plans to use it frequently throughout the trial.

It's not surprising that she ended up in prison, having carried into her trial what the *Post* described as a 'cultural emblem of elitism, privilege and celebrity... the bag that money alone cannot buy'.

And all over the world, ambitious people who would love a symbol of elitism and privilege say to themselves, 'I must have that bag.' So it's no surprise to find that Joseph Gioconda, a partner specializing in intellectual property with the New York firm of Kirkland & Ellis LLP working on the Hermès account, has a full in-tray.

'I have anywhere from 40 to 100 active investigations on my desk at any time,' he says.

> I have seen knockoffs being sold openly on Rodeo Drive in Beverly Hills. When I started, Hermès had a counterfeiting problem but it was steady and predictable. The quality of the counterfeits was poor and their quantity was manageable. In the last 18 months, the problem has exploded. I track the reports from customs and I get to the point where I come in every day and there is a stack on my desk. It used to be one a month, then one a week. Now I have eight a day. It used to be two or four bags, now it's 2,000 or 4,000 per shipment, and that's just what gets caught.

Battling knockoffs and counterfeits isn't just an aspect of Hermès' sales strategy: it is beginning to take it over. 'I talk to the chief executive of Hermès every day. He used to have more important things to do,' Gioconda says.

He adds that, if it gives up the fight and lets the avalanche of fake Birkins roll on, Hermès won't be able to sell its bag any more. And if it's possible to see where the $6,000 goes in a bag, then you can see it in the Birkin: each bag is stitched by hand; each one takes 18 hours to make in one of three, only three, tiny workshops in France.

So, Hermès has got heavy with the counterfeiters. The 160-year-old company's image of old-world sophistication jars with the brutal reality that Gioconda represents. Every day, he's issuing 'cease and desist' orders to shops and importers that are selling knockoffs, setting up stings where his undercover agents sneak hidden cameras into the shops that stock counterfeits, chivvying the police into raiding warehouses, garages, even bedrooms.

At Kirkland & Ellis, one of Gioconda's paralegals spends 20 hours a week shopping – logging on to the internet from home, checking auction sites for counterfeits.

Gioconda has even had to write to Jennifer Lopez, who was planning to give all the guests at her cancelled wedding a knockoff Birkin as a souvenir. It was a type imported from Italy, made in bright plastic and known as a 'Jelly Kelly', and was a surprise fashion hit in 2003 – so much so that prices shot up, just like the real thing.

More convincing fakes have ended up in front of a jury. 'We did two jury trials, where we had the guys on tape telling their customers that no one would know the difference, and this was in a shop just down the block from Hermès,' he says. 'Then we looked at the broader picture, and saw the same thing was happening in Chicago, Florida, Hawaii, California. There's ties, watches, scarves too. Everything my clients make is copied, and the name is also put on some things they don't even make.'

His investigators reported back on a strange phenomenon: many of the best knockoffs were not being bought by office workers and fashion victims, but by Hermès customers. They had the red, but they wanted the black too, and there was no way they were going to the back of the queue. But a $100 knockoff wouldn't do it – after all, it may be chic to admit to having a fake, but not an easy-to-spot fake.

So while China is still the sweatshop producer of knockoff Birkins, Italy has cornered the market for quality counterfeits. 'The disturbing thing is that the premium counterfeits are becoming more desirable than the real thing. In Italy, you can find the quality leather that you need and the quality workmanship. In Milan, the copies are made by taking the product, taking it to pieces, laying it out, copying it piece by piece. They copy it right down to the stitching detail,' says Gioconda. 'It's that quality that allows them to sell for a higher price. Today a good-quality knockoff sells for $1,000.'

Gioconda's also struggling against a tide of mid-quality knockoffs, without the Hermès branding, imported from the Far East. But if being on the 'A' list means that you can skip the queue for a real Birkin, then perhaps aspiring to the 'D' list means that you know the place downtown where you can take your blank and have it stamped with the manufacturer's name. Meanwhile, the blanks are in shop windows everywhere, and Gioconda and Hermès are fuming. 'The mark-up is huge. The shopkeeper pays $50 for blanks, puts them in his window. He doesn't have to put out a sign explaining what they are,' says Gioconda. 'The bags sell themselves.'

Party bags

In the US, buying counterfeit bags has become part of the social whirl in polite society.

Every week, the *New York Times Magazine* carries a column called 'The Ethicist', which debates the difficult problems of social etiquette for its readers. On 6 February 2005, Ms A Stein wrote in to ask about whether her local school should be selling counterfeit bags at its holiday fair. 'I told the principal and the head of the PTA that this was illegal,' she wrote. 'They said it must be legal because so many people sell fakes... what do you think?'

'The Ethicist' drolly replied that, if the school had 'the courage of its lack of convictions', it would sell stolen cars too. 'The plight of Prada and Coach may not bring a tear to anyone's eye, but ethics compels us to act honourably, even to the makers of inane status symbols. Besides, it would be dispiriting for the students to see their principal dragged off in handcuffs.'

Andrea Powers would volunteer to do it, given the chance. As a private investigator at Boston firm Powers and Associates, when she sees a woman in the street with a good-quality knockoff she starts a conversation. 'I'm at the mall and I see her, and I'll say "I love that bag! Where did you get it?",' she says. 'And the woman says, "I bought it at a purse party", and I say, "I'd love to hold one of those parties. Do you know who I can contact?", and nine times out of ten I come away with a number.'

'The purse party is a brilliant manoeuvre,' says Gioconda. 'These are upscale people from good neighbourhoods. It's the new Tupperware.'

Psychologist Abraham Maslow, in his 1943 paper 'A theory of human motivation',[1] created the concept of the 'hierarchy of needs'. It states that we have a few basic needs that must be satisfied before we look for more sophisticated needs. At the most basic level, Maslow says we need food, water, sleep and warmth, before we look for things like love, or consider trifles like not breaking the law. Thanks to the purse party, Maslow's list of basic needs can be supplemented for many people in the United States: food, water, sleep and warmth, and a really good knockoff handbag.

To achieve this, the hostess invites friends and acquaintances to the party. Her suppliers arrive with boxes of fake purses. Some are expensive counterfeits, others cheaper knockoffs. People make their purchases, and the hostess is rewarded with a bag to the value of 10 per cent of the turnover.

'She might invite 15, 20, even 50 people, most often on a Friday or a Saturday night,' Powers says. 'The suppliers can make $2,000 or $3,000 for four hours of work.'

The purse party is now a retail marketing tactic too: often store owners will hold a party after hours, to bait buyers into coming to the store. While they are there, they are offered the store merchandise to buy as well. It's a reward for regular customers of beauty or hairdressing salons, and the suppliers will also make sure they offer the guests the chance to run their own party, and sign at least one of them up.

It's fun, it's frivolous, it's against the law and it's Powers's job to be party pooper. The fizz goes out of the evening when the hostess realizes that she has invited Powers. That usually happens when Powers locks the door and announces that it's a raid.

Recently, she found herself at a party in a local hair salon at 7 pm. Unknown to the salon's party guests, state and local police were outside, videoing them as they arrived. 'I went early. I wanted to get a good look around,' Powers says. 'The shelves were full of products. When it's time to go, I'm on my cellphone, like I'm calling a friend. I'm actually calling for law enforcement.'

In come the police. The door is locked. If you're late, you will see a sign in the window telling you that the party is cancelled, because the police confiscated the bags and arrested the suppliers. Most of the guests know what they are buying is illegal and slink off, 'but there's always one who wants to argue', Powers jokes.

She's not usually after the organizer, who escapes with a lecture, unless she is a regular offender. It's the suppliers that the police, and the handbag manufacturers that employ Powers, want to catch. 'The first thing the hostess says to us is "Am I in trouble? Will you take my house?" she says. 'And we tell her, "We could." Because it could happen.'

Instead, the standard punishment for the supplier is a year of probation, and restitution of damages to the brand owners. Even to get that in the New England area where Powers works, the suppliers have to be found in possession of 25 or more counterfeits, as 24 could be considered for 'personal use'. For special busts, in a neat twist, Powers will sometimes arrange to be the party host, and set up her own counterfeit purse party, staffed entirely with female law enforcement officers. That makes the arrests a lot smoother, but Powers doesn't get to earn a free bag.

Infiltrating the middle classes

Like Powers, Gioconda has seen the respectable face of selling counterfeit bags mushroom in the post-*Sex and the City* era. In 2002, acting on a tip-off, he found a woman called Susan Sutherland was selling $1,000 knockoff bags from a rented hotel suite in Beverly Hills. Having personally served her with one cease and desist order, he found that she was popping up in high-class hotels from Houston to Chicago, selling her fakes. Each time, Gioconda would hop on a plane, fly to the hotel and close her down.

When eventually he raided her house, he found that she had thousands of bags in storage. Gioconda couldn't believe what he saw. 'I was shocked. The location was a multimillionaire's home in Valencia [a wealthy suburb], and she was selling the bags right out of her garage. No one was home, so we broke into the house, and there were hundreds of Hermès bags alone.'

He called the US attorney, who prosecutes federal crimes, to offer him the chance to prosecute. 'He told me, "We're a bit too busy looking after terrorist threats at the moment",' Gioconda recalls. 'In the end, we had to pay the US marshal overtime because we were doing the raid at the weekend. It cost us $3,000 in overtime alone. But it signalled to me there was a sea change, that counterfeiting had infiltrated the middle classes.'

Hermès wanted to find who was supplying the bags and, armed with the name of the Chinese American importer–exporter who traded with the manufacturer, Hermès and US customs go looking for the importer. 'He drops off the face of the earth,' says Gioconda. 'But we have the name of the manufacturer in China. That was a bit of a joke. Our Chinese counsel was very realistic with our chances of doing anything.'

When Gioconda turned his attention to the powers behind the website The Knockoff Shop,[2] he was even more shocked: not because of the replicas, which he had seen many times before, but because the owners didn't even try to hide themselves. Starting in late 2001, the site offered 'designer replica handbags and accessories'. The owners weren't hiding. In fact, they put their names – Kym Whitney and Missy Ramey – on the website, and their address – 4927 Little Cub Creek, in Denver, Colorado. They said:

> We had some extra time, so we thought we'd start a business. (Yeah, right!) Kym is the mother of two very cute little boys and Missy is the mother of two very cute big Labradors. We both have full-time careers (in addition to being mothers!). Kym is a travel agent and Missy runs a book publishing company. Extra time? Who has extra time these days???!! We'd love to hear your thoughts on this site.

The site was plastered with feedback from customers who knew exactly why they were buying. 'Thanks so much for the quick and speedy service. Everyone is ooooing and ahhhhhing over the pink "Gucci" bag,' said Lori from Denver, Colorado. 'They are beautiful and look just like the real thing!' added Marina from New York. 'Received my bag today and am totally thrilled!! Everyone will think it's the real thing. A million thank yous!' gushed Pam of Rockport, West Virginia.

Gioconda's thoughts would not have been the feedback they were expecting. 'It was astonishing: they were selling counterfeits openly and bragging about it,' he says.

'The only way to put a serious dent in this is to educate consumers who think this is a trivial novelty,' Gioconda says. 'The irony for them would be that, if they steal enough of the brand, the value of the brand goes away.'

But why is this not trivial? The middle-class moms of New England and Manhattan fashionistas are hardly career criminals, and they are hardly the natural market for the real thing. Just don't say that to Barbara Kolsun, senior vice-president and general counsel for Kate Spade, who is on a mission to rid the world of fake Kate Spade bags, one purse party at a time.

'Brand equity is the return for development costs, quality control and human rights compliance,' she says. 'With luxury brands, people don't make the connection. The perception is, who cares?' Her point: Kate Spade isn't a company that grew from a background of privilege and luxury; it's a mid-size company that was started by three people who risked everything because they thought they could be a success. It is the authentic American dream, a small company that could be put out of business by knockoffs.

These days, living the dream means paying Kolsun and a host of investigators to police the brand, and it also means adhering to a code of ethics. 'We manufacture in China, in Turkey and in the US, but we would never work with any factory that wasn't human rights compliant,' says Kolsun, whose job it is to ensure that compliance. 'We do all the things that a socially responsible company would do, but counterfeiters don't have to play by those rules. I have seen the pictures of children in China who are making knockoff bags. I don't want us to be part of that.'

So if you set up a purse party, and get caught, don't go crying to Kolsun. 'It's what frustrates me the most. There are women who are well off and who can afford the real thing,' she says. 'Last week one of my investigators reported to me that one of the guys who had been setting up purse parties had been using it to gain access to homes, to steal credit cards and identities, and drain the bank accounts of the party hosts. And I thought, "How perfect".'

But as long as we're a captive market, Gioconda's in-tray will be full. 'Add up the money you get from robbing a bank and compare it to the money you get from counterfeiting, and you would never rob another bank,' he jokes, making the assumption that bank robbers aren't reading this for career advice.

Kolsun isn't so charitable towards the middle classes and their New Tupperware. She is disgusted by the fact that we live in a world where few see counterfeiting as a crime, and if she gets the chance she's coming after your purse party. 'Some of us wish for a return to the 19th century when hangings and amputations were visited on counterfeiters,' she warns.

Notes

1. Abraham Maslow (1943) A theory of human motivation, *Psychological Review*, **50**, pp 370–96.
2. http://www.knockoffshop.com, but you won't find it any more.

PART 2

Inside the knockoff economy

5 Copying is a beautiful thing

I'm at a conference, listening to a speech about how China is toughening its anti-counterfeiting regime, and how a government crackdown on counterfeiters will soon be bearing fruit. 'Let me tell you about China,' a lawyer whispers to me. 'This is such bullshit. China is a freaking nightmare.'

'We raided a market in Shanghai two weeks ago. Yesterday I got an email from the client, and it's right back up again. You can curtail counterfeiting, you can raid on behalf of one brand, you can limit it for a while – but you can't get rid of it. With everything we do, we are just about holding our own,' says Randall Rabenold, a director of North Carolina-based investigator Vaudra Ltd.

Silk Alley

During the breakneck Westernization of Beijing in the late 1990s and early 2000s, if you visited the Silk Alley market it was easy to see why China's counterfeiting problem is so persistent. Since 1996 the informal market on the east side of the city, a block away from the US Embassy, was a tourist destination that could often match Tiananmen Square and the Forbidden City for the number of visiting Europeans and Americans it attracted. As you wandered the narrow street, traders would pull you towards their stalls: 'Sir, look, buy a watch'; 'Bag for your wife, A1 quality'. The watches, the bags, the clothing, the golf clubs, the sunglasses and even the fountain pens were almost all knockoffs, some poor, some acceptable, some overruns for the real factory, some that had simply failed inspection and others that were accurate copies of products the traders had never seen. 'Quality' didn't just mean the materials and workmanship – it's shorthand for the product's faithfulness to the famous brand it mimics. Haggling brought the already low prices down by half. Airline cabin staff on the Beijing run took orders for their friends and families, guide books and websites gave tips, and some enterprising tourists paid for their trips by filling their bags with Ralph Lauren, Gucci, Rolex, Mont Blanc, Levi's and dozens of other fakes.

On 5 January 2005, the party stopped. In sub-zero temperatures, police moved in and closed the market, confiscating hundreds of cartons of stock, closing off the street. It's common in Beijing nowadays for small gaggles of citizens to demonstrate against perceived injustices, and six traders staged an impromptu protest on the roof of the market. They were talked down by police perched on a firefighter's ladder. For a couple of weeks, the police had been turning a blind eye to the trading of any knockoffs, even the ones that they would usually have confiscated, to allow the traders to get rid of surplus stock.

As one door closed for Silk Alley's knockoff vendors, another opened. The evicted traders were allowed to apply for one of the 1,500 pitches in a bright, new five-floor indoor mall with 35,000 square metres of space that was opening next door a week later, also known as Silk Alley. Rents were double what they were accustomed to paying, but the hardest condition was the government's stipulation on what they could sell: no fakes. If that caused the traders to scratch their heads, the tourists who flocked to the new Silk Alley – up to 20,000 a day – were just as shocked and just as unhappy.

Sure enough, when the new mall opened its doors on 16 January, with the press in attendance, the fakes were hidden. But it was too good to last.

Four months later, Silk Alley is once again the biggest and the best knockoff bazaar in the world – but this time the fakes are on show in orderly little booths. Each floor, the size of a football pitch, has its own speciality: if you want a bag, that's in the basement. Watches, displayed in steel briefcases that can be snapped shut and secreted under the counter in an instant, are on the fourth floor, next to the neat racks of wannabe Oakley, Gucci, Ray-Ban and Burberry sunglasses, which in turn lead on to the counterfeit Mont Blanc pens. Sportswear is on the first and second floor, packing out almost half the mall with fake Adidas, Nike, Reebok and Puma. It's 25 degrees outside, but for some reason at least 20 stalls are offering North Face Gore-Tex jackets (known locally as 'North Fakes') – perhaps because they are being snapped up by tourists to take home in their suitcases.

One thing that has certainly changed is the Silk Alley retail experience. Now tourists can buy their knockoffs in air-conditioned comfort. There are lavatories and ATMs and floor plans and an information desk and a supermarket selling genuine food. Despite the instruction to put prices on every product (and rumours of a 5,000 yuan fine if you don't), almost nothing carries a price and, even if it did, it sells for about half of what the traders ask after a little polite haggling. That means that a mid-quality knockoff Rolex costs about £7; 'designer' sunglasses are £10, complete with matching case. Outside, hawkers offer me a copy of the *Hitchhiker's Guide to the Galaxy*, less than one week after it opened in US movie theatres, on a DVD for 40p.

In London, you can't buy a blank DVD for 40p. You can see why some companies throw up their hands in despair when they try to stop Chinese counterfeiters knocking off their products.

Waking the sleeping cat

England used to be known as the 'workshop of the world'. That mantle has long since passed to China. For a quarter of a century, its economy has been growing at 9 per cent a year. In the last 15 years, its exports to the US have grown 1,600 per cent. Its output is now $1.6 trillion of goods every year, according to the Department of Statistics, and it aims to treble it in the next 15 years. If you have three pairs of shoes, two, on average, were made in China. The average income of a Chinese citizen has quadrupled in 25 years, and 60 per cent of its exports are created by small companies and factories.

It's a long way from the days of the inward-looking, centrally planned economy that Chairman Mao presided over; but the way that China has changed gives you one clue as to why it is now responsible for two-thirds of the world's fakes that are imported to the developed world – or, if you include those that come from Hong Kong as well, three-quarters.

In December 1978, on the occasion of the Third Plenum of the 11th Central Committee of the Chinese Communist Party, party chairman Deng Xiaoping ripped up the rules that had caused China's 1.4 billion population to fall alarmingly behind the pace of development in the first world. He abandoned the policy known as the 'Two Whatevers' (support whatever policy decisions Chairman Mao made and follow whatever instructions Chairman Mao gave). In future, political success would be measured by the attainment of economic, not social, goals.

How the goals were reached mattered less than the fact that they must be reached. Or, in Deng's words: 'It doesn't matter if it is a black cat or a white cat. As long as it can catch mice, it is a good cat.'

Deng's speech woke the sleeping, er, cat. Investors anxious to exploit a new market invested in China, and licensed some of the white cats to make their products. For the black cats, this offered a slightly different opportunity.

The first point is the Chinese principles of consensus management, which meant that a contract is more of a starting point for negotiations, rather than the conclusion that Western companies thought they had reached. Anyone who has employed builders at home will know that what you end up with can often, bit by bit, become radically different from what was planned. This, for the Western companies who licensed their manufacturing to Chinese factories, made enforcing the conditions of their manufacturing contracts almost impossible.

Second, many Chinese were already accustomed to doing whatever it takes to get by, to working outside the system in order to get on, and the authorities were used to letting small infractions pass. When that was added to a Communist culture where the legal system or police had no experience of intellectual property, suddenly there was a whole set of exciting opportunities to become wealthy by making knockoffs.

Lastly, and perhaps most significantly, the Chinese are extremely good at copying. 'If you are a good artist in China, you are good at copying a Song Dynasty painting. There's not as much emphasis on creativity in traditional Chinese culture, but a lot on being able to copy well,' says Edouard Schmitt zur Hohe of Schmitt zur Hohe & Ferrante Intellectual Property, a 16-year resident of Beijing where he works to control counterfeiting for his clients, who are mostly luxury goods brands.

Combine all three, add a quarter of a century of economic growth fuelled by government-backed bank loans to business that are often never repaid and employees who work hard and expect little, and you have an industry that is flourishing, profitable and constantly developing. According to the China United Intellectual Property Protection Centre (CUIPPC), a private business that has been representing Western companies like Coca-Cola, Microsoft and Kodak in China since 1994, there are even regional centres of counterfeiting expertise: imagine Silicon Valley for fakes. So if you are manufacturing in Chaosan, in Guangdong province, your speciality is likely to be electronics, cigarettes, pharmaceuticals or CDs. For car parts, it's more likely you'll be in Wenzhou City or the Pearl River Delta. In Yuxiao County, the expertise is in manufacturing fake cigarettes; in Jintan City, it's pesticide. Meanwhile the China Small Commodities City in Yiwu, five hours' drive from Shanghai, is to knockoffs what Wall Street is to stocks and shares: 200,000 buyers, 30,000 wholesale stalls and 3,500 retailers trade around 100,000 products that are available here; 2,000 tonnes of product are bought and sold every day.

Silk Alley is just the most obvious example of how enthusiastically Chinese knockoff manufacturers and retailers have grasped the commercial opportunities available – however they reach their customers. Alibaba.com (www.alibaba.com), founded by entrepreneur Jack Ma in 1999 and headquartered in Hangzhou, eastern China, now has more than 2,000 employees plus 13 regional sales offices across China. It matches buyers and sellers across the globe: 10 million of them in 200 countries and territories, creating $5 billion in trade in 2004. Alibaba.com has become a way for China's entrepreneurs to sell to a waiting world: the company has even run seminars teaching Chinese executives to make small talk and not to smoke in meetings with Western buyers.[1]

While most of the trade on Alibaba.com is entirely legitimate – and it does vet its premium suppliers thoroughly – you don't have to search hard to find items that are counterfeits. 'We can supply all kinds of bag. Including designer bag such as Lv, chanel, gucci etc all the Year round. All of them have High quality and competitive Prices,' announces Weihai Shuangying Import and Export Co Ltd. The Beijing Hopes Trading Co Ltd supplies golf clubs to a waiting world: low-cost Callaway, Titliest, Taylormade, all from the same factory.

Back in the physical world, walk half a mile from Silk Alley across Ritan Park, where once a year the emperor would sacrifice to the sun god, and the shop signs are no longer just in Mandarin. Along Yabao Lu, traders call out to anyone with white skin in Russian; a street lined with wholesale shops selling counterfeit baseball caps, designer clothes and bags displays signs in Russian offering to make batches of product for traders who have been travelling from Eastern Europe for many years. It's not glamorous or fun like Silk Alley. The shopkeepers don't joke with the Westerners or flash counterfeit DVDs at them. It's a place for serious business.

The top of the speed

Even the domestic market is flooded with knockoffs – often less faithful and easy to spot for a Western eye. Chinese consumers have adopted Western brands, not yet having local brands to compete, but have added their own slightly surreal twist. A fake Nike T-shirt in a shop in northern Beijing combines the familiar swoosh with a less familiar slogan exhorting 'Anita! Run at the top of the speed!'

This might make you believe that China is a lawless state, a Wild West for knockoffs. Certainly, some of those who speak for the companies whose products are routinely counterfeited in China would say so. 'The problem is so widespread in China that it is almost impossible to do anything about,' says Darren Pogoda, staff attorney for the International AntiCounterfeiting Coalition (IACC), based in Washington, DC. He works on behalf of 140 members, almost all of whom have a counterfeiting problem somewhere in China.

Many companies complain of getting sucked into interminable legal struggles. New Balance president emeritus John Larsen, formerly the company president, has been battling the fakes for many years. New Balance licensed Horace Chang as its first licensee in the market, but he exported his products worldwide, breaking the agreement. So New Balance terminated the relationship; and Chang continued to manufacture products and sell them. Taken to court, he produced a contract signed by New Balance that confirmed he was a manufacturer – the courts ruled that Chang could manufacture and sell New Balance shoes for ever, licence free.

Larsen has a dim view of how the law is enforced in China. 'There really is no established rule of law in China. They have laws, but they don't have enforcement opportunities and practices there. And of course corruption in China, particularly in the courts, is from our experience pervasive,' he says.

The case is still not resolved, but Larsen has made some progress. 'I think what we've been able to do is to raise the levels of awareness throughout the quite high levels of Chinese government that what's going on is absurd. It not only impacted us, but it was a deterrent to future investment in China. People were having second thoughts about the way they do business.'

Even if Larsen wins his long fight against Chang, other manufacturers are copying his shoes in the domestic market, and he's finding it impossible to enforce actions against them. He's calculating the damage to New Balance both now and in the future. 'The [knockoff] products are never the same,' he says.

> There are no warranties. If the product fails and the consumer thinks it's our product and we say no, we're not going to do anything, then we get the blame: first of all for having a product that failed, secondly for not dealing with it. And thirdly we've lost whatever the profits are on the sale of that product originally, and fourthly we've lost a customer and any kind of lifetime profits that would result.

You don't have to be a glamorous sportswear brand to suffer at the hands of China's counterfeiters. Peter Baranay, president of Abro Industries of South Bend, Indiana, has been fighting them for years.

If you haven't heard of Abro Industries, it's because you live in a rich country. Abro produces glues, solvents and fillers for the developing world – products that perform the day-to-day tasks of holding things together. In Pakistan, 'Abro' is the word for masking tape.

It's also the brand name that Hunan Magic Power Industrial of Liuyang Province used for its glues, solvents and fillers. Oh, and it's using the Abro logo too. 'I've spent 30-plus years creating our brand internationally and these people don't have the intentions or creativity to create their own brand, and therefore they try to steal mine,' spits Baranay. 'They are doing it because they lack the creativity or the capital... or the aggressiveness to create their own brand. So they simply steal someone else's and put it in the distribution chain.'

Abro had registered its brand in China and in 165 countries more than 10 years ago, but Hunan claimed that it had the trademark for Abro, because Abro had made a mistake in its filing, and used its competitive registration papers to stop its products being raided. Having personally travelled to China to meet the government, Baranay has the ear of the politicians in Beijing – but so far this has achieved little in the regions where his products are knocked off, except to stop the manufacture of some knockoff glue.

The upshot of its long struggle to hold on to its business, Baranay says: the company now employs more lawyers than direct employees in the US. So at least the legal industry is doing well out it.

If there is one organization that ought to be able to do something about counterfeiting, but which many manufacturers have learned not to rely on, then that is the Chinese central government. When China became a member of the World Trade Organization (WTO) in December 2001, the major sticking point was its knockoff economy; China hastily had to strengthen its anti-counterfeiting law, a process that has continued ever since, so that now the country has some of the most effective and widespread anti-counterfeiting regimes, on paper at least. But laws don't stop counterfeiters alone: people have to enforce those laws, which many hundreds of miles from Beijing in a remote town where counterfeiting is the local business can be almost impossible. By lowering the barriers to international trade, critics of the WTO say, the West has helped China to flood the world with fakes.

'At central government level, there is sincerity. How much power does central government trickle down to make things happen?' asks Tim Trainer, the president of the IACC.

The big country

Fan Liming, the general manager at CUIPPC, has a picture that he claims answers that question. A thin man with a wispy beard stands in the dock of Guangzhou's courthouse, head slightly bowed. The dock is a simple wooden frame, like the outline of a packing case. It looks as if he has been put into a see-through box. His hands are cuffed in front of him. He wears a faded striped sports shirt and a cheap pair of trousers. His name is Yang Xianming, and he has just been sentenced to six years for counterfeiting Kodak 35mm film in a small factory based in an apartment in Guangzhou City.

It's not a recent picture: CUIPPC started investigating Yang on 8 November 2000, raided his apartment on Wenming Road on 20 December and his warehouse on 24 December 2000, and recovered more than 100,000 films before they hauled him into court soon afterwards. It was, however, the first criminal prosecution in the history of that courthouse for counterfeiting: a courthouse that was right in the middle of one of China's most prominent counterfeiting regions.

'We are the pioneers,' says Fan. 'By May 2004 we calculated we have conducted raids on 3,302 manufacturers and 2,707 wholesalers. We have recovered $2 million for clients, had more than 60 people put in prison. So as you can see we work hard.' That means that, since CUIPPC was founded, it has helped the police to conduct, on average, two raids a day. It handles 500 cases a year for its clients, who include Coca-Cola, Microsoft, Kodak, Philips, Canon, Samsung and Yves Saint Laurent.

'On one day in 1999, we raided more than 30 battery factories,' says Li Guorong, the general manager of client services at CUIPPC. 'Five manufacturers cooperated, and the factories were anything from several tens of people to one or two. It took 200 police officers.'

Does this do any good? Or are the constant raids simply fluff, a way to keep Western companies happy while failing to change the situation? The experience of Silk Alley, where knockoffs have been as stubborn as garden weeds, suggests that enforcement is patchy at best, and that China's counterfeiters are mostly safe, and will not meet Yang's fate.

Size matters, says Li. 'It's important for foreigners to understand the difficulties we have,' he says. 'The law is strong enough. The problem is how you enforce that law. China is such a big country. Sometimes the factory is the largest single employer in the province, so if there is a raid the local mayor might call the police and tell them not to proceed.'

But in the approach to the Beijing Olympics in 2008, when China will be on show to the world, the government is trying to create a stricter environment. In 2004, 1,000 IP cases went to court. If a Chinese manufacturer misappropriated the Olympic symbol while encouraging Anita to run faster on a T-shirt, he would certainly join them: China enacted special laws in 2004 to protect the Olympic movement's IP.[2] Radio and TV advertisements encourage the Chinese to rat out Olympic counterfeiters; 690 billboards have been pulled down and the logo was taken off unauthorized stickers attached to 67,000 taxis.

On 8 December 2004, the laws against counterfeiters were tightened too. If the value of the goods you sell exceeds 50,000 yuan ($6,000), then the police can prosecute you – previously, the threshold was double the amount. For a company, the threshold is 150,000 yuan, down from 500,000 yuan. At the CUIPPC, Li has seen it make a difference: but not in the amount of counterfeiting, just the way the knockoffs are made. 'The counterfeiters also know what the thresholds are. We see a trend now to making small batches, shipping them out each day, or shipping them out in the evening or at weekends or during the holidays.'

As one lawyer who deals with the Chinese authorities on behalf of his high-fashion clients points out, you don't solve a problem by making laws. 'If the Chinese government wanted to stop everyone counterfeiting tomorrow, they would succeed. The government has done things as radical as that in the past. But they can't this time. It would be economic disaster.'

Li says that, 'if the government cracked down completely on counterfeiting tomorrow, as it could, thousands of people would lose their jobs'.

Counterfeiting is now so huge in China that radical action would crash the economy overnight, ruining Deng Xiaoping's 27-year-old economic strategy. It would ruin local economies in the poor south of the country, and even destabilize a government where counterfeit factories and warehouses are often owned by local military and political grandees. If the knockoff economy is 7 per cent of world trade and China is responsible for two-thirds of that, then, using the most conservative estimates, China's counterfeiters are responsible for about 5 per cent of world trade. It wouldn't just be China's small businesses that would be out of business if the supply of product was cut off.

China's blitzkrieg economic miracle gives CUIPPC's Fan hope that market forces will finish off counterfeiters. You might think he would be just the person to despair at the steadily spiralling knockoff business, but not so. 'China is a developing country. Our businesses need assets to grow. The businessmen are small, but making counterfeits lets them grow, and when they have enough money to make genuine product they will, because that is what they want to make,' he says. 'The best way for all of us is to cooperate in this.'

The most important thing for Western businesspeople, he adds, is to be realistic, and not try to embarrass the government by forcing it to do something it simply can't do. 'Counterfeiting is not a criminal problem, a law issue. It is a phenomenon of our economic development. It is part of our social stability. After 20 or 30 years, it will be curbed. If we do a good job at CUIPPC, we put ourselves out of business.'

Be patient, says Li, a message that might resonate with China's 5,000 years of culture, but won't find favour in US boardrooms where directors have to report financial progress every three months.

> China has too many people, too many farmers, and not enough land. They don't have stable work and they are not well educated. What do we expect them to do? Every company that invests here now knows that its money will be repaid one day. So for this period they won't make a profit, but they should still do the job.

Copying in China is still beautiful: 'We tell our clients: our job is to maintain good control, not to eradicate the problem completely,' says Fan. 'If your counterfeiters have a 20 per cent share of your market, then great. But zero per cent, that's not going to happen.'

Notes

1. *Wall Street Journal*, 13 January 2004.
2. *South China Morning Post*, 10 January 2005.

6 A greater Europe

In the 14th century, the Elector Palatine in the Holy Roman Empire hanged a wine seller who was trying to sell counterfeit product. In 1544, Emperor Charles V decreed that anyone who put a false mark of authenticity on Flemish tapestry would have his right hand chopped off. Charles IX of France introduced the death penalty for counterfeiting in 1564, and 102 years later Carcassonne's counterfeit drapers would be sentenced to the pillory.[1]

Europe's a much more civilized place now, most of the time. In 2004, when the European Commission was debating Directive 2004/48/EC on the enforcement of intellectual property rights (eventually adopted on 29 April 2004, in the nick of time before 10 new members acceded, and the process would have had to begin again), one of the rapporteurs – staff who attempt to create constructive dialogue between representatives with different national interests, languages and opinions – was surprised to receive a package at her home one morning. She was even more surprised to find that someone, who presumably wasn't in favour of stronger enforcement, had sent her a box of pigs' ears.

Europe has hundreds of years of experience fighting counterfeiting. Its countries have systems of laws to dissuade counterfeiters that are the envy of much of the rest of the world. It has industries that need protecting: fashion, luxury goods, pharmaceuticals, car parts. It has sophisticated, relatively wealthy consumers.

It has also all the problems that are creating healthy markets for counterfeiters across the globe: consumers who don't care about the crime; organized criminal gangs with international connections; islands of poverty that have created an underclass that cares more about food and housing than adhering to the letter of the law; and a reduction in trade barriers that have fulfilled on the promise of a common market, but which – as more states are pulled into the 25-member Union – create an ever-bigger opportunity to create and move counterfeit goods.

The Italian job

In Europe today counterfeiting is not one problem; it is many. It's not exclusively a criminal problem, but is rooted in the social problems of its member countries. The attempts to combat it are stymied as much by the squabbles and indifference of the politicians and business-people in Europe as by the cunning of the counterfeiters.

'In Italy,' says Roger Warwick, sitting in his office in Bologna, 'we do things in a different way.'

This is a phrase that anyone who has ever done business in the country will find familiar. As an expat Brit in northern Italy, Warwick knows exactly how different southern European business is for Anglo-Saxons, whose business culture emphasizes rules and regulations. He quit London and a safe job as a duty-free shop manager at Heathrow Airport in 1978 to come to Italy to help a company crack down on retail theft ('I couldn't stand the weather. It was December. I thought I would go for a few months, and never came back'), and now is the managing director of anti-counterfeiting gumshoe agency Pyramid International. For two decades he has been seeking out knockoffs, finding the culprits, tracking them down and acting as a cultural go-between for his clients – three out of every five are US clients, sometimes they are British and on rare occasions Italian – and the Italian authorities. He spans two cultures, and he doesn't just translate the language. Often, he has to translate attitudes – and that can be much harder.

Almost 30 years of dealing with Italian consumers have taught him that knockoffs are now, and will always be, as much a part of the Mediterranean culture as the mild weather. Ten per cent of clothes bought in Italy are knockoffs. 'The Italian customer is pretty wide awake,' he says. 'He or she is perfectly happy to buy a Fendi bag or a

Rolex watch, knowing that it is a fake. There is no stigma. Italians say, "It's commerce." It's a northern European idea to think that morals are something we should all be worrying about. In southern Europe, morals are for your priest to worry about.'

The law in Italy backs this up. If you have a market stall selling fake Gucci bags, that's OK – as long as you tell your customers that they are fakes. In the markets of northern Italy, where you find the small workshops that make the high-quality leather goods and designer clothes that characterize the knockoff business in Europe's largest producer of fakes, the stallholders have a small but essential accessory – a printed sign that admits they are selling counterfeit. That doesn't mean they are the sort of cheap copies that come in on the boats from South-East Asia. On the contrary – for Italian designers, the domestic counterfeit problem often stems from a policy of intentional overruns. A factory that is contracted to make 1,000 will make 1,500, Warwick explains, and won't sew the labels into the last 500, knowing that when they reach the market stall the stall owner will lean over and whisper in the customer's ear: 'It's original.'

Of course, this doesn't make the manufacture and distribution of knockoffs any more legal than it is elsewhere in Europe. Italy has many police forces, and most, if not all, could claim a stake in the fight against counterfeiters, from the Guardia di Finanza (the customs police) to the feared Carabinieri (military police), taking in the Polizia di Stato (state police), Polizia Municipale (metropolitan police), Polizia Provinciale (provincial police) and others. If knockoffs are flourishing in Italy, it is not through a lack of personnel. It's because, says Warwick, it is part of the national psyche.

So why is it different in Italy? First, Italy has always had crafts-people who have organized themselves in small family businesses. 'There are a lot of branded products made in Italy, and there are a lot of small businesses. For a large company to get involved in coun-terfeiting is quite hard; it's relatively easy for a small company. So anything involved with counterfeiting is limited to these hundreds of small outfits,' says Warwick. Those outfits have a long tradition of doing what it takes to generate business, and live in a culture where the authorities understand.

Second, thrift has been a fact of life for a country that was, until recently, relatively poor, but with a chic culture. 'It is quite fashionable to say, "Look at my bag! I know it's a fake, but look how little I paid,'" Warwick says, laughing.

And third, the combination of self-reliance and weak local law enforcement long ago created a sophisticated network of organized crime. Around Naples, the Camorra has a long history of involvement in counterfeiting. On 13 December 2004, two Italian Carabinieri officers boarded a flight in Toronto, with a companion: 64-year-old Giovanni Bandolo, the head of a local Camorra group, and wanted for trademark fraud and mafia crimes in Italy. His crime in Canada, which eventually got him extradited, was selling bogus Versace leather coats.

The coats were part of a knockoff operation that was brutally straightforward and sophisticated. Across car parks in the Toronto area, visiting Italian con artists would beckon to Canadians, calling them over to a car, and ask them for directions. To thank them for their help, the con artists would pretend to have excess stock because they were visiting Versace salespeople from Italy, and show a genuine jacket. Their marks, impressed, handed over C $500 and got a jacket pulled out from the back of a car, wrapped in plastic on a fancy hanger. When they pulled off the plastic, they found it was a fake.

Making crime pay

Warwick's experience is that the Camorra and the Sicilian Cosa Nostra have been profiting from knockoffs, especially since the Italian police have become more skilled at investigating their traditional money-earning method. 'For many years the criminals financed themselves with kidnapping. Now it is a lot easier to get involved in counterfeiting. It is no accident that Naples is surrounded by thousands and thousands of cottage industries. For 200 years, the region has been economically depressed, like Eastern Europe, and that has bred organized crime. But when you have an organized crime structure, it needs finance,' Warwick says.

With the largest production of counterfeit goods in the European Union, Italy is a perfect example of the way we embrace knockoff culture while bemoaning its consequences. Indicam, the Italian association of manufacturers against counterfeiting, calculates that the consumption of counterfeits in Italy has increased by 1,700 per cent in the last 10 years. Today, weekend visitors to Venice find the 500-year-old Accademia Bridge has a permanent unofficial market on its steps. If the canals, historic architecture, wine and food don't impress you, look out for the quality of the fake Louis Vuitton bags. They are some of the best made in Europe.

Warwick long since gave up trying single-handedly to change Italian culture. Instead, he tries to accommodate it. Just as selling knockoffs is business for the Camorra, taking them off the market is business for him and his clients. 'The Italians are very fatalistic. They think that you can't stop someone from copying. I tell them that you can't, but you can put a procedure in place to drop a ton of bricks on them when they do,' he says. 'I employ ex-coppers, but ex-policemen aren't always right for the job. They still think they are out to arrest people. I know that my job is to protect the bottom line of the company I work for.'

Understanding the social pressures in Italy is the key to understanding counterfeiting, Warwick says. Pyramid took a job in 2003 from a firm that was suffering because someone had counterfeited its selective weedkiller that was sold to farmers. The problem farmers were finding was that the counterfeit wasn't selective. It killed everything. Farmers across Italy had bought the knockoff on the black market to save cash, but had found their crops ruined.

'We set up a hotline for affected farmers to call us, and published it in the agricultural press,' Warwick recalls. 'We had one call.'

The problem? Most of the affected farmers were buying the weedkiller on the black market because their farms were, at least officially, organic. Organic produce commands a higher price, and Italy is the largest producer of organic vegetables in Europe, according to researcher Organic Monitor. Most of that produce uses the opportunities that the EU provides to ship to Europe's two largest consumers: Germany and the UK. To admit that their vegetables had been treated with this type of weedkiller, legitimate or fake, would destroy their part of the $1 million EU organics business, as it would be four years before they could use those fields for organic produce again.

To attract the attention of the multiple Italian law enforcement agencies, he makes the argument that those companies that are involved in counterfeiting are putting legitimate small companies out of business. He's seen it happen regularly as organized criminals set up legitimate business operations funded on the proceeds of crime.

> It's harder to spend the illegal cash they have earned today, so now it makes sense to get a stake in a legal business instead. And from what we have seen so far, it was far better when they were just spending the money. They have so much cash that there are no problems offering loss-leaders to their customers. They don't need to go to the banks for finance, so the overheads are low. There's enough money to put a rival legally run business out of business, and that should worry every one of us.

The involvement of sophisticated criminal operations has meant some extremely sophisticated scams. In 2004, he was tipped off that a legitimate company was shipping knockoffs with its deliveries of sporting goods. On the surface, the company he was investigating was legitimate. 'But our surveillance found that there were truck-loads of unexplained boxes moving in and out, so we set up a raid. That wasn't easy, because the company had cunningly set up a head-quarters in one province and the warehousing in another, so we needed to do two simultaneous raids in two different jurisdictions.' This, under Italian law, is no simple matter, but with the aid of a sympathetic local magistrate they were able to raid both addresses simultaneously.

The managing director of Pyramid International, his client and the police triumphantly marched into the warehouse – and found nothing. They searched the stock. It was all genuine. It had been a ghastly mistake. Confused, Warwick and his associates went outside for a walk and, this being Italy, a smoke. Looking at the building, he realized what the problem was: the inside walls didn't match the outside walls. The warehouse had a false inside wall to store the knockoffs, with a hidden door.

Alessandro Masetti, an attorney at Barzano & Zanardo in Rome, talks approvingly about stricter penalties for counterfeiters and a more streamlined process for court cases that have previously taken years, rather than months. There have been more new laws to improve prosecution in 2005 than in the previous 50 years, he says.

He also knows that Italian judges are also Italian consumers, and that means that knockoffs are part of their lives too. 'It's a political issue,' he warns. 'The judge may say "Hey, poor guy, it's better that he sells counterfeit on the streets than sells drugs."'

The dark side

Across Europe, the free movement of goods is proving a boon to the people on the street who sell knockoffs, and the people whose businesses supply them. The Union des Fabricants reports that we're suffering from 'the dark side of globalization' as criminal networks work across borders. 'Sometimes products are partly manufactured in one country, assembled in another, transported through a third one and eventually sold in a fourth,' says a report into the links between counterfeits and organized crime. The EU gives counterfeiters from the Far East a choice of hundreds of ports of entry for their products. Once inside the EU, they can reach their destination by road.

This means unlikely outposts of counterfeit gangs are popping up in European cities. Belgian police have discovered Albanian gangs in Antwerp, reselling counterfeit products from Asia. Italian street vendors in Paris are selling fake Canon cameras supplied from Italy. On 8 July 2002, when Spanish police arrested 37 people and seized 28,000 knockoff CDs as part of a crackdown on a Europe-wide counterfeiting ring, 12 were from Pakistan, 15 from Bangladesh, one was Chinese and seven were children from Pakistan and Bangladesh.[2]

Europe's not only getting more closely integrated; it's getting bigger. Since 1 May 2004, when 10 new states joined the Union, it has had a border area in which the knockoff economy is a matter of survival, for many an essential part of life: Poland.

The Wild East

In Warsaw, 693 miles north, 10 degrees colder, where the GDP per head is less than half that of Italy and unemployment more than double, counterfeiting has a different face to the chic markets of Bologna. When I told my Polish colleague that I was going to look for knockoffs at Warsaw's Stadium Market, she looked at me as if I had told her I was popping over to Chernobyl for a barn dance.

'Take a bodyguard,' she said, 'a Russian one.'

The Stadium Market, also known to locals as the Russian Market, is Europe's Wild East. Every morning the Stadion Dziesięciolecia, literal translation the 'Tenth Anniversary Stadium', hosts one of the world's odder flea markets. If you want to buy tear gas, a rifle, Russian army surplus, caviar, Russian dolls, extremely hard pornography, vodka in a plastic bottle, lots and lots of socks or some second-hand tubas, it's here. Rumour has it that, after the fall of Communism, there were some hardly used rocket launchers available, but they long ago sold out. Every day the stallholders set up around 6 am and try to make a living until lunchtime. Prices are not extravagant. At the military headgear stall my Russian army hat cost £3. I was the only customer.

Yet there's a steady trade for a more specialized group of vendors, most of whom don't even have stalls. Walk into the market and you notice groups of portly people hanging around. This in itself isn't odd: despite sub-zero temperatures, the market had plenty of people who weren't going anywhere fast. As you approach, they lean in, whispering the Polish for software, CD, DVD. They aren't hard to find, as groups hover by the entrances, positioned directly under large signs warning you not to buy or sell counterfeit goods. The Stadium Market is Poland's knockoff central: despite the efforts of the government, who repeatedly raided the market as a condition of entry to the EU in 2004, if you want a counterfeit watch, CD, DVD or software package these are the guys you need to know.

The location of the market and the persistence of the knockoff vendors tell you a lot about the reality of life in post-Communist Eastern Europe. If crumbling concrete had a value on the open market, then the Communists would have left a valuable legacy in the Stadion Dziesięciolecia. It was built in 1953 in 13 months using rubble from houses destroyed during the Warsaw Uprising in 1944, and in its pomp held 100,000 spectators, two-thirds of whom sat on wooden benches that surrounded the giant oval bowl. It had its own park and railway station. One day, the Poles hoped, it might be the centrepiece of a Warsaw Olympic Games.

The games never came and, after a life dedicated to staging Communist Party rallies and football matches, the decrepit stadium was abandoned in 1983, but rented in 1989 by a company called Damis, seeing an opportunity for some free trade. The Jarmark Europa market was born.

During the 1990s, the market flourished. It acted as a magnet for displaced traders from all over Eastern Europe: Poles were joined by Belorussians, Ukrainians, Kazakhs, Latvians – and, overwhelmingly, by the Russians. On their way out, the Russian army stopped to sell their excess inventory. More than 5,000 companies were registered with the crumbling stadium as their address, and the market became a magnet for the informal economy, where people sold whatever they could get their hands on to others who had little money to pay. In 2001, the Centralne Biuro Śledcze agency in Poland estimated that the market's turnover was 12 billion zlotys (approximately £2 billion). This compares with Polish government statistics for the same period, which only count legal trading, of 500 million zlotys, 24 times less.

Luckily I found a tourist site on the internet that had a guide for Westerners visiting the market, including helpful explanations: 'Ponieważ w wiekśzosci sa to rzeczy produkowane i sprzedawane nielegalnie, mówi sie o nich "lewe", na przyklad: "lewe programy" albo "lewe kompakty"' ('As most of these things are produced and sold illegally, they are called "bootlegs", for instance: "bootleg software" or "bootleg CDs".'). There was also a brief language tutorial for those of us who were in the market for 'lewe':

- Ile pan chce za ten kompakt? (How much do you want for this CD?)
- Dlaczego tak drogo? (Why is it so expensive?)
- Tyle pieniedzy za coś takiego? Chyba pani żartuje! (So much money for such a thing? You must be joking!)
- Kupilbym to, ale nie za tyle. (I'd buy it, but not for that much.)

However, counterfeit retailing being a service economy, most of the traders in the Stadium Market spoke English. This is a mystery, as its situation next to Warsaw's top street for murders tends to discourage visiting tourists.

You see why the loiterers all looked so fat when you show an interest in their product. Marta, almost spherical in her tight anorak, leads me down the steps, away from two bored-looking policemen, to crowd into a chilly corner by a small café. She's about 20 kilograms lighter than she looks at a distance, because four inside pockets conceal at least 120 DVDs, which she flicks quickly through. Around a half are currently in the cinema, or have just left. All the titles have English soundtracks, sometimes with two films on one disc.

The price? Thirty zlotys (£5) for three. Marta doesn't like doing business at the Stadium Market. 'I'm from Armenia,' she says. 'This is a shit place.'

Back in the market, another fatty taps me on the shoulder. As I turn round, he pulls his hand a few inches away from his jacket, holding two knockoff Omega watches, and opens the jacket enough to show me a mini jeweller's shop inside, with row upon row of heavyweight designer names.

A chilly Nigerian has set up an informal market stall. It's a tabletop with three of this season's Nike trainers on it, or at least extremely good approximations, at one-tenth the price of the genuine article. 'Don't worry,' he says, 'I got your size', nodding at two other people sitting 20 metres away, both holding bulging back bin liners.

In between the socks and rifles, the knockoffs are less exotic. Johnny Walker whisky isn't, I believe, generally packaged in plastic bottles, nor is it bright orange; but the labels, at least, looked genuine. Chanol Number 5 perfume sits next to two different knockoffs of Timotei shampoo, which at least spell the name correctly. Browsing at a stall selling nasty cheap Breitling, Seiko and Adidas watches, I'm joined by a bored-looking policeman, looking for his own souvenir.

Raiding the Russian Market has denuded it of its more exotic products, but the locals acknowledge you can't change a culture with a raid. 'We weren't a country for 100 years, and then we were under the Communists for another 40, so people got used to doing things without the help of the state,' says Michal Siciarek, a lawyer at Polish firm Taszczuk & Wspolnicy. 'My father was working illegally in Sweden, for example, and someone reported him, and you would, and he got deported. In Poland, that would never happen. No one would report anyone working illegally, and also no one would report anyone for selling counterfeit goods. That's going to take a generation to change.'

'We didn't have brand names, but we craved them. Crossing the border and going to West Germany was like visiting a funfair,' says Marek Lazewski, a trademark lawyer at S Lazewska & Son in Warsaw.

The result is that we still see the black market as entrepreneurial people. There's a perception that the black market acts against the state, so how bad can it be? We used to be a centrally planned economy. We were told what will be produced, how much will be made and what it would cost to the consumer. That's all decided for you. So in their minds there is no need to have anything called intellectual property.

Crossing borders

That should chill the hearts of anyone whose products might be found in the Russian Market. Poland is now the eastern frontier of Europe, and its border is the point of entry for knockoff goods, which once they find their way across the border can circulate more or less unfettered in a market of 450 million people. Poland has 407 kilometres of border with Belarus, 206 kilometres with Russia, 526 kilometres with Ukraine and, one customs expert commented, very unhappy customs employees. Before Poland acceded to the EU, the border guards were posted on the German border, in the more prosperous part of the country. Almost overnight, large numbers were transferred to the eastern border instead.

Charters MacDonald-Brown, who specializes in European intellectual property law for London-based Redd Solicitors, comments that the effect is 'an increased risk of fake products getting into the EU and then enjoying free circulation... a significant amount of counterfeit cosmetic products have been coming out of Poland and each year an estimated 200 million illegal CDs... In some software industry sectors, new fake products are available in Poland within weeks of release in the US.'[3]

Today in Europe the lowered trade barriers mean goods can travel uninspected from country to country – from the workshops of Italy to the retailers of Finland, from the eastern border of Poland to the street markets of Spain. We don't hang counterfeiters or chop off their hands; instead we give them the free run of a European market that has just expanded to include millions of people whose poverty makes the rest of the EU a promised land, and whose access to knockoffs gives them the perfect opportunity to exploit their new opportunities.

Whether the goods are supplied by organized criminals or opportunists, the frontier between them and us is manned by the international customs service. It's a frontier that's in imminent danger of being overrun.

Notes

1. Robert J Abalos (1985) Commercial trademark counterfeiting in the United States, the third world and beyond: American and international attempts to stem the tide, *Third World L J*, **5**, June, Boston College.
2. Union des Fabricants (2004) Counterfeiting and organized crime.
3. INTA Anticounterfeiting Forum (2005) Parallel imports: what lurks beneath the surface?

7 I thought I had seen everything

Michel Danet, Chevalier of the Legion of Honour, secretary-general of the 165-member World Customs Organization, flops into his chair in his office on the top floor of the WCO secretariat building on the Rue du Marché in Brussels, and makes a gesture that can only be called a Gallic shrug. 'I thought I knew everything about counterfeiting,' he says. 'I thought I had seen everything, and now they tell me that someone has counterfeited a petrol station.'

In fairness, Danet's 35 years of experience in French customs leading to his appointment as the world's top border cop in 1998 wouldn't have prepared him for this, unless someone had tried to smuggle one of the counterfeit petrol stations across the French border. The three that he is aware of were not going anywhere: two 'BP' stations in Bulgaria and Romania, and a rather less convincing 'BiPi' garage in Azerbaijan. But they weren't exactly hiding from the law either, as a petrol station only works when as many motorists can see it as possible. When counterfeiters are content to build monuments to their ability next to a main road in the hope that they get noticed, it vexes Danet, who is leading a body whose members inspect, record and approve 97 per cent of all international trade. The suspicion is that, whatever international customs does, however well it trains, however many seminars it holds, it is losing the battle against the tide of knockoffs.

It's war

The secretary-general isn't going down without a fight. 'Now we have to go to war,' Danet says.

> We don't know if we can eliminate counterfeiting, but as long as our society is driven by profit there will always be someone to sell it, and someone to buy it. In reality, our legal arsenal is weak. We should start by strengthening laws, but is this a government priority? Are the politicians interested? No, the police have too much to do already. So the people left to fight this are us, the customs officers.

And not all the customs officers either. We think of customs as the group of people who eyeball us as we guiltily walk through the 'nothing to declare' channel on the way back from holiday. In reality, a large, and for some countries economically vital, part of their job is collecting duty on goods that enter and leave the country. Looked at from that point of view, customs officers are primarily tax collectors.

That's a conflict of interest. If the priority is to collect duty, then the job of a border is to get as many goods through as quickly as possible. For example, at Roissy, where a large proportion of the counterfeits that reach France enter the country, the duty to look for those counterfeits conflicts with the need to serve the interests of business. 'The configuration of Roissy airport, where goods transit times are becoming shorter and shorter, is a plus for counterfeiters,' says Jean Bieche. He should know. He's the head of the customs targeting unit there.

Today, every land border, every port, every airport and every post office is a potential conduit for counterfeits. When 8.3 million general goods containers are shipped every year through the port of Rotterdam alone (and almost as many through Hamburg, Antwerp, Singapore, Bremen and tens of other major ports) and 1,300 customs officers work in the port, even if they ignored all the coal, crude oil, cement, scrap metal and other cargoes and searched for knockoffs they would still have to inspect 18 containers a shift. Inevitably, only about one in 30 containers is inspected.

Finding counterfeits might be easier if the officers making the inspections knew what they were looking for. 'There are 5,000 containers a day landing from China into Europe,' says Christophe Zimmermann, head of sector, Counterfeiting and Piracy, DG Taxud at the European Commission. 'We win by targeting the right ship-ments. Even if we had the strongest regulations, unless we know which shipments to check and which ones to pass we will never get the chance to use our regulations at all. We have to know who and what we are fighting.'

Any customs post that looks at random for illegal counterfeits isn't going to be very successful. Look at the hundreds of containers that are being unloaded from an inbound ship, and they all look more or less alike. So sharp-eyed customs officers look for telltales that the containers have been opened and their contents changed since they were loaded: locks that have been forced, labels that seem the wrong colour, adhesive tape that's a little off colour, indicating it's not from the country it claims to be from.

'We've got a huge collection of tapes in the office,' Zimmermann says. 'China is a different yellow to Korea.'

Problem two: you open the container and see a collection of bags, or shirts, or toothpaste. The documentation claims that they are bags, shirts or toothpaste, but how do you know if they are real? 'Only the manufacturer can say, "This pen is counterfeit", or at least tell us how to recognize a counterfeit pen,' Danet says. For a 50-year-old male customs officer in Hamburg who isn't trained in the subtle advantages of the Hermès Birkin bag, one criminally counterfeit Birkin looks very much like another genuine one – and the irony is that, the better the counterfeit, the less likely it is to be spotted on inspection. The customs officers have to know it's a knockoff before they look for it. If a pharmacist can't tell a fake Viagra from the real thing, how will a customs officer do it?

There are, however, many ways to outwit the inspection. The most obvious is to send 'blanks'. If Lacoste polo shirts are distributed without the little crocodile on the front, and the sew-on crocodiles are sent in the post, then the container looks like a pile of polo shirts and has to be let through on that basis.

That's why, worldwide, Danet's customs officers rely on inside information. To find knockoffs, they need to know where to look. To know them when they see them, they need to know what to look for, and every luxury goods, consumer goods, sportswear or shoe manu-facturer in the world has a constant staff hopping from port to airport to border patrol to instruct the customs officers in the finer points of stitching, logo and finish.

'It's the cost of doing business today,' says Joe Gioconda, the attorney at Kirkland & Ellis who protects Hermès products. 'What's the point in having rights on paper if you don't enforce them? So I go out and take the bags along and I sit in a room and I interview and train the agents. I sit down with cops and the customs, and I'll train them until they recognize the bags.'

He takes half a dozen bags, stills from films featuring the bags, for sessions that take up to six hours to explain the finer points of a small number of products. Perhaps the problem is that customs is still a male-dominated profession. 'The women agents have all definitely heard of the bags,' he says.

Problem three: you might disagree if you have ever had your bag searched, but looking for contraband isn't just a fishing expedition. To look for illicit products, customs has to know that there is a problem, and not everyone is facing up to it. For example, if you look at the EU figures for counterfeit seizures in 2004, there isn't even a category for counterfeit drugs. This doesn't mean that there are no counterfeit drugs coming into the EU. It just means that customs isn't looking for them.

Zimmermann puts the responsibility on Big Pharma, which he says is simply not cooperating with customs by supplying the documentation giving the officers the right to confiscate suspected counterfeits. 'It's not that we don't discover counterfeit medicines because they don't exist. We don't discover them because we don't have the application forms,' he says. 'We have 25 states in Europe, but there are less than 20 application forms filled so that the customs in those states know to watch for counterfeit medicines. It's a pity, because that means we can't stop the goods even if we have a doubt that they are genuine.' The result is that counterfeit medicines have a very low chance of being intercepted. In the UK, the world's keenest importer of counterfeit anti-impotence drugs, where 50 per cent of internet orders are fulfilled by a counterfeit, consumers are experiencing the flaccid results of this failure to enforce.

Problem four: if you can't get it in here, get it in somewhere else. Zimmermann shows some intercepted telexes from a counterfeiter who was trying to get his products into Europe, having shipped them through Bangkok, Hong Kong and Benin – the counterfeiter's port of choice on the route from Asia to Europe, where goods can be unloaded, reloaded and given documentation that makes the container seem less suspicious than if it was coming direct from Thailand. In Brussels, customs were checking incoming shipments that they suspected were bringing in the counterfeiter's goods – so he sent a last-minute message, and the captain rerouted through Zurich, where he could expect an easier passage.

Which leads us on to problem five: if you don't want your stuff to be found, you hide it. Zimmermann shows pictures of a petrol truck that customs inspected as it crossed a land border. The truck was full of counterfeit cigarettes. The neat flat-pack shape of 200 cigarettes also meant a shipment of lumber was more than it seemed – some of the wood had been hollowed out, like a giant coffin containing hundreds of packs.

'At 2 am in the morning, what can a customs officer do if he hasn't got any information about where to look?' Zimmermann says. It's also a favoured trick to bury the knockoffs under a layer of the genuine article: for example, a spindle of counterfeit CDs, with the top one looking like a blank CD ROM. Often, there's no way to tell them apart by the naked eye. 'If you're not smoking the cigarettes, you don't know if they are counterfeit or not. The packs are totally identical. When you start smoking, oh! then you realize,' Danet adds, presumably from bitter experience.

Under the surface

Some of the more bizarre schemes for outwitting customs are straight out of James Bond. In Hong Kong, where there are 500 officers assigned to rooting out counterfeiters, they were fortunate to find a shipment of CDs coming out of Macao in April 1999. With the authorities having discovered that the counterfeiters were sealing the CDs in oil drums and leaving them at the bottom of the sea for smugglers to pick up, the crime gang responsible raised the stakes. The Hong Kong authorities intercepted a fishing boat as it entered its waters, having set off from Macao. It was towing a submerged object. When it was floated, the authorities found a 14-metre concrete bridge support, which had been customized to become a disc smuggling submarine. In the centre compartment, HK \$5 million of counterfeit CDs. On each side, air pockets and ballast kept it submerged at a constant level. When the ship reached its destination, air was pumped into the pockets and it rose to the surface.

This all supposes that the local customs cares about catching counterfeits either leaving or entering their country, which raises another of Danet's shrugs.

> In poor countries, the priority is to fight poverty, and someone builds a factory. It's a good thing, whether or not it makes counterfeit goods, because it's a source of jobs. Who actually knows what's actually happening in the remote Chinese provinces? Beijing doesn't even know what is happening in the remote Chinese provinces. In France, every year the administration finds five or six officers are corrupt. These are usually individual cases. The same applies in Germany or the UK. When you find that their corruption is individual, it makes you realize that, overall, it's not a corrupt system. Customs reflects society. In other places, the society is corrupt, and the entire customs organization is corrupt too.

Or, it doesn't have the power to be corrupt:

> The difficulty in developing countries is that the customs organization is only 10 or 15 years old. You don't want to give too much power to an organization that hasn't proved its ability or loyalty yet. No one thinks the French customs can overthrow the government. In other countries, a strong customs can be a very scary thing for the government.

As with traffic wardens and undertakers, we only notice customs officers when there's bad news. Projecting a positive image for the job of confiscating products and collecting tax isn't the easiest job in the world, even if your local customs manages to resist the temptation to stage a coup.

'We recognize that we have to change minds and hearts,' says Will Robinson, policy adviser on security and facilitation at the WCO. 'In the third world there's not much political pressure to start looking for counterfeit.' Another customs officer says how much he hates the television stunts where confiscated goods are burned in a field as satisfied, wealthy businessmen look on approvingly: 'We are destroying goods when there are people who don't have anything – that's not a good image.' Those wealthy businessmen, if they want customs officers to impound goods that are counterfeiting their products, often have to pay for the cost of storing them. In a 2004 bust in Malta, 14 containers of counterfeits were seized, stored securely while they were investigated, and ultimately destroyed. The bill to Maltese customs: $129,000. In the developing world, there simply may not be the money, let alone the appetite, for anyone to seize the goods, whether the motivation is economic, political or simply the search for an easier life.

And yet the under-strength, overmatched customs officers are the true front line in a global war against criminals who may also fill their containers with heroin. Or illegally trafficked people – the one cargo that that is as lucrative as knockoffs.

The explosion of counterfeits, and their sophistication, means Danet is still getting nasty surprises after four decades in the job. 'I've got a friend who is the president of a company that manufactures luxury goods,' says Danet. 'Last week he was called by one of his old colleagues. This colleague was on holiday in China, and he says: "I'm overwhelmed by the beautiful shop you opened in Beijing. It's amazing. I'm standing outside it right now." And my friend says, "But we don't have a shop in Beijing."'

8 Where buyers and sellers meet

'I find out who they are, what they do, where they live, what car they drive, whether they live with their parents,' says Rob Holmes, 'and I identify every single one of them. Then I assess them personally, give the client a profile of exactly who they are. Some of my cases take six months, but I will find them sooner or later: that's my promise.'

Rob Holmes, one-time stand-up comedian, now a private investigator based in Hollywood, describes himself as an 'internet bounty hunter'. His crime scenes are on his desk all day every day, as long as he has his internet browser running. 'The average case takes three days,' he says. 'Half of the cases take a week or two weeks. Only 5 or 10 per cent are really elusive, but I get them all', he promises, 'eventually.'

For five years, his nemesis was a dealer in knockoff handbags he knew only as 'Janice', real name Win Yan Wong, real location Hong Kong. 'Her modus operandi was to let people order from a photo site hosted on Yahoo. The only place you could see her was as the owner of the photo album. I have been chasing her since 1999, and we arrested her at her home with her mother, who worked for her,' he says. 'She was one of the top 10 suppliers of counterfeits on the internet over the last five years. Her arrest has had a major impact on the industry: there's now a shortage of counterfeit handbags.'

Other hard nuts to crack have come from the Russian mob, strongest in the tri-state area around New York on the East Coast of the United States, and the Chinese and Arab communities. 'When you have names that are written in a different alphabet, then to put them into the Western alphabet they are transliterated. So the same name can be spelt lots of different ways, and suddenly the same person has three or four identities,' he says.

Holmes is tracking a new type of criminal engaged in a new type of international crime: using internet auction sites and bulletin boards to offer knockoffs for sale.

The global marketplace

If you have a warehouse of counterfeit luxury goods in the Far East, or Russia, or Italy, or Hollywood, you have a logistics problem. You need to find buyers, and you need to protect your identity from local law enforcement – and from your customers. You need to move your stock without it being spotted, and receive secure payment. At some time in the early 1990s, career counterfeiters might have sat in a bar, imagining how much easier their life would be if there was a global electronic communication system where consumers from San Francisco to Sydney could buy their products, and where they could hide behind assumed identities. If this global bazaar was really popular, then their criminal activity would be swamped by thousands of other messages, so only those in the know would know where to look for the knockoffs they wanted. If it worked really well, they could even use it to turn their best customers into wholesalers. It was just a shame that nothing like that existed.

Then, on 4 September 1995, eBay launched. It was swiftly followed by hundreds of other online auctions, bulletin boards and sale shops, and the knockoff globe shrank a little. Also, Holmes was in business. The first ever case of an elusive eBay counterfeiter who needed to be tracked down landed on his desk in the same year. He caught that one, too.

To quote eBay's trademark, it is 'The World's Online Marketplace'. You might be forgiven for thinking it was an auction site. According to eBay, it's not.

'Apparently there are no auction sites on the internet,' says Brian Brokate, an exasperated attorney at New York's Fifth Avenue firm of Gibney, Anthony & Flaherty LLP, the general counsel for Rolex in the US, and one of the leaders in the fight to make companies like eBay accountable for the fakes that are sold on their sites. 'Listen to eBay, and it doesn't call itself an online auction site,' he says. 'Apparently it's a "venue where buyers and sellers meet".'

It may seem like a fine distinction to you or me, but for eBay, or any one of thousands of sites offering goods for auction on the internet, it's fundamental to their business plan. That's why you will never hear an eBay employee describe his or her employer as an 'auction site', even though at any time 135 million members are offering prices in the auction of 40 million items, and posting around 3.5 million items a day. The legal difference is this: if you're a traditional auction house, you see what you are selling. It is in your possession when it is sold. You evaluate it and, if you sell a counterfeit, you take the legal liability once the mistake is spotted.

eBay never sees the goods it sells. It 'sees' the listings, in that they are visible on the site, but there isn't a very tired person at a desk in eBay headquarters in San Jose, California, vetting 40 listings a second before they are posted. In most cases, an auction is offered, conducted, settled and the goods are dispatched without eBay taking any action at all – apart from collecting its fee.

The legal basis for this is the US Digital Millennium Copyright Act, which offers immunity to websites if they don't know about copyright infringements on their sites and they act to take down the infringement as soon as they are informed of it. It's called 'notice and takedown', and it shifts the onus for policing the site to the companies whose products are being knocked off, which then have a choice: either commit time and resources to policing eBay, or let the knockoff auctions go on unchecked. Some commit to monitoring eBay. Others decide they haven't got the resources to commit.

If you want to sell knockoffs, this is obviously a tempting business model.

Trust and safety

'We are a platform for buyers and sellers to trade,' states Garreth Griffith, head of trust and safety at eBay UK, and obviously not about to describe his employer as an auction site, 'but the bottom line for us is that members who think eBay is just a bunch of fakes won't come back. We're pretty watertight these days.'

Griffith places his faith in a programme that eBay has been running since 1997, called the Verified Rights Owner Programme, or VeRO for short. eBay's very proud of VeRO – Griffith calls it a 'wonderful creation' – and it has undeniably been effective at cutting the number of fakes sold on the site.

VeRO asks the companies whose products are faked to spot those fakes when they are up for auction on the site. If you make designer jeans and someone posts an auction for what looks like a knockoff of your jeans, you get an alert, and can request to eBay that the auction is taken down. So if you want to sell some counterfeit goods on eBay, and you place an auction that either hints or states that they are not real – for example, describing something as a 'copy' – then the brand owner knows about it immediately.

The problem for vendors, 10,000 of whom help out with the VeRO programme, is that they do almost all the work and, for some, there's a lot of it. In August 2004, Tiffany launched a lawsuit against eBay, claiming that eBay got the benefit from vendors selling counterfeits. A crucial piece of its argument was that eBay had bought sponsored links on Google and Yahoo. That means that, if you did a web search for 'Tiffany jewellery', a link would pop up to guide you to eBay.

Tiffany's research showed that, when you got there, you wouldn't see a lot of Tiffany jewellery, but you would see a lot of knockoffs. It did a test-buy of 186 products claiming to be Tiffany. Of those, 73 per cent were fakes and 22 per cent fell in a grey area – for example, in real life they claimed to be 'Tiffany inspired', so weren't really counterfeit. Only 5 per cent, or one piece in 20, was genuine.

Tiffany had been a member of VeRO for five months in 2003. It had taken down 19,000 auctions, but had to pay two people to work full time at doing it.[1]

'Since they are making the money from it, the public is being defrauded by it and Tiffany is being damaged by it, the question is who should bear the burden of policing it,' James Swire, the lawyer representing Tiffany, told the Reuters News Agency.[2]

Brokate resents what he perceives as eBay refusing to take responsibility for the counterfeits sold under its name.

'Statistically, any sale on eBay of five items or more is 99 per cent likely to be counterfeit goods. You would think there would be some way you could hold eBay liable for trademark or copyright infringement. Well, you can't,' says Brokate. 'The ability for eBay to control the sale is there. The benefit to eBay is enormous. OK, it doesn't have a warehouse for its goods, but it might do for its money. eBay benefits enormously from the sale of counterfeit goods. Every trademark owner knows this is a huge problem and it's not stopping.'

eBay is extremely profitable: 147 million members trade $40 billion of goods every year. Its revenues are around $1 billion a quarter, and still growing steeply.

Figures like that make eBay bigger and more profitable than all but a few of the companies whose goods are knocked off by counterfeiters in the site's auctions. 'Because it created the market, it should bear the burden of the risk of selling the counterfeit goods offered,' says Anthony Keats, a partner at Keats McFarland & Wilson LLP, whose office is in Beverly Hills.

The problem for big brands is that it's a huge investment to stop people from buying knockoffs, which, if eBay didn't exist, the buyers would not have otherwise been able to find. Having created fertile ground for knockoffs, VeRO is taking down an auction every 20 seconds. Cunning listers know just enough to list in a way that won't trigger the automatic filters, or simply claim the product is real, before supplying the fake. eBay doesn't claim the system is perfect. (In a reversal of fortune, eBay has even been sued by eBay seller Michael Meddors after several of his auctions were incorrectly taken down under the VeRO rules. Meddors claimed VeRO was 'out of control'.[3])

Brett Healy, eBay's senior intellectual property counsel, defends his employer. 'It's not feasible for us to try and block items before they are listed. Likewise, we can't become experts in all products, trademarks, copyrights and patents of every rights owner on the globe,' he says. 'eBay is fundamentally committed to helping companies protect their IP. We know that counterfeiters can be crafty, and we have more than 50 employees dedicated to checking for infringing items ourselves.'

In Europe, Griffith has 'between two and 230 people' at any time looking into the fakes being sold on the site, and he promises that anyone who is a persistent offender gets their details passed to the police. 'The happiest days in my job are when someone emails me from the National Hi-Tech Crime Unit and says thank you,' he says.

'We want a floodlit internet highway with no dark alleys. On the other hand, we don't own the shops in our virtual mall. We simply rent out space. We can't grab someone in the restroom and arrest them. We want to have the police patrolling our mall.'

Healy adds that eBay makes a distinction between career counterfeiters and people selling one item, who aren't likely to get pinched in the virtual restroom: 'We think they may be well intentioned but misinformed. We think those people can be rehabilitated.' Try and sell one knockoff on eBay, and you get a polite tutorial by email, and a warning, and a note on your file. Try it again and again, and your career as an eBayer will be curtailed.

The problem for the companies that complain about eBay is that, even if counterfeiters are thrown off the world's largest online marketplace, there are plenty of smaller, less regulated ones that will take the business. That's where Holmes makes his business.

Anything goes?

eBay isn't the only place on the internet where buyers and sellers meet. What the others lack in scale, they more than make up for in permissiveness. On smaller auction sites, sorry, smaller trading platforms, on bulletin boards, on specialist websites, buyers and sellers have found plenty of dark alleys just off the internet highway.

'The guys know that they are better off going to smaller websites,' says Griffith. 'I don't want it to be the case, but it's true that what eBay has done is more likely just to drive them somewhere else.'

Holmes spends his days trawling the other places where buyers and sellers meet. He says:

> We see two types of online counterfeiter. One does it as a full-time job. They will never get out of the business. That's only 20 per cent of the sites I see. The other 80 per cent, it's just to supplement their income. Every weekend in every major city in the Western world, the 80 per cent are doing business. It's someone in your town. You aren't going to turn your own neighbour in to the law; it's the suburban mentality. You don't want someone from your street to get into trouble.

His promise to clients is: whether your counterfeiters are in the 20 or the 80 per cent, he will find them.

There's no shortage of work. A site like ioffer.com regularly carries offers to buy suspiciously cheap goods or set up business as a retailer in knockoffs.

'I pose as an unsuspecting customer,' he says. 'My investigators are busy making purchases, anything from one product to becoming an entire marketing scheme for counterfeits.'

Holmes worries about the numbers of part-time counterfeiters he sees who take the deals on offer, not knowing that their suppliers are often connected to Chinese gangs or the Russian mob.

> These are the places where people offer you the chance to set up as a retailer. You reply by email, and you get all the instructions you need. You might get just a few photos. Or you might get the chance to set up a site where you are shielded by a web hosting company, and you can trade anonymously. Your cash buys a starter kit, you get a catalogue and you're in business. If you live in the suburbs, you can easily get a side job selling counterfeits.

As a front for the counterfeiters, these suburban moms show their friends and neighbours the catalogue. They give her orders, which she can place. Or she can set up a small trading post on the internet, and take orders from anywhere.

On the internet, it's easy to hide your true identity and, as Holmes works undercover to try to trace the suppliers, he finds the best ones are always hidden.

> The average person would be able to find a way to contact the counterfeiter in about 25 per cent of the cases, but it costs $10 a year to be completely anonymous unless I get a subpoena to find out who you are. I find them through other sources. Every one of us has a back door into his or her life. It might be that the email address I captured at the time of purchase can tell me more. I can sometimes find out more about you if I know where you are from.
>
> The woman who sold me a handbag over the internet yesterday belongs to her local dog rescue centre. I can use that to find a number for her, and address.

Like a good gumshoe, the Holmes Detective Agency is in an unassuming brick building, rather than the shiny glass-and-steel towers favoured by the lawyers who get in touch when their attempts to track down internet counterfeiting rings backfire. It's hardly surprising their batting average is so low, Holmes explains.

Imagine you catch the eye of a company's IP lawyer, and suddenly there may be 20 people from the company who visit your site on the same day. You're going to ask yourself why 20 people from the same place visited you, and catch on pretty fast. Investigating by just visiting the site means you're leaving your fingerprints all over. So finding counterfeiters on the internet – the difference between me and the average investigator is that I know how to tiptoe. It's like the difference between a cat burglar and an amateur cat burglar.

VeRO might have pushed the knockoff problem underground, but not very far. The internet has made it almost too easy to flog fakes. If you were going to build an ideal place for buyers and sellers of counterfeit goods to meet, you couldn't have built a better one than the internet.

'eBay will always be a problem, because that's the nature of the market,' Holmes says, 'and the guys who are selling knockoffs on sites like eBay aren't stupid. They noticed that law enforcement and brand owners like to work nine-to-five weekdays, and so they think, "Why don't we start running auctions on a Saturday morning?" It's simple. That's what they've done, and that's why I have to work weekends these days.'

Notes

1. *Jewelers Circular Keystone*, 1 August 2004.
2. Reuters, 21 July 2004.
3. *AuctionBytes*, 12 July 2004.

9 War and peace

In 1994, Alexei (not his real name), disaffected by the chaos in the Russian military, retired from the KGB's counter-intelligence unit. Like many of his colleagues who left the service, he found a niche for his skills in Russia's nascent private sector, landing what he thought was a cushy job as security manager for the Russian office of a US sporting goods company. His first job: kick his employer's counterfeiters out of government-owned shops.

'The products were sold, openly, in every government department store,' he says.

> In 1995 we raided [the department store] GUM. Next thing I knew I was contacted by one of the big men in one of the criminal organizations. In his organization, he was the number two. He came to see me. There were three of them altogether, sitting in my office, and he said, 'Alexei, I understand that you have to do this, but those are our products you have taken. We had 200 items in that store. So this is what we will do in future: we will move all our products from the shops, and we will sell them in the flea markets instead. Then if you find any of your company's products in the shops, let us know, and we will find who is responsible.'

Alexei took the deal.

That bargain, struck when the Russian anti-counterfeiting laws were full of holes and the shops full of knockoffs, was the first time – but not the last – that Alexei had to strike a business deal rather than rely on the law. Today, as an independent anti-counterfeiting investigator working in Russia and the other states of the former Soviet Union, he has a simple way to interest the police, customs and prosecutors to enforce the law on behalf of his US and British clients. He bribes them, often $10,000 or more, and hides the cost of the backhanders in his fee under a 'don't-ask-don't-tell' arrangement with his Western employers. 'They don't know exactly where the money I spend goes,' he says, 'but then again they don't ask that question very often.'

'How much it will cost us depends on how clever the police are, how greedy they are and how high up in the organization you have to go,' he says. 'I don't like it, but if the police do something for you and you don't give them something back they will never do anything for you ever again, and they will tell others too, and they won't help either.'

Money talks

The reality of counterfeit investigations in the former Soviet states is that the highest bidder usually wins, which is bad for Alexei, because he's working to a budget. He is in a lop-sided bidding war: on his side, the anti-counterfeiting budget of the manufacturers who often resist investing too much in regions like Russia, where profits are low; on the other side, the almost unlimited resources of Russian criminal gangs with exotic names like Complex 29 and The Naumovites, or of their shell companies, who ship and sell knockoffs as a way to launder drug or kidnapping money.

'You're a counterfeiter, and you make jeans. To do this, you have invested at least $500,000 to set up the manufacturing and the imports,' says Alexei.

> How much will the company being counterfeited pay for my investigation? Perhaps $50,000, if I am lucky. Even if we give the police $10,000 of that, the counterfeiter will have a minimum of $50,000 put aside for the police. Now most of the police are honest, so the first group he approaches might not take the $50,000, but when you have that much money you will always find someone crooked enough, sometimes in the prosecutor's office, to take it in the end. You only need one group of people connected with the case to take the money, and your criminal problem goes away.

If you are a counterfeiter, it is money well spent. When the prosecutor or the police lose interest in a criminal case, the worst that can happen to a counterfeiter is losing one consignment of stock and paying a fine. The fine is 500 roubles. That's $19.

In a speech to the Russian parliament in March 2005, Interior Minister Rashid Nurgaliyev described the extent of Russia's organized crime network and the extent of its commercial influence:

> Seeking to gain additional revenues, the criminal communities are actively spreading their influence beyond the national borders, having set up financial and economic bridgeheads in more than 40 foreign countries. Simultaneously, foreign mafia organizations are intensively penetrating the Russian market. At present 116 criminal groups are active on Russian territory. They have interregional and international links and they have more than 4,000 active members. They control at least 500 major economic entities.

In 2004 Russia's Federal Financial Task Force stopped 2,000 instances of money laundering. On average, the Russian police uncover two organized crime networks a day. The government claims that, in 2004, the Interior Ministry prevented 12,000 'economic crimes' funded by organized crime, 85 per cent of which were classified as 'serious' or 'very serious'.

Where are the good guys?

It's a convenient fiction that fighting organized crime is a simple matter of cops and robbers, good guys against bad guys, where the good guys are easy to identify because they wear uniforms. In reality, the financial rewards of the knockoff economy blur the boundaries between the two. For example, imported counterfeits are rarely discovered on their way into the country by honest inspectors: Russian law doesn't allow customs officers to seize products ex officio simply because they suspect counterfeiting, as would routinely happen in Europe and the US, and so there is always a reason to let a shipment pass. Alexei wearily says:

> Unless we look after them, customs officers do nothing, because every day they see 10 trucks from the same criminal importer, who pays

them cash to make a decision inside the hour. They are interested in the business he gives them, so do you think they will notice the counterfeits in his trucks? I don't think so. In my experience, in 70 per cent of cases, even when customs find counterfeits, they never tell the police or the prosecutor. They just give the product to someone who can sell it and earn the money for themselves.

No prizes for guessing who can sell counterfeit products: the same people from whom they were confiscated.

Alexei explains that, even if they are told to look for product, the customs service often won't find counterfeits because the counterfeiters know how to work around the law so that the paperwork doesn't raise suspicion.

'You want to bring counterfeit into Russia to sell it,' says Alexei,

so you go to Istanbul to buy. You purchase the goods and ship them by land using a cargo company. There are no containers going by sea, no invoices to hide, no description of the goods on the paperwork.

You have a partner cargo company in Istanbul who ships for you. The manufacturer in Turkey packs them up for you. The cargo company picks them up from the manufacturer, and mixes them with another customer's product in a truck, and sends it to Moscow. The trucks belong to the cargo company, it has good connections with several customs posts and it pays them to look the other way. The customs stamps the form and releases the product.

In Russia, the entire consignment, which often mixes goods imported on behalf of several criminal gangs, is sold to a shell company set up by the cargo company. The shell company splits the consignment according to which gang owns it, and 'sells' the consignments to other shell companies set up by the counterfeiters who bought the product in Istanbul, whose name is on no documentation at all. Because the importation forms never mention the goods by name either, the paper trail is vague enough to disguise what the products are, who bought them and who received what at the Russian end. By now, it's a matter for the police, as the goods are inside the country.

From Alexei's point of view, the police are little better. Two months ago, he raided a warehouse in a joint operation with the police, and the police seized 11,000 counterfeits. The evidence was tagged, logged and passed to the prosecutors who were taking the case to trial. The week before we met, Alexei had found out that the entire warehouseful of evidence had unaccountably gone missing. Case dismissed.

The corruption that follows counterfeiting stretches as far as the company's own staff in some of Moscow's brand-name *prêt-à-porter* boutiques, which Alexei has investigated when working undercover.

> They don't order the quantity they can sell. They order 30 per cent of the quantity. The other 70 per cent they make as counterfeits to sell as the real product in the shop, and it costs them much less; they employ people to make the counterfeit product to order. I know two people, one in Turkey, one in China, whose job this is.

The in-house counterfeiters rely, he says, on the disinclination of the fashion houses to look too closely at what is going on outside Europe and the US. Meanwhile the knockoff traders at infamous counterfeit markets like the Yabao Lu market in Beijing speak fluent Russian to every white face, despite the rarity of Russian tourists in China.

Alexei's decade in the private sector has disillusioned him about the corruption that's endemic in the Russian version of capitalism.

> It's my Soviet education. My parents were Communists. My father was a party boss for his district. I was a party member for some time, and I still have my Communist Party card at home. I don't like people who are involved in corrupt trade, and what Gorbachev and Yeltsin did to Russia I don't like either. At least in the old days the authorities had great power, that was lost, and we didn't have such corruption, such a gap between rich and poor.

Ultimately, he adds, the state is in collusion with the gangsters, even if it protests otherwise. 'Why is a customs officer paid such a small amount of money in our society? If everything is done legally, the officials would have nothing, so every government post is a way to enrich yourself.'

Not every country has the corruption problem that Russia experiences today; but it is far from unique. Transparency International (TI), a non-profit organization that provides a yearly report ranking countries by how corrupt they are for business, ranks Russia 90th out of 146 in its 2004 report, noting President Putin's campaign against corruption and the March 2004 decision to raise civil service salaries, adding drily that 'public opinion remains sceptical this will be effective'. There is also a presidential commission in Russia with the remit to find the causes of corruption – but TI reports that it hasn't actually met yet.

When governments allow corruption to fester, it is left to the companies that suffer to protect themselves. They may twist the arms or cross the palms of the counterfeiters and the local government, using whatever means they are prepared to employ. While few would boast about breaking the law, Alexei's existence is proof that some are prepared to pay a third party to do it.

As well as its higher budget, organized crime has another advantage in a business negotiation: it can use violence and intimidation, because that's not against the rules in its business. When companies take on criminals without involving the law, then that violence may one day be turned on them. One executive whom I contacted to talk about how his company fights organized criminal counterfeiters refused to let me use his name or even his company's line of business. 'I was a federal prosecutor in New York dealing with organized crime and I never feared for my safety. Now I don't have a government behind me, and I absolutely do fear for it,' he told me.

When I asked him for proof, he emailed me a picture. It was of a counterfeiter he had been tracking in Bulgaria. At least, it was most of him. The previous month, a rival counterfeiting gang had caught up with him and blown his head off with a shotgun.

Tough Love

While bribery and corruption are the dark side of civil anti-counterfeiting, using business as an incentive can prove to be remarkably effective in rehabilitating counterfeiters. It depends on the motivation of the fakers – and what you have got to offer to satisfy their needs. Greg Rogers worked as Vice-President for Home Entertainment at Walt Disney Co's South-East Asian subsidiary in the early 1990s. When Disney arrived in the Far East, it discovered that its fame had preceded it, as Mickey, Donald and friends were already widely counterfeited throughout the region. The scale and the organization of the counterfeiting – and its links with the state – gave Disney's executives a problem they had never previously faced. Rogers explained:

In some cases in China, it was a nationally organized entity. The Chinese army owned factories for a long time, and I don't know who knew exactly what was being made there, but we all knew the factories were heavily involved in counterfeiting. And the Chinese government knows where its power lies, so it's not exactly going to go against the wishes of its own army. We became aware of the counterfeiting, and we also became aware of the fact that intellectual property wasn't understood by the counterfeiters. For them it was just a business opportunity. They saw that the cost of raw materials was $10 and our product sold for $300.

Disney is accustomed to playing hardball with its intellectual property. You misappropriate Mickey at your peril. In 1998, Disney had successfully lobbied Congress to pass the Sonny Bono Copyright Term Extension Act, which extended copyright on their creations for companies from 75 to 95 years. For Disney, those rights would have expired in 2004. The 20-year extension will be worth many billions of dollars to Disney. And nine years earlier, in 1989, Disney had turned its ire, and its lawyers, on three day-care centres in Hallandale, Florida that had painted pictures of its cartoon figures on the walls. On 3 August, the Associated Press reported the heart-rending tale of five-year-old Wayne Allen, who cried as Mickey and Minnie were whitewashed at the Temple Messianique day-care centre. 'I don't want Mickey to go away,' he had sobbed. 'I will miss him so much.' Warner Bros stepped in, and painted Yogi Bear and Bugs Bunny on the walls instead. Warner Bros won the publicity battle, but Disney was fighting a bigger war: no one messes with Mickey.

Disney didn't want China flooded with fake Mickeys, but it certainly didn't want Yogis of any type to replace him in the affections of the 290 million Chinese children under 14. The priority wasn't to stamp out all Disney production; it was to license it effectively.

'When we opened the Asia office, we were confronted by the same problem every single day,' Rogers recalls. 'If we took one business out by raiding the premises, that business simply transferred to someone else's name. The new business would be in the same town. Often it would be in the same square mile. We realized that it's not just about taking something out of a market; you have to put something back.'

Disney didn't start offering bribes – it offered incentives. Like its mouse, the company had big ears, and it listened to what the counterfeiters and the government wanted. The counterfeiters often weren't career criminals: they wanted to earn a living. The government wanted foreign investment.

'We took the view that, if we could convince existing counterfeiters to be licensees and bring the quality of their goods up to Disney standard, that was the only way we could make a difference,' says Rogers. This had a neat spin-off: the ex-counterfeiters policed the counterfeiters better than the police policed the counterfeiters, and regulated the situation without the authorities getting involved. 'If we successfully recruited an ex-counterfeiter, then he wouldn't let another counterfeiter open on his patch,' Rogers said. He calls the strategy the 'Tough Love approach'.

Tough Love worked with the government too: Disney could get the attention of the authorities, because it could offer something the government dearly wanted – the right to build a Disney theme park. 'We said, "We would love to open a theme park in your country, but we can't until you have sorted our problems out",' Rogers says. 'And so the answer comes; it just takes a very long time. Disney had the advantage that it was a highly recognized brand. Everyone knows Mickey and Donald. Not everyone knows Cartier watches. The scale of what Disney brings to the table helped concentrate their minds.'

Later Disney could open its Beijing office, which was responsible for on-site visits to approve manufacturing and monitor working conditions. In September 2005, Hong Kong Disneyland opens on Lantau Island. There's another Disney theme park planned for Shanghai in 2010. Disney has 1,000 stores and concessions across China, and the government got its theme parks. Like a Disney story, it has a happy ending, but Rogers remembers some very un-Disney scenes along the way. 'It was like a bad movie, like *Scarface*. You're in an empty warehouse somewhere in China with three burly guys, and you're talking about Disney towels, trying to convince them there's no future for them in counterfeiting. Luckily in China, everyone just wants to do business.'

Closing the deal

Selling a proposition is also what makes private undercover investigations work. Randall Rabenold, a director of North Carolina-based investigator Vaudra Ltd, found that, when he became an undercover counterfeiting investigator, it wasn't his career in the US Secret Service ('a lot of boredom, a lot of politics') that suited him to the job – it was his subsequent experience as a salesman. 'Everything ultimately comes down to their greed. If you convince them that you have money for them, then you've got their attention,' he says. His job has led him into situations where he poses as a buyer anywhere in the world. He has had to slip out of Korea under an assumed name on behalf of his employers, he has used their money to make down payments of shipments of counterfeits so they can see the goods, and he's ended up in situations where Secret Service training has been useful after all.

> I always remember my police training. Always let someone know where you are and stand by the door. In the Secret Service, we were told to watch their hands. It's what's in their hands that can kill you, so you keep your eyes open and never drop your guard. I've sat around the kerosene heater in Korea, all three of us smoking, talking, cussing a little, waiting for when that black limo draws up.

Rabenold's experience in dealing with big-time criminals has shown him the difference between the theory of dealing with counterfeiters and the harsh reality.

> We will never pay anyone to conduct a seizure, but what you find is the most successful programmes in many countries where there is a lot of counterfeiting are naturally the ones that involve payment. We don't get in that area. Other companies may do it creatively, with computers and fax machines to move the money, but they do it. I go to government legal seminars, and they all seem to be saying the right stuff about stamping out corruption and moving in the right direction, and then I talk to my friends in those regions. They tell me, 'Randy, it's all bullshit.' It's frustrating, because I'm usually talking to them because I am working for a brand owner who has just dumped a ton of money somewhere like Russia.

The long-term failure of the authorities to prioritize the fight against counterfeiting in many parts of the world – and, while Russia and China are the most obvious examples, TI's research shows they are far from unique – pushes the onus to deal with counterfeiters back on to commercial companies, which are faced with entrenched corruption and official tolerance of large-scale criminality. When companies like Disney have something the government or the counterfeiters want, it can change the situation – the counterfeiters are brought into the legitimate economy, or the government suddenly rediscovers its political will to enforce its own laws. But entities like the Russian criminal gangs, who exist almost completely above the law, aren't very susceptible to incentives and, if you recruit them, they might not make the most reliable business partners.

In that case, the manufacturers and the gangs are simply engaged in a nasty trade war, and the weapons are purely financial; raids are about confiscations and petty fines, not criminal prosecutions, and profit margins are so great for counterfeiters that these actions aren't much more than mosquito bites. The criminals are better armed and able to use violence and intimidation. Also, manufacturers aren't in it to reduce counterfeiting: just to reduce the amount of their product that is counterfeited.

The best a manufacturer can achieve is often that its counterfeiting problem simply goes away for a while, because it has made itself enough of a nuisance that the much-bitten counterfeiters start to knock off the manufacturer's competitors instead for a few months. It's often tempting for companies that can't get police support to put the whole problem of knockoffs into the too-hard basket and just abandon a region to counterfeiters.

In Moscow, even some companies that are superficially committed to cracking down on counterfeits have long since given up on being able to make a difference without the full-blooded support of the police. 'It is frustrating, because many Western companies don't want the public to know that their products are being counterfeited, in case the public panics and doesn't buy their goods any more,' says Olga Barranikova, the Russia representative for the Coalition for Intellectual Property Rights, which works in the former Soviet states on behalf of many Western companies. Sometimes the Russian office is more interested in not creating problems at headquarters than fixing an insoluble problem in Moscow.

> I know some of the investigators who prepare the counterfeiting figures for several big companies in Moscow. They don't go out and check; they just put a figure down. They know the local managers aren't interested in fighting counterfeits; they are interested in reporting to their bosses. They say, 'Let's not make the decline too steep or they won't employ us any more.'

They tend to settle for a figure, she says, of around 10 per cent reduction a year, whatever is really happening on the street.

Russia has been attempting to join the 148 countries in the World Trade Association since the mid-1990s, and much of the government's motivation for cleaning up corruption and pursuing counterfeiters has come from its desire to sweeten the WTO. But with several ex-Soviet states – already WTO members – as examples, Barranikova thinks this charm offensive will make little ultimate difference.

> After we join the WTO, I am afraid we will forget about IP. Take the example of Moldova. They joined in July 2001, and afterwards they have done almost nothing to enforce IP. It's a political show. The WTO should do much more for countries like us, but I am not sure they care. They come, they organize workshops for a day and they disappear again.

In Moscow, organized crime is probably not cowering in fear of a workshop.

The problem when the state and intergovernmental bodies consider counterfeiting as solely a commercial crime is that it leaves the companies affected to rely on commercial solutions. Those solutions often don't work if there's a stronger commercial incentive to break the law.

Also, enforcing the law is commercialized too. Justice is sold to the highest bidder.

The knockoff economy creates a culture of lip-service to the law, while money laundering, bribery and corruption take root just below the surface. If this goes unchecked, sweeteners become the way things get achieved, and the people who pay best are effectively above the law.

Then someone gets his head blown off, and we realize it's not just about money after all, and we do have to draw a line somewhere.

Alexei defends his role in the ad hoc privatization of justice in Moscow: 'I say: a bad peace is better than a good war.' But when the going rate for getting the police to do their job starts at $10,000, how bad has the peace become?

PART 3

You can't compete with free

10 Illusions

Where School Road meets Aga Khan Road in the dry heat of Islamabad, Pakistan, you find the Super Market shopping centre, a luxurious Western-style mall combining electronics shops, clothes and food shops – and in Block E there's Illusions, a brightly lit video and DVD retailer that you would find in any main street in Los Angeles, New York, London or Paris. It has some differences: for example, staff are proud to boast that, whatever you want, new or old, they can get it in a week. And prices are keen: the local equivalent of $3 or less for any film, even the blockbusters that would cost $20 in the US or £15 in the UK.

Some of the new titles are extremely new: films that are still unavailable in Europe on DVD are old stock here. The most popular items on sale have reached the shelves in Pakistan before they reached cinema screens outside the US. Some have barely opened in LA and New York. That is because Illusions is well named: the store – as in many similar stores across Asia, South America and Africa – contains many examples of fakes, illegal copies, perfect in every detail, thanks to digital copying technology that means it is identical to the master.

The one difference is that the regional protection – which stops DVDs intended for Asia being used in the United States or Europe – is missing. Illusions is an international business. The staff know which DVD will play in which region, because its customers need to know: many of them pop across the road from the adjacent diplomatic compound, home of the British High Commission and the US Embassy.

Even at its prices, Illusions is still pricey for the average Pakistani. Wages in Pakistan average $470 per year, so Illusions is selling to an affluent middle and upper class and the expats who live nearby.

Illusions is just one small cog in a giant machine. It's part of a massive global business that in many countries has proved too powerful for any rival. It's not surprising. Illusions gets its product before its rivals, it has lower prices and never has a shortage of supply. Its suppliers can always supply the top titles at bargain prices. It always makes a profit, no matter how low competition drives the prices.

That's because Illusions sells knockoffs. If counterfeiters have created a knockoff economy, then digital content piracy is its ultimate expression.

The content crisis

Digital piracy is all about knocking off what the middle managers in the entertainment industry call 'content', but what we think of as our favourite bands, or the computer game for which we have been waiting for months, or that actor we hate, or that bloody noise, or you-must-see-it-it's-unbelievable.

Today, because films on DVDs, computer games, software and music on a CD are all stored as sequences of bits and bytes, copying of 'content' is easier than it has ever been. Put simply, if you transfer all the bits and bytes accurately in the same order, you will end up with the film, music or software as well. It doesn't just look or sound the same; it actually is the same, identical in every way to the original.

The entertainment and software business today relies on this for its success: it has created a global network of ways in which to copy content and make it available. CD and DVD pressing plants are in every industrialized country to duplicate every type of content in every language. Global information networks are geared to sending and receiving the same content. Digital satellite and cable television uses the same principle.

Counterfeiters or, as they are rather dashingly known in the content business, 'pirates' know this too. Music, films, software and games can be copied, packaged and transported in hours, not weeks. Pirate copies of films are routinely on the market before the original is out of the cinema, and sometimes before the original is in the cinema.

In 2001, actor Dennis Hopper flew to Shanghai to film the TV series *Flatland* immediately after finishing adding his voice track to his previous film. Two days later, he saw a pirate copy of the same film – at that time nowhere near a commercial release – on sale in a street market. He bought it and found that the voice track he had recorded less than a week previously was already on the pirate copy. If you had wanted to see the Bond film *Die Another Day* early, you should have moved to South-East Asia. It was released in commercial theatres on 22 November 2002 – one day after the pirate DVD went on sale in Malaysia.[1]

Illusions is in the middle of a region with 50 per cent of the world's optical disc plants. In Pakistan, 58 per cent of discs are pirated. Its disc pressing plants created 180 million discs in 2003, 50 per cent more than in 2002. The domestic market would buy 20 million of these. 'In 2003, the average monthly export of optical discs from Pakistan was 13 million discs, a quantity exceeding the demand of many developed music markets,' says the International Federation of the Phonographic Industry (IFPI).

The myth is that counterfeiting is just a Hollywood problem. To be honest, we don't really care about the fortunes of Sony. But it's the smaller studios and record companies that hurt more, because they have less power to hit back. In India, the world's second-largest film production centre, knockoffs are hurting Bollywood too – in fact, the impact is financially more dramatic there, where the domestic release of a film can be killed by widespread piracy before the release date. India's excellent internet connections and growing global trade mean that the international release of a film can also flop when pirate copies are uploaded to the internet or simply emailed out of the country.

In September 2003, upcoming director Kaizad Gustad was surprised that he could see his Bollywood film *Boom*, one of the most hyped releases of the year, on cable television in Hyderabad and Mumbai, or hire it for 60 rupees at the Mira market in Mumbai. This was surprising because in September 2003 he hadn't even finished making it.[2] The pirate copy was a 'rough cut' that had been stolen from the office of the film's producer, and which everyone agreed made no sense. It still didn't stop thousands renting it, most of whom will never see the finished version.

Yash Chopra, chairman of the entertainment committee of the Federation of Indian Chambers of Commerce, has a solution: 'We have launched a movement and have decided to form our own anti-piracy squads, as the government has said that it does not have the force to fight piracy,' he says.[3] Chopra's answer to rampant piracy was a levy: everyone in the film industry paid by making a 1 per cent donation from their earnings, from the star actors to the most junior members of the crew.

Lavinia Carey, chair of the Alliance Against Counterfeiting and Piracy (AACP), finds laughable the idea that piracy hurts Hollywood most. If the counterfeiters carry on at this level of success, she says, 'the Hollywood studios will last the longest, so even in the short term we're poorer for it, because there will just be less choice. Wherever you are in the world, your local industry won't be able to afford to make movies.'

The rewards of piracy have attracted some nasty customers, as we will see. 'In 2002 there was a raid in Malaysia, and the investigators didn't carry weapons. As they left the premises, the counterfeiters chased after them and beat them up,' says Tim Trainer, the president of the International AntiCounterfeiting Coalition (IACC). Also in 2002 the Malaysian Minister for Domestic Trade and Consumer Affairs reported that his life had been threatened. The president of one of the municipal councils had a similar death threat. If that didn't get his attention, the pirates promised to rape his daughter as well.

Pirates ahoy

Piracy is several types of counterfeiting under one name. Large-scale commercial production, small-time garage industries and secretive internet-based gangs all produce the raw material. Small shops and market traders sell it. It all adds up to a massive headache for the industry.

The main problem is that we don't perceive the value in the content that the industry wants us to pay: the explosive growth in illegal file sharing over the internet demonstrates this. On the internet today there are 870 million illegal music files. In the developed world, the IFPI reports that CD sales are down 22 per cent in five years – around the time that downloading has become popular; Forrester Research concluded in 2004 that 36 per cent of downloaders buy less music as a result. In the UK, one in five people download illegally.

Whose fault is this? Many would blame the industry's sluggish response to the download craze. It took several years to create legal, paid-for services; now they exist, a generation has become used to the idea that music can be theirs cheaply, whether they get it online or whether they buy knockoffs at a market.

For many years, the software business has had to fight similar levels of counterfeiting, as have games developers. The music business points out that 15 per cent of its revenues go into finding new talent, which is three times what Microsoft, for example, would invest in R&D.

If the problems in the developed world are tricky to solve, they are mostly based around consumer behaviour: if we suddenly started to care, the counterfeits would disappear too. In the developing world, where earnings and disposable incomes are lower, there is another problem: price.

A silent spring in Hanoi

At the IACC, Trainer has no sympathy for the authorities in poorer countries who demand low-priced CDs and DVDs for their own markets. The problem, he says, is that those discs will simply be reimported to higher-priced markets. It would make the damage done by counterfeiting seem minor by comparison. 'I was talking to a judge in Cambodia, and she says, "Lower the price of your goods. We can't afford them. Give us a break and there won't be as much counterfeiting",' he says, 'but I said to her, it has to be a trade-off. I can't do "I lower my price and you do nothing". So what are you going to do to really make a difference to the level of counterfeiting? The fact was, she had no answer, and that's why nothing is happening.'

Others disagree. Bruce Lehman, the chairman of the International Intellectual Property Institute, and the US Assistant Secretary of Commerce from 1993 to 1998, thinks it is the music business that is living in an illusion. He says:

We were working in Vietnam to investigate how much of music is pirated. All the local shopkeepers admitted that they stocked pirated discs. They told me: you just can't get legitimate recordings here. Go to Hanoi, and there are music stores everywhere selling albums that come out of China for $1 apiece. It's a highly organized business. If the US government forced Vietnam to stick to the letter of the law, it would be a silent spring in Hanoi, and the reason is that the industry hasn't bothered to set up an alternative. You have to set up a market for a market to function.

His argument: until the industry invests in setting up alternatives to the pirates that use broadly similar outlets and price points, digital piracy is never going away.

If you tell the local people in Hanoi that they can have all the CDs they want for $15 a crack, you would need your head examined, so you have to develop a price model that offers different prices in different countries. That's not going to be easy for the record companies – but, until they come up with an alternative, they are crying wolf, because they are never going to fix the problem.

At the AACP, Carey's spectacularly messy London office is buried in counterfeit goods, like a metaphor for her business. She shows off some of the knockoff videos she has received from her investigators. On the back of the packaging the pirates have printed little messages to the companies the pirates are ripping off. 'Piracy does not support terrorism', says one. 'Piracy creates jobs', says another. She also has doubts about the commitment of some companies that should be helping in the fight against digital piracy. As she sees it, some companies are sticking their heads in the sand. 'For me, it's warfare. I don't care,' she says. 'But I am surprised at how little money is invested by companies who have major brands to protect, how little they invest in lobbying government, how little value they see in their brands that they don't put resources into protecting them. It's almost like they're not hurting enough yet.'

When you see the scale of the global manufacturing business for knockoff CDs and DVDs, you wonder how much 'enough' could possibly be.

Notes

1. Testimony of Jack Valenti to US House of Representatives, 13 March 2003.
2. *India New England News*, 15 September 2003.
3. *Khaleej Times*, 9 October 2002.

11 Lifting the stone

TZ hands me a CD of Whitney Houston's 'Greatest Hits'. 'This was bought from a record shop in central London,' he says. It's a fake, but one of the best the forensics lab at the IFPI – the trade body that represents the recording industry internationally – has ever seen. 'See how we found it?' he asks, pointing to a small blue sticker on the front, listing the hits on the disc, promising '&4 new songs'.

'That's it,' he says. 'There's no gap between the "&" sign and the "4". This has the booklet, it has a sticker on the front – it's identical right down to the codes embedded on the disc.'

The IFPI's secure forensics lab sees new counterfeit CDs every day, bought by members in markets, shops, bazaars and bars and on the streets in every country where the IFPI has members. Most are poor copies. Some don't even pretend to be the real thing, and are curiosities, mostly interesting as clues as to which gangs are supplying which region this week.

On the other hand, some are virtually perfect. Whoever made the copy of Whitney Houston's 'Greatest Hits' wasn't trying to supply a country that had limited access to the real thing; the production costs of typesetting and printing the insert, the disc, even a direct mail reply card, are many times the cost of a simple knockoff. The printing, the packaging, the disc are, to the naked eye, indistinguishable from the genuine product. Some counterfeiters would have cut costs by scanning the little sticker on the front and reprinting it, but a sticker made using that short cut looks a little blurry when sitting on the shelves next to the real thing. These forgers had typeset their own stickers, using the same font, carefully matching the colours. Hours of painstaking forgery had been undone by one typographical error, a single missing space.

A hidden problem

We simply don't know how many of the CDs on the racks in your local music shop are counterfeit, because when they are of this quality there's no way to tell using the naked eye – though, because of the cost of manufacturing a counterfeit to this standard and the difficulty of getting it into a large retailer that buys from a few well-known distributors, it is probably relatively few. With the easy pickings available when you sell obvious knockoffs in a local market, few criminal gangs will have the patience or the facilities to ape these forgers. On the other hand, provided you can sneak the counterfeit discs into the supply chain, making identical copies is a high-reward business model. 'They are businesspeople, after all, and professional counterfeiters will go to the best people possible. You can sell 5,000 discs at £1 each, but it's much better to sell 1,000 at £10 each. It's a matter of profit,' says TZ.

TZ doesn't want to give his name or much background as to how he came to work in his locked laboratory, surrounded by probably the world's most extensive and certainly the world's best-quality collection of counterfeit CDs. The lab has been working for five years, part of an initiative to match the increasing sophistication of counterfeiters and their ability to manufacture in one country and distribute across the entire world. Counterfeit discs manufactured in 35 countries have been identified at the lab so far, none created in the back streets or on home computers. These discs started life in CD manufacturing plants; it's TZ's job to work out which one, using telltale evidence that will lead the IFPI's investigators back to the businesspeople responsible.

His tools: a microscope and a box of legitimate discs, sorted by country of origin. 'It's similar to ballistics, matching a bullet,' he explains, focusing on the surface of one of the thousands of counterfeits he has been sent. In fact, it's better than matching a bullet, thanks to the precision of the CD manufacturing process.

Every commercially produced compact disc, or DVD, has the same basic structure. Unlike a CD burned in a home computer, every disc is moulded in an industrial CD pressing machine using a template called a 'stamper', in a process that takes 3.5 seconds. The stamper is the pattern of bumps and dents – 'pits' and 'lands' in CD pressing jargon – that a laser in your CD player bounces off to create the signal that a CD player turns into music. It's the same on a DVD, although the pits and lands are smaller – so there are more on a disc, and more data can be stored.

The stamper is placed inside the mould into which the machine squirts liquid polycarbonate plastic, at a temperature between 300 and 400 degrees Celsius. Immediately, cold water is flushed over the mould to cool the plastic into the shape of a CD with exactly the pattern of pits and lands that it takes from the stamper. This clear plastic disc is then metallized by applying a thin layer of aluminium that the laser bounces off. A layer of lacquer seals in the metal, preventing oxidation or damage, and creating a flat top surface for printing. Although it looks like the bumps are on the bottom of the disc, it's not the case. It is a flat, clear plastic surface, called the mirror side, through which the laser shines, to bounce off the sealed top surface, and the mould that makes the mirror side never changes.

And the mirror side is the key to TZ's work. 'The disc plant by definition has to copy the disc accurately,' he says.

It needs to have an accuracy of 0.0001 millimetre, so you get a high enough yield. Any imperfection leaves its trace on the moulding, and the traces form a unique fingerprint that can be 0.001 millimetre long and 0.0001 millimetre deep. The moulding is so much better than matching footprints, because the whole process is about creating an exact copy, so it's a forensic scientist's dream: they are copying something so precisely that any accidental damage is bigger than what you are trying to copy.

Under the microscope, the mirror side of every disc from the same machine looks identical in a way that's invisible to the naked eye. Simply by looking at them, TZ can match, precisely, two discs with the same origin. For TZ, every line on every pressing plant has its own fingerprint.

Under the microscope, the marks are as clear and distinct as a signature. TZ tees up a copy of a Sarah Brightman CD from Ukraine and, next to it, a counterfeit Guns n' Roses CD from Germany. On the human scale, and certainly when you play them, they have nothing in common. Under TZ's microscope, they are identical, undoubtedly from the same pressing plant.

'We had some plants in the Ukraine in 2001 and 2002 that were a big problem. We didn't have a copyright law locally that meant we could raid them, so manufacturing wasn't illegal there. However, exporting the CDs was,' says TZ. When undercover investigators tipped off German customs in Frankfurt to seize a consignment in January 2001 on its way to Latin America, TZ begged a sample. It matched to so many pirate CDs found all over the world that the IFPI had all the evidence it needed. In the way things are done, it passed the evidence to the US trade representative. The US trade representative passed the evidence to the Ukrainian government with a firm hint. The Ukrainian government took the hint and closed the pressing plant down.

In the corner of the lab, there's a small container of unmatched discs, commercially pirated counterfeits that TZ can't identify – yet. He calls them his 'Moby Dicks', after the novel in which a ship's captain obsessively pursues a great white whale. TZ works on a smaller scale, but no less obsessively – the previous week, he had a minor victory when a CD he has been trying to match for four years finally gave up its secret. 'There are a few discs here I haven't matched in five years,' he says, 'but I've not given up on them yet. I'm still hoping.'

Sometimes, even incontrovertible evidence isn't enough. Having made a match in the early years of the lab's existence, the IFPI had identified one of the world's most active counterfeiting plants in Ukraine. The damage it was doing to the recording business was great enough for President Bill Clinton personally to take the initiative and ask the Ukrainian government to close the plant.

A short time later, TZ was analysing the first batch of knockoffs of that week's releases. His microscope told him unequivocally that the Ukrainian plant was back in business, because the CDs that had been counterfeited were not released commercially until after it was – apparently – closed.

One in three

It's that kind of power and influence that TZ's boss Iain Grant has been battling every day since he joined the IFPI as head of enforcement in August 1997. A tough Scot, Grant had 20 years of experience in the Hong Kong police, finishing his career there as head of the drugs squad; but he had 20 years of prejudice about the importance of counterfeiting, which he had seen every day in his old job, to jettison. 'If someone had come to me in Hong Kong and asked, "What are you going to do about these counterfeit watches?", I'd have said, "I'm too busy." It's not as important as drugs or weapons in their eyes.'

Grant is no longer too busy, nor does he accept that argument from the police and customs he works alongside. The IFPI estimates that illegal music sales were a $4.5 billion business worldwide in 2003 – and that's at the prices the counterfeiters are charging. It's bigger than every national market except the US and Japan. One in three CDs sold on the planet is illegal. Add cassettes, and 40 per cent of world trade in music is against the law – and we haven't even touched illegal downloading.

In Taiwan, the local disc burning business is a good one: it has a capacity of 7.9 billion units. The local demand for the discs it produces is 270 million units. In China, 4.9 billion discs are made in commercial pressing plants, with a local demand of 1.1 billion. In India, 1.9 billion are produced for a market that needs 400 million, and in Thailand 570 million discs are produced, for a legitimate local market of 27 million.[1]

The 1,040 optical disc processing plants worldwide had, in IFPI's estimate, an overcapacity of 19.4 billion discs. That's three discs for every person on the planet, and we're not adding in the amount of counterfeiting that's done by small factories using recordable CDs and home computers.

To see what this does to the local market for music, take Brazil as an example. In 2003, the value of the music market dropped by 17 per cent. Unit sales were down by a quarter. The IFPI's research shows that 44 per cent of shoppers in Brazil buy counterfeits. 'Brazil remains in the list of the IFPI's top ten priority territories because of the inefficiency (or non-existence) of coordinated police efforts at a national level,' says the IFPI's 2004 Commercial Piracy Report.

'Police corruption is rife, and court judges are slow to use criminal procedures against pirates.'

Or Mexico, where music sales dropped by 50 per cent in three years, between 2000 and 2003. Or Russia, whose pirate discs have been traced by TZ's lab to 26 countries. Or even Spain, where 24 per cent of sales are counterfeit and, in 2003, 2,800 people were arrested and charged with stealing intellectual property. Spain's best-selling musicians are campaigning against the pirates under the slogan, 'Music is dying – help us'.

However, you might think that it's not music that is dying, but the musicians and, let's face it, they could handle a pay cut better than we could. This ignores, Grant says, the role that music plays in local economies, and it also ignores the role played in production and distribution by organized criminals.

As he travels to other countries, Grant hears the same problem many times: if you're a legitimate CD shop in a high-piracy country, you can't make a living. IFPI members have declined to set up large shops in areas of the UK where there are large numbers of counterfeit discs until the problem is brought under control.

The people making the profits, meanwhile, are reinvesting those profits, often in an incredibly sophisticated logistical operation. Jack Valenti, at that time the president and chief executive of the Motion Picture Association of America, whose members suffer from DVD piracy from the same production facilities, testified to the US House of Representatives in 2003[2] about one factory that his investigators had discovered:

> Pirate factories go to great lengths to conceal and harden their operations. One raid in October 2001, near Bangkok, revealed an underground tunnel linking a factory to a residential house. Pirate products were moved out of the factory on a meter-wide, specially installed electric rail system that ended under the kitchen sink of a nearby home. The products were trucked away from the back of the house, effectively hiding the movement of pirated goods out of the factory.

The counterfeiters invested in security as well:

> The pirates employ sophisticated security systems, such as hardened front doors and surveillance cameras, to delay entry by enforcement officials into the factories. These security devices give the pirates the

10 to 15 minutes they need to destroy the evidence of their crimes in vats of acid kept specifically for this purpose. Local police have been forced to adopt equally sophisticated responses. In the raid on a factory in Thailand the police, accompanied by our anti-piracy enforcement team, broke through the roof of the factory and rappelled down ropes in order to maintain the element of surprise.

Organized criminals

It's not all James Bond excitement, but increasingly the IFPI is uncovering large, organized networks of crime rather than individuals out to make some extra cash. One of the IFPI's major successes against organized crime occurred in 1999 and 2000, only a couple of miles from Grant's London office. The City of London police had contacted him, having found that a large number of counterfeit CDs were being offered for sale on local markets. 'They said, "There seem to be these Russian guys involved. Are you interested?" And I said we were,' says Grant. He put an undercover investigator on the case. His job was to make contact and find out where the CDs were coming from. 'They were based in St Petersburg and using a courier network throughout southern England,' Grant recalls. Vladimir Stroguine was taking orders: his UK distributors would tell him which CDs they wanted and give him a copy of the genuine article. He would courier it to Russia, and three weeks later the counterfeits came back.

Grant's investigator got another message back: it wasn't just CDs. 'It was obvious he could lead us to other types of criminal activity, such as importing guns and drugs. Then we went back to the police, and at that point they are willing to take on an investigation.'

One year of investigation uncovered, among other things, a massive credit card forging operation based around a counterfeiting factory in North London. Stroguine's associate Alexander Tanov was running a credit card 'skimming' network based in the restaurants and hotels of London. When you paid with your credit card, the waiter would use a small machine to 'skim' the details of your card by reading the magnetic stripe. The waiters passed the details back to Tanov. One of those skimmers, unknown to Tanov, was working undercover for the IFPI. He pretended his machine wasn't working, and was taken back to Stroguine's address in West Hendon to download the information. All the time, Tanov was being tailed by undercover officers of the Cheque and Credit Card Unit of the City of London police – when he left Stroguine, they followed him to his home address.

On 27 January 2000, police raided both addresses. Stroguine's flat was packed with knockoff CDs. Tanov's was a full-scale credit card factory, with 4,000 black pieces of plastic, an embossing machine, a printer, a machine to encode a magnetic stripe and a Russian machine to place a hologram on the cards to create convincing MasterCards or Visa cards.

The sentences were handed down at London's Southwark Crown Court. Both received four years and were deported. Grant's investigator had uncovered evidence that CDs and credit cards weren't the end of their import–export activity, which also included gunrunning. When you go to a market this weekend and pick up a knockoff copy of the CD you want, it is gangsters like Tanov and Stroguine who get the profit, he says. 'In my experience about 75 per cent of music piracy involves, at some point, an element of organized crime. It could be the buying; it could be the selling; it could be the manufacturing. But with the profits on offer, organized criminals are not going to leave it all to some guy in a garage, are they?'

The 'organization' extends to intimidation. Grant's 40 experienced investigators run the same risks as his narcotics investigators did in Hong Kong, he says, not least because Grant now sees some of the gang leaders he once investigated for heroin trafficking moving their muscle into CD trafficking.

> If I went to a market and set up a stall selling dodgy gear, I wouldn't be there very long, and it wouldn't be the police moving me on. When you are involved in organized crime, you have to control the street, and these guys know that because they are astute businessmen. Our investigators do end up in danger. You're taking the livelihoods of the people you're investigating, and these are people who can be violent with each other.

While many police forces would struggle to declare an enthusiasm for anti-counterfeiting work, fighting organized crime is top of the priority list in most forces. So why do we need Grant and his global network of 40 investigators? 'With an international dimension, you need an international response,' he says, but perhaps the real reason is to be a conscience, to nag the police and to keep putting cases in front of them until they take action. Half of Grant's time is spent travelling the world to countries where there is a counterfeiting problem and sitting down with local law enforcement to remind them gently of their duties. 'I don't go complaining. I go to offer help,' he says. 'If you catch them and don't prosecute, it breaks down. If you prosecute but don't sentence, it breaks down. If you sentence, but don't take their money, you'll have a problem. So what is very important is that you need to engage the full spectrum of criminal justice.'

And here he hits two barriers. First, not everyone wants the criminals to be prosecuted. In 1998, in Bulgaria, a police officer was pursuing a criminal gang's efforts to export large quantities of CDs to Western Europe. Soon after the story broke, the officer was arrested for corruption, on faked charges, though with Grant's help he was later cleared. Russia is a continuing source of frustration. 'It's difficult to get things done. The case falls off the rails. Evidence gets lost. There's a perverse judgment in court. You can't dictate to people how to do things in their own country but, no matter how bad things seem on the surface, there's always someone who isn't tainted who will take it on for you,' he says.

Counterfeiters have also grasped the full potential of a global economy in a way that law enforcement has not. 'Take Israel: the criminal gangs there somehow don't have the same difficulty in working with the Palestinians that the government does,' Grant says. 'In 1999 in Paraguay, there was a pressing plant run by Hong Kong Chinese.'

In Lagos, Oluwat Sabair of Abraham & Co, a law firm that specializes in the fight against counterfeiting, has seen the influence of international criminal gangs:

> They just closed one CD manufacturing plant here with 11 lines and another with five lines. They found 17 Chinese guys there. The spotlight has been on China, and the competition between counterfeiters is intense. But when they put pressure on counterfeiters in China, no one is looking at the danger of them moving to places like Nigeria. If they become strongly rooted in our country, they will be impossible to get out.

'A global problem requires a global solution,' says Grant, but the criminals are better at globalization than law enforcement. The IFPI's lab, packed with knockoff CDs from all points of the globe, shows the scale of the problem. Ultimately though, it's not the job of a private club of recording companies to enforce the law. 'We can disturb the debris around the stone,' Grant says. 'It's for governments and law enforcement to lift the stone, and see what's under it.'

Notes

1. Source: Understanding and Solutions Ltd, quoted by IFPI.
2. Subcommittee on Courts, the Internet, and Intellectual Property, Committee on the Judiciary, US House of Representatives, 13 March 2003.

12 Ordinary criminals

Napoleon said the British were a nation of shopkeepers. Today, the Brits are a knockoff nation of stallholders and market shoppers. The Sunday morning market at Wembley is bristling: 500 stalls in the shadow of Wembley Stadium, one of London's largest and most successful street markets. Between 9 am and 3 pm, tens of thousands of shoppers gather to buy clothes, sportswear, household goods – and especially CDs and DVDs. Perhaps one stall in five is selling films or music, and every one is offering counterfeits.

'It's moved on from the people on the market who did a bit of counterfeit on the side,' says Giles Speid, the principal trading standards enforcement officer at the London boroughs of Brent and Harrow trading standards service. 'In the 10 weeks leading up to Christmas, apart from the food stalls, we're talking about 90 per cent of the market being knockoff stuff of some type.'

Speid spots a market stall with a small mountain of pirate copies of DVDs. 'What have we here, gentlemen?' he asks, quickly moving on to the stall, taking it over with his body language. Having 'front', he explains, is essential for avoiding trouble; that, and the stab vests that he and his colleague Mohammed Tariq – a trading standards officer from Birmingham on secondment in London – need to wear when they raid markets. Five years ago, Speid admits, he wouldn't have considered wearing a vest, but there's a different sort of counterfeiter in the market these days.

Snide

Today's raid has an unexpected bonus. As Mohammed – an expert in Bollywood cinema – sorts through the bounty to find at least three films that opened in London's Asian cinemas less than 48 hours previously, Speid lifts the tarpaulin at the back of the market stall. Behind it, four customers freeze, caught in the act as they shop in the DVD pirate equivalent of a speakeasy. Speid has discovered a secret stall-within-a-stall, which you couldn't spot if you passed 2 feet away. It has £5 copies of Hollywood films, one of which still hadn't opened in UK cinemas, and most of which are still showing.

'Is this your stall?' Speid calls after two market traders who are walking away, doing a poor impression of innocent men.

'Can I still buy this one?' a confused customer asks Speid, holding a knockoff DVD out as the two of them bundle the entire stock into a giant plastic bag on the market stall.

As the two trading standards enforcement officers stroll through the market with the proceeds of their raid, which will be logged and recycled (counterfeit CDs and DVDs become polystyrene cups), word is going round the market that they are on the warpath. 'I can't serve you,' says one trader, swiftly grabbing a CD back from his customer and sweeping his stock into a brown cardboard box. 'The trading standards are here.' In fact, the trading standards are looking over the customer's shoulder. Mohammed listens to the shouts in Punjabi that bounce from stall to stall, warning every trader in the market to hide their stock. 'They don't know I understand what they are saying,' he laughs. As they stop at another music and film stall, it's virtually empty, with just a few legitimate discs. Mohammed lifts the cloth that covers the table on the next-door clothing stall. Underneath are at least 1,000 fake discs in an untidy pile where they have been swiftly hidden. 'These yours?' asks Speid, who can't help but laugh. The market trader acts surprised, giving a 'how-did-they-get-there?' look.

Today is the stallholder's lucky day: the guys literally have their hands full with the heavy bag of discs they confiscated from the speakeasy. It's the weight they can carry – and the people available to do it – that often dictates the extent of a raid, Speid admits. 'We hire vans for the occasion, but when we raid the first four stalls, sometimes, the van's full. Last time we raided, we took six vans, plus police vehicles, and by 1 o'clock we had to stop because they were all full,' he says.

The market traders have a word for counterfeits: they call it 'snide'. 'If I couldn't sell snide I'd be back to painting and decorating, like I used to,' says Ricky Jones, whose successful stall occupies five times the space of most of his competitors. He tried selling CDs and DVDs, but the variable quality made him move into knockoff sportswear instead. Speid respects Jones because, every time he raids, Jones asks his staff to help Speid bag up the goods he's about to confiscate. The two have a grudging respect. The occasional seizure and the risk that one day he will be prosecuted is the cost of business, Jones admits. 'But without the snide, there wouldn't be a market,' he says.

As we talk, it's not just the stallholders who are spreading the word of the approaching trading standards raid. The market security staff – whose job should be to enforce legal trading – are on their walkie-talkies, warning the stallholders at the other end of the market to hide their counterfeits. The stallholders pay an informal tax to the security to do this, says Speid. 'There's no one better than the market security to do an early warning,' he says. 'It's like holding back the sea here. It does get frustrating at times.'

Jones appreciates the warnings from the market staff: he doesn't want to lose an entire week's stock to Speid and his team. 'I've got a lot of gear here, so I'm never going to get rid of all of it in time, but the security come by and say, "Hide the valuable stuff",' he says.

The frustrations of Brent and Harrow trading standards are echoed all over the UK, Europe and the United States by whoever is enforcing the law against knockoffs. Today, almost everywhere there is a market you will see pirated CDs and DVDs. The UK is also the home of the car boot sale, a pastime that brings frowns and sniggers from other Europeans and mystified looks from Americans. Who would want to pay to drive into a field at 5 am to sell the stuff they don't need in the middle of the British winter, and claim they are doing it because it is enjoyable?

Global cottage industry

A few years ago, I was a regular Sunday guest on a national talk radio show. My slot started at 7.30 am, immediately after an antiques specialist who was advertised as 'Mr Car Boot Sale Man'. Every week, the switchboard lit up like fairy lights as excited punters called in to discuss their latest car boot sale purchase. Callers were instructed that they could only get on the show if they agreed to shout 'I've got a car boot sale bargain!' when they were put on air. At 7.30, after Mr Car Boot Sale Man took his last call, the lights on the switchboard died, and we were left in eerie Sunday morning silence as the nation returned to rooting for bargains.

Yet increasingly the car boot sale isn't the place to find a valuable antique; it's one more route to market for knockoffs, especially CDs and DVDs. The British Film Council estimates that there are 60 million in circulation and, even though police and trading standards confiscated 1 million DVDs alone in 2004, the lost sales are already at £500 million for law-abiding British shopkeepers.

For 30 years, the British Phonographic Industry Limited, better known as the BPI, has been battling the counterfeiters who satisfy the appetites of bargain-hunting Brits. And on the evidence of Wembley, they are losing.

The BPI was set up in 1973 to counter the growth in bootlegs. If you are over 30 you might remember going to see a band and standing next to the guy who wasn't jumping up and down in the centre front of the crowd because he was holding a tape recorder and a microphone, checking nervously for bouncers as he recorded the concert for posterity and profit. The ultimate in lo-fi, bootleg tapes were often unlistenable, barely repaying the effort of seeking them out in the dingy back corner of your local independent record shop.

Today, a pirate CD is literally note perfect. It's an exact copy of the original. Who needs a bootleg when you can have the real thing? As David Martin – the BPI's director of anti-piracy – points out, the growth in counterfeiting in the UK is six times faster than the growth in the legal music market, and bootleggers are history.

For a while, the BPI's focus was on the professional counterfeit CDs that the IFPI's forensics labs are investigating and that we might buy without knowing it was a counterfeit. But one look at the cheap imitations that are flooding Wembley market – and markets across the developed world – tells you that Western consumers don't care about the packaging quite as much as they care about getting a cheap copy.

'Our biggest problem today isn't imported pirate CDs any more,' says Martin.

> Today it's a cottage industry and we have to go after a guy making five CDs a week as well as a guy making 10,000 a week. My guess is that there is a counterfeiter on every street in Britain now. In 1993, when I joined the BPI, there were 12 major cassette counterfeiting factories in the UK. We knew exactly where they were. In 2005, those 12 have become about 100,000 CD factories. The recordable CD has killed off the bootlegger.

As well as in street markets and car boot sales, you can pick up a knockoff CD or DVD at work, in pubs and bars, on a street corner or over the internet. On the UK's high streets, it's not hard to find people with plastic bags of knockoffs, or a guy with a photocopied price list who will fetch your order from a nearby car. The knockoff business is tempting, even for businesspeople who already have a legitimate business. Jayanti Amarishi Buhecha was one of them. When police raided his Bollywood film distribution business based in Cambridge, they discovered that he was now in the knockoff business. They found 18,000 cheap counterfeit discs that he was distributing all over London. In February 2005, he received a three-year sentence in Harrow Crown Court, to Mohammed's delight. But if he thought that jailing one of the south of England's most prolific pirates would solve the problem of counterfeiting on his patch, he was soon brought down to earth. 'I walked out of the court after the Buhecha case, and I went to get a sandwich. I was stopped in the street by a Chinese woman who wanted to sell me counterfeit DVDs,' he says.

'I was having lunch in the pub last Friday', says Bill Bilon, the deputy director of trading standards at Brent and Harrow, 'and someone tried to sell me knockoff CDs.'

'If you want to make pirate discs, you don't have to go to a CD manufacturing plant any more,' explains Martin. 'It doesn't have to look professional, because the public is happy to pay £4 for the disc. They think they are getting a bargain. There's a machine outside my door that can make 500 CDs an hour. If you have a couple of thousand pounds, you can go to a wholesaler and he will sell you one.' The machine is the size of a pedal bin. You could put it in the boot of a car or keep it under your stairs and at night manufacture CDs for a unit cost of around 60 pence. Even counting the cost of the cheaply photocopied label and the shrink wrap, your profit margin is at least 300 per cent, as the content costs nothing.

'It's a law enforcement void,' says Martin.

The lowest priority

The agency for policing intellectual property in the UK is trading standards. This owes less to a master plan to outwit pirates than the simple problem that no one else fancies the job: the police have other priority crimes, customs work at the borders, and there is no special force to protect intellectual property. And so it falls to Speid, Bilon, Mohammed and their colleagues, who are not employed by national government, or the police, or the courts, but by their local authorities.

Bilon sees the problems that trading standards have in many parts of the country. 'We are the lowest priority, which isn't surprising when they are funding education, social services and housing from the same budget.'

For many years, trading standards were a very British institution, whose job was to ensure that your grocer gave you a full pound of carrots and your publican sold a full pint of beer. In a country where few police officers carry a gun and the law limits the number of crimes even a police officer can arrest you for, it's no surprise to find that your local trading standards officer doesn't have the ability to throw his or her weight about. 'They have no power of arrest, and a small overtime budget, so often they can't work at the weekend. But of course, the weekend is when the counterfeiters come out to play,' says Martin, who after 22 years in the RAF's intelligence service spent a year in Derbyshire as a trading standards officer.

> Councils will say intellectual property isn't an issue for us. Food safety is a problem; animal health is too – but not knockoff music. God bless trading standards for what they do, but they are just not equipped. When you see the sort of people they are trying to stop, the sort of

people who are behind these markets, they could give trading standards officers two good hidings for daring to interfere. You see it – the officer walks up to the counterfeiter, asks 'What's your name?', and the counterfeiter says 'Mickey Mouse'. And he can't do a bloody thing about it.

If the structure and powers of trading standards come from a kindlier, gentler age, then the market traders they are forced to confront don't feel the need to play by the old rules. The counterfeiters who thrive in the street markets and car boot sales in the UK today are using technology to their advantage: they don't carry stock for trading standards to confiscate. 'Barras Market in Glasgow is a typical example,' says Martin, who occasionally puts on a bobble hat as a disguise and a stab vest as protection to check up on the most notorious counterfeiters. 'They use kids as young as 11 who stand behind stalls. You can buy £10,000 of software from them for £10.'

Wise to the trading standards and the limitations of their powers, the stall holds no stock. The kid runs off and returns 10 minutes later. The person who is really in charge of the store has just burned a CD ROM with the music, software or film you ordered on it. It's as simple as, and quicker than, ordering a pizza, and when the trading standards raid there's little to snatch and no adults to arrest.

That was the case in a raid that Martin helped coordinate on Scotland's Ingliston Market, in the shadow of Edinburgh airport, on 14 December 2004. More than 100 police flooded the market, which had been linked to criminal gangs selling knockoffs to raise money for outlawed Northern Irish terror gangs and local organized crime and had even been blamed for the Edinburgh public's reluctance to go to the cinema. Police arrested 18 traders and confiscated £10 million worth of counterfeit goods.

'We went back to the market three hours later, and the counterfeiters were back. The kids were back behind the stalls. They know we're not going to send police in to arrest children,' says Martin. A year later, the police raided again on 21 November. This time, £3 million of goods was confiscated, another £2 million of CDs and DVDs was looted by the market customers after the traders ran off to avoid arrest, and the operation was hailed by law enforcement as a 'serious blow to organized crime' and 'a fantastic success'. A couple of weeks later, most of the traders were back once more.[1]

'A few months ago we raided a stall in Paddy's Market in Glasgow,' Martin says.

> The stallholders went with police to their mobile home, where they had a complete factory set up. It was being run by the bloke, his wife and their two daughters. Two days after we confiscated their equipment, we checked on them and they had re-equipped. Three days later, they had to be arrested again because they were back in business.

Even the threat of deportation doesn't deter counterfeiters, says Bilon.

> On 13 April 2005, we raided a video shop and took away more than 8,000 counterfeits. The police arrested him and found he was here illegally, but they let him go. On 21 April, we went back. We couldn't believe we found the same quantity of stuff. He was arrested the next day, and that night he was on a plane to the Punjab.

Many of the UK's markets are effectively unpoliced, as over-stretched trading standards officers rarely conduct observations. Speid says that sometimes it's because they simply don't have the staff; sometimes it is because the trading standards staff claim that the policing of the world's fastest-growing crime wave isn't a job that they should be doing – but often it is because the markets are effectively the province of criminal gangs, and a group that can't even make an arrest is taking a risk just by being there.

Martin would like to see the police involved with more cases, but accepts that few forces see counterfeiting as a priority. It's frustrating for him, because he believes that action against counterfeits will have a knock-on effect in bringing down other crimes. He says:

> Because a police force isn't rewarded for catching counterfeiters, but is rewarded for bringing down burglary, then often large counterfeiting cases get bounced back to trading standards. Counterfeiting might never make it to priority one – but if it made priority 10, then stallholders and car boot sale pirates could expect more raids and arrests. I'm not advocating we send everyone involved in counterfeiting to jail. Well… not quite everyone.

The second part of Martin's plan is to try to get to the source of the supply. The source today is thousands of small factories. 'One factory we raided in Scotland was using college kids who were paid £40 for working an eight-hour shift. They ran three shifts so they can keep the factory running 24 hours a day,' he says.

It's even harder when the cheap knockoff copying is done outside the UK. 'We have aircrew coming from Pakistan bringing the DVDs now,' says Mohammed. 'A DVD from Pakistan costs between 30p and 40p, and a CD 20p. If you have a suitcase and there are 4,000 or 5,000 discs in it, it's a huge profit. I guarantee that every flight from Pakistan has at least two of these suitcases in it.'

When he was last in Pakistan, he posed as a tourist to ask a video shop owner if he could get a supply of knockoffs for his shop in the UK. He was shocked to find that they knew exactly how to ship the discs, down to the staffing schedules of UK customs. 'They were telling me everything. Like when to bring them in, because the customs wouldn't check at these times. They are saying, "We can supply all you want, no problem",' he says. For times when customs are more alert, the discs come in to Belgium, and the wholesalers rent a van and pick them up by ferry.

But the most important part of the problem, cutting public demand for knockoffs, isn't something that Martin seriously considers. Faced with an endless supply of cheap CDs, he admits that it will take a generation to change the attitudes of the otherwise law-abiding British public, and maybe almost as long to change the emphasis in British policing of counterfeiters. 'I'm not despondent,' he says, 'but there will be no improvement in the next few years.'

It's worse when the police get to see one of their own colleagues has set up as a counterfeiter – as happened when former police superintendent John Stewart set up a stall with his son offering counterfeit CDs in the Pontefract Lane Market in Leeds. A former high-flyer in the force, Stewart had been head of discipline and complaints in West Yorkshire police and was qualified to become a chief constable. Two car accidents meant he had to retire through ill health, at which point he started his criminal career. You might have expected him to be aware of the risks.

Perhaps the temptation of easy money was too great. In 1999, his son Karl had a thriving market stall in the council-run market, and Stewart was roped in to help: purchasing a CD copier, helping out on the stall, cutting the paper covers he had copied. Every week, Karl sold between 600 and 700 CDs at the Sunday morning market, which was run by the city council, and every week Stewart would copy some more stock.

By 2002, the police had enough and prosecuted their ex-colleague on charges of conspiracy to defraud. Found guilty, he was fined £20,000 and given a prison sentence of 16 months, suspended for two years. Disappointed at the leniency of the sentence – they wanted Stewart to go to prison – the BPI weighed in with a suit for civil damages, and the disgraced ex-cop had to pay another £90,000 in December 2004.[2]

Some coppers don't even wait to leave the force before going into the knockoff business: 'We just did a job in the North-East. At 5 am, we kicked in the door of a house and raided the CD factory inside,' says Martin. 'At 7 am, we went back to the police station to have breakfast. I was sitting there in the canteen, I look up, and on the wall there's a poster advertising pirate CDs: "Get the top 40 CDs cheap!" It even had the name of the police officer to contact. When they think that's OK, what the hell is going on?'

Notes

1. *Scottish Daily Record*, 23 November 2005.
2. *Yorkshire Post*, 29 December 2004.

13 Turning guns into CD burners

The car bomb contained 40 pounds of Frangex – similar to Semtex – high-grade explosive, purchased in Belfast. It was packed with live ammunition, nuts and bolts, to cause maximum damage. The car was to be driven to the market, parked, and detonated at the right moment to cause maximum death and carnage and maximum impact one Sunday in January 2003.

The bomb plot, hatched by dissident Republicans, never came off. Exposed by Belfast's *Sunday World* newspaper, the story was one more depressing chapter in the story of the troubles in Northern Ireland, and for the visitors to the market not a particularly surprising one. However, the intended targets were unusual: the paramilitaries were hunting a unit of the Police Service of Northern Ireland whose job was to patrol the market looking for knockoffs.

Northern Ireland's Sunday markets – Nutts Corner in a Loyalist area, Jonesboro in a Republican district, but also countless other markets like Clogher, Bangor, Lisburn, Newtownards and St George's – offer the same spread of knockoffs that you might see anywhere else in the UK. But, in Northern Ireland, the knockoff economy is thriving more than most: despite having a population of only 1.7 million people – about 3 per cent of the population of the UK – there are more knockoffs seized in Northern Ireland than in the rest of the UK put together. It's not that they are getting everything. That represents, according to the Police Service of Northern Ireland (PSNI), about 5 per cent of the counterfeits on the Northern Irish market.

Northern Ireland is a case study in what happens when terrorists, and ex-terrorists, need cash and are looking for the easiest ways to get it: because if you are experienced at avoiding the law, there are few easier ways to make cash than selling pirate CDs, DVDs and software.

The Lion Kings

According to the 2004/05 'threat assessment' issued by Northern Ireland's Organised Crime Task Force (OCTF), in 2003/04 the police seized £7,625,000 of counterfeits. Of that, £5,175,000 – around two-thirds – was made up of games, music, films and software. That's 10 times the size of the alcohol bootlegging trade in Northern Ireland and more than three times the trade in knockoff clothes.

Terrorism and piracy have gone hand in hand for many years in Northern Ireland. In 1995, Disney's launch of the video of *The Lion King* was spoiled by 1 million advance pirate copies flooding the market, earning £4 million for the suppliers. After investigating, Disney discovered that one of the biggest suppliers was the IRA.[1] Today, the OCTF reports that 'Paramilitary gangs carry out 80 per cent of organised intellectual property crime in Northern Ireland. Both Loyalist and Republican gangs are equally heavily involved.'

It is only in the last few years that the extent of the link between the paramilitaries and counterfeiting has become explicit, as the OCTF has set about measuring the scale of the problem, and since in Northern Ireland the lead investigators of counterfeiting are the police. A series of high-profile raids has followed. In September 2003, for example, information gathered from informants led the police to a CD factory in Thailand, where they confiscated thousands of CDs, labels and duplicating machinery. Closer to home, the PSNI and the Garda (the Republic of Ireland police force) have cooperated to raid CD factories close to the border.

In Dromahair, for example, on the south side of the border, a raid on 22 April 2004 discovered a farmhouse with one occupant, but 37 burners, thousands of recordable CDs, printers, scanners and labelling machines. The occupant told the police he was making counterfeits to sell at Clogher and Jonesboro markets. The CDs were being sold with the cooperation of the paramilitaries, reported the IFPI: 'It is thought the operators pay a percentage for protection, but if caught are under strict instructions not to implicate their protectors.'[2]

The scale of the paramilitary piracy business in Northern Ireland is shocking: the PSNI has identified 230 organized crime gangs, of which it considers 85 to be 'top-level' gangs. 'They generate large criminal profits, are violent, and many employ specialist techniques to run, protect and enhance their criminal enterprises,' says the OCTF, which has traced their criminal contacts to Turkey and Thailand.

Some are exporting their expertise. When the Scottish police raided Ingliston Market in Edinburgh in 2003, the police reported a connection to Irish terrorism. 'The Ulster Volunteer Force was behind much of what we seized. It's big business in Ulster,' said an unnamed police officer to the press. 'They supply the cash and the know-how to Scottish criminals and then cream off the profits. People who turn their nose up in disgust if asked to donate to the UVF have been happily filling terrorists' pockets for too long.'[3]

Detective Superintendent Andy Sproule, the head of the organized crime squad for the PSNI, has had 28 years of policing in Northern Ireland and knows the methods used by the paramilitaries to create counterfeiting businesses. The techniques are no different to running a terrorist organization, he says.

> There are the individuals who would be the brains behind it, technical people who when they are not building mortars are building multi-bay CD burners. There are enforcers, who would ensure that the pitch at a market was left alone to do business. There are investors, who can take care of the money and make sure that the Assets Recovery Agency [the government body with the power to confiscate the proceeds of crime] can't get their hands on it. And there are individuals who have skills in smuggling. The route they once used to bring guns in to the country is the route they can now use to bring in CDs. Then if you look at where they do business: one of the biggest markets is Jonesboro, and that's in South Armagh. Nothing happens there without the paramilitaries having an overview of it.

The terror gangs are accustomed to making international contacts, he explains. 'Some will go to Thailand to send back or bring back CDs and DVDs. They are doing business in China, Singapore, all over the place.'

Raymond Leinster is now the director-general of the Federation Against Copyright Theft (FACT), but received his training for the job over 28 years in the police in Northern Ireland, most recently investigating counterfeiting as part of the OCTF.

'They have been selling counterfeit products that I know of for over 20 years,' he says. 'The paramilitaries have a keen eye for a profit. The main sources of income have always been films, music and software. But 20 years ago, the IRA was selling counterfeit toothpaste. They are just the people with the acumen and the sophistication to do it.'

He explains that 80 per cent of the piracy in the region is directly linked to dissident Republican groups, the Irish Republican Army (IRA), the Irish National Liberation Army (INLA), the Ulster Defence Association (UDA), the Ulster Volunteer Force (UVF), the Loyalist Volunteer Force (LVF) and their criminal offshoots. 'The other 20 per cent of counterfeiting only occurs on their largesse. You're going to come up against them and, if you do, you're literally going to be outgunned.'

Leinster and Sproule agree that, while 97 per cent of Northern Irish residents thought that organized crime was a problem – and when you add cigarette smuggling and counterfeiting together, it was the second most common crime that they associate with the problem – there's an undercurrent of sympathy with the people selling counterfeits. 'The paramilitaries have a totally disproportionate influence over their communities,' says Leinster. 'Socially, it's good for them to be seen as providing goods at a cheap price. It's perverse, but everybody loves a bargain.'

'I saw a TV programme shot at the markets, and there's a woman giving out to the camera,' Sproule says. 'She's saying these people are providing a social service. If we can get the goods at one-third the price, that's good business. For people who don't have much, it's hard to argue.'

Everybody loves a bargain

Northern Ireland is the clearest link between terror and fakes, but there have been other reports, notably supplied by Interpol. When Ron Noble, the secretary-general of Interpol, testified to the United

States House Committee on International Relations in 2003,[4] he was clear that terrorist links existed in many places, not just Northern Ireland.

'In Kosovo, there is a long-standing relationship between criminal organizations and local ethnic-Albanian extremist groups. This relationship is based on family or social ties. It is suspected that funds generated from IPC [intellectual property crime] benefit both criminal organizations and extremist groups,' he said.

He also pinpointed examples of counterfeiting that fed terrorism in the Middle East:

> In February 2000, an individual was arrested for piracy and suspected fundraising for Hizbullah. The individual sold pirated music CDs, Sega, Sony and Nintendo game discs to fund a Hizbullah-related organization. Among the discs recovered were discs containing images and short films of terrorist attacks and interviews with suicide bombers. The discs were allegedly used as propaganda to generate funds for Hizbullah. Interpol is in possession of some of these films. This individual is currently a fugitive.

And, not surprisingly, al-Qaeda:

> The investigation into a shipment of fake goods from Dubai to Copenhagen, Denmark suggests that al-Qaeda may have indirectly obtained financing through counterfeit goods. Danish customs intercepted a container, containing counterfeit shampoos, creams, cologne and perfume. The sender of the counterfeit goods is allegedly a member of al-Qaeda. A transnational investigation involved agencies from three countries: Denmark, the United Kingdom and the United States.

Osama Bin Laden popped up on an unlikely counterfeit in November 2001: two music compilations on sale in Paraguay. They contained brightly coloured inlay cards with images of the twin towers of the World Trade Center on fire and a picture of the terrorist with 'Osama! Heroe' on it. The origin seems to be the Middle Eastern community in Paraguay's capital of piracy (and therefore the piracy capital of the whole of South America), Cuidad del Este. There is no evidence, however, that the profits from the CDs went to Osama Bin Laden, or that he even likes Latin American music.[5]

In another of the world's terrorist theatres, Chechen sympathizer Ziyaudi Terloyev was found to be running a pirate CD plant in Niginsk, outside Moscow. When Russian police raided it in September 2000, they found 5,000 pirate discs. At his home, they discovered explosives, grenades, detonators and ammunition. Their estimate for the earnings from his counterfeiting business: between $500,000 and $700,000 a month.[6]

Considering the profile of counterfeiters worldwide, it would be odd if some of them at least were not involved in terror and violence. Looked at another way, it's perhaps stranger that we haven't found more of them.

Part of the problem, Noble told the US government, was that investigations into counterfeiting are usually based around discovering, impounding and destroying goods. For the police or the companies involved, the destination of the cash raised – which might be hard to find – is not important.

Also, there's little direct evidence to show that bombs are being built on the profit from fake DVDs. Sproule explains that the Irish paramilitaries are acting more like racketeers than people who are raising money for a cause. 'Certainly for the Loyalists it's a case of "Here's one for me, and here's one for the cause",' he says. 'They aren't necessarily going out buying guns, but it may be a Mercedes and a holiday, and the money is also invested in buying drugs, that kind of crime.'

Another problem in making a link is that the funds are often raised by sympathizers, who then donate, rather than being directly traceable to terrorists. 'In terms of radical fundamentalist militants, these persons may for long periods of time not be directly involved in terrorist activity. During these periods, while not on active service duty, they support themselves through criminal activity… A portion of the money earned in these activities is kept while a portion is remitted to radical fundamentalist terrorist groups in cash form' was how Noble described it. Can we call this a strong link to terrorism? Probably not. It is, however, a support for a community that fosters and approves of terror.

A black hole

At the US Department of Justice, deputy chief of the computer crime and intellectual property section Michael O'Leary isn't about to launch a terrorist search on the proceeds of counterfeiting. 'We invited Ron Noble to provide evidence to support his statements. We are still waiting. Statements are statements, not evidence,' he says. 'We have cautioned against overstating the links between IP crime and terrorism. I can tell you, having looked at some of the cases that allegedly have links, they do not. It's often a case of a guy who gets caught in a bind, and then starts naming names to help himself.'

One record company executive disagrees strongly with that opinion: he says that, in his experience, law enforcement chooses not to follow up on leads he supplies. 'In our investigations we have discovered wire transfers from al-Qaeda. When that happens we call in the FBI', he says, 'and it goes into a black hole.'

Should we split hairs? Whether the money goes directly to terrorists themselves or to criminals who support terrorists but might also import drugs or go on expensive holidays, it's all bad news. The lessons learned in Northern Ireland show that two things will help cut the ties between counterfeits and terrorist funding.

The first is more enforcement – not by raiding markets, says Sproule, but by finding the groups responsible for supply and taking them out. In business, he says, the sectarian divide is far less obvious: there are even some wholesalers who supply knockoffs to both Loyalist and Republican gangs. Progress has been made by the OCTF where, with customs and police working as partners, it's easier to identify the big players and go after them at ports and on the border, not when the fakes get to market. 'There is no quick fix,' he warns. 'It's a war of attrition. It's very hard to appeal to a sense of civic duty when the public just wants something cheap.' He adds that the culture of lawlessness and intimidation that the terrorists on both sides have created will take many years, and not just many raids, to break down.

The second would be if the public made a strong connection between their cheap CD and the problems of their community, a connection that Sproule, Leinster and others know to exist but find it hard to communicate. Says Leinster: 'Unless someone strikes pay dirt and finds paperwork that says the profit from the sale of those CDs is going into a bank account and that account belongs to the UDA, it's just not going to happen. When you deal with an extremely honed, professional organization, it's very tough to make any difference.'

Notes

1. *Guardian*, 16 September 1995.
2. *IFPI Enforcement Bulletin*, June 2004.
3. *Sun*, 16 December 2003.
4. United States House Committee on International Relations, 16 July 2003.
5. IFPI (2004) *Music Piracy: Serious, violent and organised crime*, 4th edn.
6. IFPI (2004) *Music Piracy: Serious, violent and organised crime*, 4th edn.

14 Making a scene

When *Harry Potter and the Prisoner of Azkaban* premiered in London in March 2004, there were some people in the cinemas who weren't looking at the screen. The Vue cinema chain had equipped its staff with night vision goggles so they could scan the audience.[1] They were looking for the modern equivalent of the bootlegger at a rock concert: the film pirate who sneaks a camcorder into the cinema to record the film, so it can be put on to a pirate DVD or sent across the internet.

Anyone who has watched a bad bootleg, known in the industry as a 'cam', knows it's a grim experience, with the occasional wobble as the photographer shuffles in the seat, or the sudden intrusion of a voice from the cinema audience, or the eternal promise that any second the video camera's tape will run out and you'll never see the end. You can't imagine that, in many countries, someone has risked prison to get it. Thanks to the Family Entertainment and Copyright Bill 2005, for example, those in the United States caught filming in the cinema are committing a federal crime. They can be sent to jail for up to three years.

These second-rate copies go to satisfying the incredible appetite of the world's most sophisticated and hungriest knockoff distribution organization: The Scene.

Behind The Scene

The Scene isn't located in one place: it doesn't have any premises at all. It doesn't have employees, and the people that make it work never meet and have probably never spoken. They don't get paid for what they do, though The Scene does have a strict hierarchy and its members are highly specialized. More than Amazon or eBay or any legitimate internet site, it's living proof that the net has changed the very nature of how products are distributed. It is eating the profits of software companies, music publishers, film studios and computer games developers so that some consider the only way to survive is to adapt to The Scene's rules. And it's populated by a bunch of kids, many of whom should be spending more time doing their schoolwork.

What, then, is The Scene? It's a collection of people who share the same goal: to get their hands on as much copyright material as possible, for free, and exchange it using the internet. That means movies, preferably before their cinema release and certainly before they are commercially available on DVD. It means computer games – again, most valuably, if the game has not been released to the public. It also means computer software – almost anything, including business software that most members of The Scene could have little use for.

The raw material is everywhere. Software and computer games can be found on the servers of the developing companies and downloaded by enterprising hackers. That's what famously happened to Half-Life 2, one of the most eagerly awaited computer games there has ever been: by exploiting a security flaw in the developer's email software, the hackers sneaked in and sneaked out with the code for the game in October 2003.

That's big news: computer game debuts are as big as cinema openings. For example, the PS/2 game Gran Turismo 4 sold 635,000 copies in its first week on the market in Japan alone. For its European launch, the company stocked shops with 3,182,535 copies.[2]

Gabe Newell, the chief executive of Valve, the company developing Half-Life, enlisted the help of game fans to track down the hackers. 'It was extraordinary to watch how quickly and how cleverly gamers were able to unravel what are traditionally unsolvable problems for law enforcement,' he said[3] after the FBI had arrested some of the culprits in June 2004.

Films are even easier to find. There are many ways to get hold of a movie; by making a 'cam', hoping your usher doesn't have night goggles on, or by using contacts inside the studios or DVD pressing plants, or in a cinema, where you can make a high-quality copy by recording the film while using sound direct from the projection system. Music uses insiders too: in July 2004, U2 were doing a photo shoot in Nice. Guitarist The Edge had brought along a rough cut of the album that was to become 'How to defuse an atomic bomb'. It mysteriously went missing: the police were called and U2's record label panicked – if it had turned up on the internet, within hours a large proportion of the album's buyers could have downloaded it for free, thanks to the efficiency of The Scene.

'The package came sooner than any of us expected,' says Brian Sandro. 'Preparing a film for release takes about eight hours – basically an eternity for people who are into immediate gratification.'

Brian's talking about his life in a release group. The package is a pre-release copy of 'Alexander', which he has just received from his contact. He's part of The Scene – or, as Brian describes it, 'an elite group of technocrats [who] silently work the controls'.

Actually, Brian doesn't exist. He's a character – the star of 'The Scene', a web-based soap that's about his release group, free to download.[4] It's written by people who used to be part of The Scene and, to be honest, its dramatic content is interesting mostly to them. But don't take my work for it. The episodes are only 20 minutes long: about the attention span of the target audience.

From the top

The Scene is a giant pyramid. At the top are about 30 giant servers, computers with vast capacity attached to the internet, but using technology to hide their whereabouts. Only the people who administer these 'topservers' know where they are, but they may be distributing more than half a million movies every day. The topservers may be deliberately obscure, but their effect isn't. According to Envisional, a consultancy that monitors internet use by pirates, the distribution of stolen content is now between 50 and 65 per cent of all internet use. Read that again: almost two-thirds of the internet is devoted to the knockoff economy.

If you are swapping knockoff films with your pals using peer-to-peer technology like Kazaa – in which you make the content you have available to everyone else who has the software and they do the same for you – you can't get them direct from a topserver. That's where the beautiful efficiency of The Scene helps you.

A limited number of Scene members can log in to the topservers and upload the content they have filched. Security is tight – only users who are known can get in, and only from a specific location. These users head 'release groups', who compete to get the best content as early as possible and to crack any copy protection on their new toys. The competition between release groups is fierce; a major score like Half-Life 2 earns lifelong bragging rights.

Immediately below the topservers are the 'dumps' – less exclusive servers that can download from topservers with which they have an affiliation. As your movie, game, song, TV programme or software pops up on one of these servers, an army of thousands of the worker ants of The Scene, the couriers, gets to work.

If you're one of the 3,500 (a US government estimate) elite couriers, your job is to find the new content and send it to as many other servers as possible. It's a race against other couriers: if you get there first, you score a credit, which you can cash in to download whatever you want for your own use. Couriers are constantly watching for new content and, when it arrives, there's a global flurry of activity. By the time the new content makes it to one of the peer-to-peer networks where everyone can join in, there are thousands of copies of the file. It means that anyone who wants it can get it without a wait, and thanks to the ant army of 'curries' this takes hours, not the weeks of normal distribution.[5]

An example was the botched cinematic release of *The Hulk*, which two weeks before it made it to the cinemas was available on all the major peer-to-peer networks. From a pre-release print of the film being illegally copied in New York to the film being downloadable worldwide from the peer-to-peer networks took 72 hours. Inside 24 hours, the couriers had created around 50,000 copies on servers all over the world.

Faced with a problem on this scale, there are two ways for the industry to respond: try to destroy the pyramid, or use it to your advantage. At the moment, there's a lot of the first going on and not much of the second. Not surprisingly, because the essential feature of The Scene is free distribution. No one is getting rich out of it; they are just getting stuff that they want, and often they are working for kudos. In the early years of The Scene, it even had its own email newsletter, the Courier Weektop Scorecard. It tracked the number of credits the different courier groups had won, and published courier league tables featuring curries with poetic names like 'Avalanch', 'Cadence' and 'Darkwolf'. It even interviewed Scene celebrities:

> Hodd: I joined in 1996 as a complete newbie and traded with reachout and all that crap... I learned a lot from them but felt like I was missing out on the real scene... a guy in the group Buffy, told me that PHX was looking for more traders and they had a 120gig site at the time and in 96 that was huge shit...

You don't understand it? That's the point. There was even a public website dedicated to The Scene known as iSONEWS.com, run by Scene member David Rocci, with more than 100,000 registered visitors. (Today, iSONEWS.com has been closed down after Rocci was prosecuted for violating copyright laws.)

The Scorecard is also history, but the frantic competition to distribute knockoff material to as many Scene servers as possible still exists. The couriers call it 'The Races'.

The obvious place to start if you're trying to halt The Races is by making content more secure. No courier will spend an entire evening uploading copies of a commercially available DVD or CD. It's the exclusivity which gives The Scene its thrill.

Protecting your valuable property isn't that easy. Kevin Mitnick, who served four years for hacking in the US and has now created a career as a security consultant, is often asked to try to break in to computer systems by the company that owns them: he always succeeds. He was never affiliated to a topserver and never acted as a courier, but he used to download computer programs so he could mess around with them, as a pastime. 'They just want to free the software for some reason. It's kind of strange, but it's just what they want to do. I think it's more the thrill of breaking in, well, what can we do with it? So they just release it. I admit I'd be really pissed off if I was the victim. That's a serious issue,' he says.

Mitnick's speciality as a hacker was social engineering, which is a fancy phrase for working a con trick: getting someone to give you what you need, or getting access to somewhere that you can pick it up and walk out with it. That's how *The Hulk* was stolen, and it's almost impossible to stop. 'My girlfriend and I have a friend gives us some movies that aren't released on DVD because he works in the industry. If you work in the industry, you get pre-release copies. If I had wanted to, I could have released one. I didn't, but you could. So how can they track the source? It's really very difficult,' says Mitnick.

One method often trumpeted by the movie studios is copy protection, designed to make a DVD impossible to 'rip' – that means to copy to your hard disk, so it can be copied again to a blank DVD. Today, ripping is painfully easy. You can buy software to do it – at the time of writing, Surplus Computers of Santa Clara, California was offering me either 'Complete Video Studio 4000 Pro' for $9.99, or the even more obvious 'I Copy DVDs 2' for $15.99. If you don't want to spend $16, there are many free utilities.

Stop, thief

Stopping the rip is too little and too late as a way to deal with The Scene. First, by the time it is on the DVD, The Scene has finished with it. Second, for movies at least, anything that can be played can be copied. 'Anything you can play and re-record, just not in the digital format. There's literally no way to stop it. If you have a digitally protected CD and you can film it, how are you going to stop it?' says Mitnick.

The other alternative is to criminalize The Scene and arrest its leaders, find the topservers and take them down, and dry up the flow from the top of the pyramid. That was the rationale behind Operation Buccaneer, the first global police sting, which arrested, prosecuted and ultimately jailed 40 members of a release group known as DrinkOrDie (DOD).

DOD originated in Moscow in 1993 and, like most of these ad hoc organizations, it has a hierarchy. There were four types of member: suppliers, who obtained software illegally; crackers, who disabled the copy protection; testers, who used their networks to check that it was working; and packagers, who would upload it to The Scene servers so it could be distributed and downloaded.

Most of DOD's fame was in its early career. It was DOD that managed to put out a pirate copy of Windows 95 two weeks before the launch. At that time, the group was topping the charts for its activity. By 2001, it was nowhere near as visible, but it was large, active, and the FBI wanted to bring it down – and send a message to other groups that they were not safe from prosecution.

The case against DOD is just one that has landed on the desk of Michael O'Leary, now deputy chief of the computer crime and intellectual property section at the Department of Justice. His workload is huge. There are, he estimates, 200 cases of this type open. 'Working in the Department of Justice is a bit like working in a casino. You don't know what time it is outside. You don't know exactly where you are.'

The case against DOD started when the Department of Justice took a peek online at sites like www.iSONEWS.com. 'You would find thousands of people discussing piracy and counterfeiting, and what ran through the conversation was very little fear of prosecution,' he says.[6]

The online discussions gave the FBI, US customs and the Department of Justice all the evidence they needed to take down suspects. O'Leary and his team enjoyed reading about the raids on bulletin boards afterwards. 'They would say, "They searched Jimmy's apartment. They took his TV. They took his car" – a lot of what they said wasn't actually correct, but it works to our advantage. It made us look better than we are.' At one raid conducted by the Dutch police at his request, O'Leary was delighted to find that the friend of one of the suspects had set up a webcam, which was broadcasting on the internet. 'It was great,' he laughs. 'We got to watch what was going on at our own raid.'

Buccaneer owed its success to the willingness of gang members to turn informant on others – after all, the government had impounded their computers, which were full of chatroom logs and other evidence, and it wasn't as if their fellow couriers and crackers were personal friends. On 11 December 2001, police in 27 US cities, plus Australia, Norway, Finland and the UK, were served with more than 100 warrants directed at 62 people. A hundred and thirty computers were seized, and US customs claimed each computer had between 1 and 2 terabytes of stolen software on it. A terabyte can store the equivalent of more than 1,000 CD ROMs.

Law enforcement officials were astounded to find that DOD was not just a bunch of kids making fun in their bedrooms. Many of the 62 had good jobs. Some ran networks where they tested the software. Others worked in the IT business and stole the software to order.

The DOD suspects quickly folded. Leader John Sankus was sentenced to 46 months in prison. Before he was arrested, he was working for the computer retailer Gateway Inc. He lived with his parents in Philadelphia. On 11 December, 40 US customs agents had burst into his store and handcuffed him. 'I felt like someone who had just murdered 50 people,' he told the *New York Times*. 'Most of the people I have been around with are not out to cheat anybody.'

'They are just out to make a name for themselves for no reason other than self-gratification,' David Grimes, another member who was working for CheckPoint software – which ironically builds software to keep hackers out of your network – told the same reporter. By that stage, he was serving 37 months in prison.

Many other DOD members around the world have gone the same way. Some were jailed, others were fined and a few took a deal to become prosecution witnesses. At the time of writing, one remains: Hew Raymond Griffiths, internet nickname Bandido, is in Australia, fighting extradition. He was co-leader of the group with Sankus.

It's like an addiction

DrinkOrDie may be history, but it's a small blip on The Scene. The world's law enforcement are still monitoring the activities of the members, trying to bring down the topservers. Buccaneer has been followed by many other raids: in August 2002, Glendon Martin, a 25-year-old Texan, went on a hacker bulletin board to warn others what would happen, while he awaited sentencing for stealing software:

> I was up at 6.30am happily burning Midtown Madness [a computer game] when I heard a knock at the door. 'FBI open up!' I wasn't quite sure I had heard what I just heard, so I looked out my window and saw the back end of a police car. Naturally I went running to the front door. I saw a few people outside, one of them with one of those black battering rams.[7]

In fear of his parents' front door being wrecked (like Sankus, Martin lived with his parents), he let the agents in.

> They stormed my house, 12 of them from the front. They woke my nine year old brother up at gun point. They had me against the wall with an M4 [machine gun] to my face... My parents were in the backyard watching the sun come up and eight more of them jumped over the fence and walked my parents in to the house at gunpoint.

Martin admitted he was in The Scene 'for the rush of being a courier'. 'It really is fucked up, it's like an addiction.'

At the US District Court in Chicago, four members of Fastlane couriers pleaded guilty to conspiring to commit copyright infringement. With no prior record, Martin got three years' probation, 90 days in a halfway house and a $100,000 fine, but he got lucky. One of the others was sentenced to four years in prison.

O'Leary and the other senior figures in the prosecutions found that the release groups are unlike any other criminal gangs they had dealt with. 'The sophistication of these guys online is amazing. They fall into the category of offenders who think this is a big game,' he says.

> We had some defendants who met their co-conspirators for the first time when they were sitting outside the grand jury waiting to testify. And of all the people in a room, the defendant has a clearer idea in his head than anyone else of what he is up against. In these kinds of cases, he's often explaining the case to his attorney.

O'Leary admits he isn't going to win, even if he raids every supplier in the US, as there are plenty more to take their place. While the level of prosecutions increases, The Scene is so efficient that the actions of a few couriers and crackers can seem like the actions of a million.

While feature films are a Scene highlight, the trafficking takes place in anything that can be ripped and sent across the net: music, computer games, software. The content, which often seems secondary to the release groups compared to the thrill of The Races, is collectively known as Warez, pronounced 'wares'. To reduce the trading in Warez, the people complicit in it have to imagine that they are doing something wrong, and imagine it powerfully enough for it to match the thrill of The Races and the kudos of not being caught.

Meanwhile, at least one company is using The Scene as a way to distribute free content for its marketing, taking advantage of unofficial contacts to place its files on a topserver.

Like the internet, The Scene is designed to be incredibly resilient. It can be slowed but not, at the moment, stopped. The problem with digital piracy is that it's a way to counterfeit that gives great content at no cost – or the finished product at next to no cost. Whatever the record companies, the software houses and the film studios do, they can't compete with free. When you add the power of the internet to the global distribution of criminal gangs, the market manipulation of organized crime and the easy availability of street markets and back-room factories, you have what Brian Sandro, the hero of internet soap 'The Scene', calls 'a massive global infrastructure that exists solely to acquire and disseminate content'. All the raids in the world can't stop it, nor will they. It certainly isn't going to be stopped by cinema ushers in night vision goggles.

'If I could snap my fingers this afternoon and prosecute every IP criminal in the US, take them off the streets, it wouldn't solve the problem,' O'Leary admits.

Notes

1. BBC News, 31 May 2004.
2. *Computer and Video Games*, 9 March 2005.
3. *IGN Insider*, 10 June 2004.
4. http://www.welcometothescene.com/download.shtml.
5. 'The shadow internet', *Wired*, 13 January 2005.
6. Speech to INTA Forum, Washington, DC, February 2005.
7. Article submitted on www.iSONEWS.com.

15 From Russia with Windows

'Russia is becoming quite normal, you know.'

As chairman of Microsoft Russia and CIS, Olga Dergunova is in charge of the subsidiary of the world's largest software company in a region that covers 11 time zones, takes 12 hours to fly across ('On the other hand, you can sit in a traffic jam in Moscow for four hours, so it's not so bad') and has a population of 279 million.

Walking towards Microsoft's office in a residential suburb of Moscow, you assume it must be the giant new glass-and-concrete building, purposely designed to ape the Stalinist skyscrapers that dominate the local skyline. When you arrive, you discover that Microsoft Russia is across the road, behind a school, sharing office space in a small three-story block. It doesn't even have its name on the door.

One out of three ain't bad

In Russia, Microsoft is a big name with a relatively small business. Although the company does not say what its revenue is for the region, we have a good idea of what product counterfeiting is doing to Microsoft: according to researcher IDC, 87 per cent of the Microsoft software used in Russia is pirated, whether it is pre-installed on a new computer or bought at a market or in a shop. 'In

Moscow, piracy is now down to 60 per cent, at a guess. Of course, in the far east of the country, you can go to places where you won't find one legitimate copy of our software,' says Dergunova, who admits that '70 per cent piracy is our dream'.

For a car salesperson to dream that, one day, one out of three cars sold gets paid for, or for a supermarket manager to express satisfaction because 13 per cent of the people who visit the shop pay money rather than walking out with the goods, is ridiculous, but this is the software business and, across the world, 36 per cent of software isn't legally bought. That's product that would have sold for $29 billion.[1]

Russia is now joint fifth in the global piracy table, with that pillar of respect for the rule of law, Zimbabwe. It's doing a better job at legalizing its software business than China and Vietnam (92 per cent piracy), Ukraine – also under Dergunova's remit – (91 per cent, not helped by the fact that the national laws don't yet have a definition for counterfeiting, though it is illegal) and Indonesia (88 per cent). But nowhere in the world is especially compliant: the citizens of the US install 22 per cent of their business software illegally, the Brits 29 per cent and those in Switzerland, home to the World Trade Organization and the World Intellectual Property Organization, 31 per cent.

For Microsoft Russia, 87 per cent is a major achievement. In 1997 I met Microsoft's first anti-piracy tsar, Eugene Danilov, who at that time was proud to have brought down the piracy rate in the country to 91 per cent. 'In Russia this year there will be 1.5 million PCs sold,' he told me. 'That's as many as in Australia. But in Australia we sell $300 million of software. In Russia, it's $25 million.'

The difference in the last 10 years may seem small, but if you look at it another way it's huge. In 1997, Microsoft received revenue for 9 per cent of its products. In 2004, it received revenue for 13 per cent – a 50 per cent improvement.

In 1997, Microsoft was having trouble making any progress at all. It was desperate enough to offer a free printer for buying software with your computer, and gave free palmtops to companies that admitted they used knockoffs. Danilov had struck a deal with a counterfeiter to offer legitimate software alongside counterfeits on his website, because the margin for legitimate product was better, even if it hardly sold. Government support was patchy at best: to save money the Moscow City Department of Education had even just kitted itself out with pirated copies of Windows, bought from a local dealer and shipped from an illegal CD ROM pressing facility in Cyprus. Consumers would have to work for four weeks to earn the cash for Microsoft Office, but Danilov's solution to that wasn't exactly caring capitalism. They should, he told me, get a better job.

Evolution, not revolution

The knockoff software market in Russia was as old as the PC, which arrived in Russia before US software companies could legally set up subsidiaries there. Illegally imported US software was sold on the street in markets, just as it is today. Large-scale downloading hasn't yet taken off in Russia because few have a fast internet connection, so even today by far the major piracy problem, says Dergunova, is counterfeit CD ROMs – for which the going rate is around $3. Half-hearted copyright enforcement after the Russians introduced their current constitution in 1993 did nothing to solve the problem. Many software companies that were new to Russia tried an amnesty similar to Microsoft's, where existing counterfeit software users handed in knockoff product and for a nominal charge in roubles got a genuine copy of the package and the promise of limited support. The roubles could not be taken out of the country and inflation swiftly destroyed their value, so for example in the offices of Borland, a US software company that owned the rights to a program called dBase that was popular in Russia, the roubles sat in a cardboard box in the Moscow office, available by the fistful for any visiting executive who could find a shopkeeper to take them.

Today dBase is ancient history in the IT business, the rouble is Russia's only legal currency and visiting US executives have no problem spending it, and inflation is under control, but government departments, companies large and small still use counterfeit software, Dergunova admits. 'Is everything perfect here? No. Will it evolve? Absolutely,' she says. 'Seventy years ago, the value of property was destroyed in this country. Property, even physical, was not a concept that people had in their minds. It has taken 15 years to change that mentality. In the beginning, people didn't pay us because they didn't know they should. Now they know.'

They know because the government, despite its poor record on buying knockoffs, has become a vocal supporter of a legitimate software business in Russia. The process began when Russia was attempting to join the 148 members of the World Trade Organization; it became a priority when the Ministry of Finance spotted how much it was losing in potential purchase tax revenue. Russian Microsoft product sells for 70 per cent of the price of US and European versions, and the Russian government stands to make 18 per cent of that in VAT. To encourage Russians into a legitimate software buying habit, the Ministry of Education – the ministry that had no problem in buying knockoffs in 1997 – has recently completed a programme to distribute computers to schools throughout the country. This time the PCs were all supplied with legitimate, pre-loaded Microsoft software, bought at a discount through an official dealer.

Sergey Alpatov, who runs the marketing for small businesses for Microsoft in Russia, admits that compliance with the law is patchy. Small companies, as is the case in the US, Europe or anywhere else, are still more likely to buy a knockoff than the large ones whose books are under scrutiny. 'But our research shows that, bit by bit, people are changing their behaviour,' he says. 'We have good legislation. And the police see what the problem is now, where a couple of years ago they couldn't see it.'

Some things have certainly changed. Microsoft no longer supplies product to any dealer who would sell counterfeits – providing they know who is selling the counterfeits. Some of the retail kiosks have been raided, some of the 30 CD replication plants have been inspected, and large businesses desperate for overseas investment have to open their accounts to inspection by outsiders. 'Big companies need capital and foreign investors. Look at their books – if they ordered fake software, it's pretty obvious. There are people in business and government for whom the way Russia is perceived across the globe is very important right now,' says Dergunova.

'Russia is a country in transition,' she reminds me as I leave. At the top of the road, you can see that the transition is far from over. At the kiosk opposite the shoe shop that sells 'genuine style' training shoes, with this season's Nike counterfeit selling for 850 roubles ($35), I pick up counterfeit copies of Windows XP and Microsoft Office 2003 Professional for 80 roubles each. 'The software is guaranteed for two weeks,' the shopkeeper tells me, asking if I am interested in his full range, which covers most commercial PC software sold in Western Europe, from anti-virus products to computer-aided design software at 80 roubles a disc. Smaller items that would sell for about $50 in the US are loaded together on to multiple application packages, often around 10 or 15 packages to a CD ROM.

Under the counter

At the Coalition for Intellectual Property Rights, Russia representative Olga Barranikova quietly despairs that Microsoft will ever get paid for 30 per cent of its sales. 'It's not difficult to change the law but it is difficult to change the people's understanding,' she says.

> Every four years we have new deputies in the Duma, and we start from the beginning again. First they all decide they want to create a law, because they don't realize we have the laws already. It takes between one and two years to educate them. Meanwhile, when the legal production facilities make the counterfeit discs, they do it at night. Come the day, it is a legal production factory again.

Russian police raids on the production facility cannot legally confiscate the equipment used to make counterfeits. Barranikova points out that the counterfeiters lose one day of production at worst. She is pressing for laws that force producers to account for the volume of polycarbonate they use, but this sort of change moves slowly, she says, even with the carrot of WTO membership to concentrate the minds of the politicians.

'If you went to the market a few years ago, they knew you were from Microsoft but it didn't bother the stallholders. Now they will start to collect the counterfeit Microsoft CDs and hide them under the counter,' Dergunova assured me. At Gorbushka Market, housed in an old television factory in the west of the city, they would have a lot of hiding to do.

On the first floor, at least 50 small shops compete to sell software, DVDs, computer games and CDs at rock-bottom prices. This is no flea market: with shops selling washing machines, video cameras and satellite dishes nearby, it is much like any Western mall, stripped of its fast-food concessions and bored children. Gorbushka started as an informal market in the 1970s, as a group of would-be rockers gathered near the Gorbunov House of Culture to trade tapes of their favourite Western music, defying the authorities for the chance to experience forbidden culture like Deep Purple and Black Sabbath. The market grew until it featured traders in music, DVDs and lots and lots of software.

When it moved to its new location in 2001, the authorities attempted to crack down on the counterfeiters. Some raids followed. Modern Moscow still has a respect for large government slogans plastered on gaudy posters; today, the posters exhorting citizens to work hard and build a strong Communist state have been replaced, in Gorbushka at least, with Russian slogans that translate as 'Listen up, you pirate, I choose copyright!' and 'Stop imitation, down with the fakes!'

Perhaps because of its tradition of beating the system, perhaps because the genuine items on sale look expensive next to their knockoff neighbours, compliance is patchy, and the genuine CDs and CD ROMs – often sold at knock-down prices by the Russian subsidiaries of games and record companies – attract little interest. Whether you are looking for a knockoff EA Sports FIFA Soccer 2005, a bootleg copy of Half-Life 2, CDs featuring five albums from one recording artist squished as MP3s on to one disc, or the standard parade of Microsoft software packages – some of which, like Microsoft Money, are not even officially available in Russia – it's all there, and nothing costs more than $5.

The two problems in policing counterfeiting of digital products in Russia, as in many similar countries at the top of the Business Software Alliance piracy list, are lack of awareness from customers that they might be breaking the law, and a feeling from counterfeiter and customer alike that it's foreign product anyway, so who cares?

For many Russians, and their neighbours in Ukraine, Georgia and all the other ex-Soviet states, the counterfeits are more real than the real product. For example, in Soviet Russia, families for many years got the chance to watch Disney's *Snow White and the Seven Dwarfs*, which state TV had acquired from a poor-quality pirated tape filmed in the West. A generation of Russians grew up believing that the time code in the top corner, a series of numbers showing how much of the film had elapsed, was part of the authentic Disney experience. When a genuine copy was shown on Russian TV for the first time, scores complained that it couldn't be real because they couldn't see the little numbers.

The same applies for Russian computer purchasers. At Gorbushka you will spend the same as you would spend in the West on your computer, and usually almost next to nothing on software. It is the way it always has been.

The knock-on effect is that Western software companies are often wary about investing in Russia. They don't bother to set up the expensive 24-hour support that users in the West are accustomed to. In Russia, you can get basic office-hours telephone support for Microsoft products, but at nowhere near the level of sophistication that you would find in the West. 'One of my friends bought a licensed Microsoft product. He had some problems, he phoned technical support and they couldn't help, because the quality of staff in Moscow isn't good,' says Alexander Matveyev. 'If there is no service, and I can buy either the licensed product for $300 or the counterfeit for $3, what will I do?' His friend turned to one of the local market traders who sold him software that had been counterfeited and 'improved' by a Russian hacker.

Finding a patent attorney who understands people who buy counterfeit software isn't an everyday experience, but this is Russia. 'I'm not just a patent attorney. I'm a consumer too,' says Matveyev, who works in his father's firm in central Moscow. 'If you're a company like Microsoft, your trademark can work for you, but it cannot work instead of you,' he warns.

Matveyev says that Microsoft should earn 'honest money, not easy money', or expect to be counterfeited. 'Fighting against counterfeiting isn't just about controlling counterfeit products. It's about letting people see you are in control of quality,' he says.

But as Barranikova points out, unless Russians start paying for software, there is never going to be a 'quality' Russian software industry, because no one has the incentive to invest locally in the staff that it would need. The biggest losers, she says, are Russian software companies. 'We are trying to protect the rights of Russians too – for example, we have a special accounting system, and that needs special accounting software,' she says, 'but they counterfeit that software too.'

As it is too complex for Microsoft or any other company to adapt existing financial software packages for Russian standards, this should be a profitable niche for Russian software companies – and Russia has some of the most talented programmers anywhere in the world. But it isn't. In some sectors Russian software developers could compete with Microsoft, but they can't compete with nearly free versions of their own product and, unlike Microsoft, they don't make revenues of more than $40 billion a year (of which profit is approximately $18 billion) to sweeten the pill.

Because Windows and Office are the big sellers on the $3 racks, the counterfeits that you might romantically think are a well-deserved dent in the $18 billion money mountain are hurting would-be competitors even more than Microsoft. Ironically, thanks to counterfeiters, Microsoft's de facto monopoly in Russia is assured for a generation. If you're going to pay $3 for software, you might as well get the market leader.

Quick! Send for the ferret

Back in the US, the Business Software Alliance, as well as – you will recall – making children cry by forcing them to steal each other's paintings, is trying to educate the lucky mites about the financial consequences of the knockoff software business. US and Canadian teachers can download a comic from BSA's 'Play it safe in cyber-space' website called 'Copyright Crusader to the Rescue' to use in their classroom, featuring one of the more unusual superheroes in comic-book history. He's a ferret in a mask called Garret, who pops out of a computer screen to lecture children about copying software illegally:

> *Garret the Ferret*: It's big Shawn. Companies lose billions of dollars every year. It also means people can lose their jobs.

> *Shawn*: My friend's dad lost his job at a software company last year. I never thought about the bad things that can happen when I copy software.

Five months after it was released, more than a million kids have overcome misgivings that Garret the Ferret's ('Take a look at the box Shawn... That is the copyright symbol. It means the program is protected by copyright laws') name doesn't quite rhyme, and have either downloaded or read his comic-book adventures. It's too early to say whether the kids took any of it in, or just played along so they could get out of school early and see if they could pull down a copy of *Grand Theft Auto*.

The BSA's Debbi Mayster argues that, if the global software business is going to hold back the tide of illegal software, it has to catch the next generation young.

'It's going to take time, but we want to catch them when they are developing a code of ethics,' she says. 'The other intellectual property associations have taken to suing kids who download music or films. We feel strongly we need to educate them instead.' Educating them at college, she says, is too late. They presumably haven't got time for comics, as they are downloading pre-release movies in their dorm rooms instead.

The ultimate problem for Microsoft and its competitors anywhere in the world is that, when we look at a single CD ROM, we don't see much value – certainly not the value that Microsoft puts on it. Large companies don't even get hundreds of CD ROMs for their money – they already have the software on their server, and they buy a piece of paper that permits a set number of staff to use it – so either accidentally or on purpose, it's not unusual to find that a few more have been sneaked in at the edges.

In Western Europe and the US, technology that means you can't use your copy of Microsoft Windows until you register it, and after you register it no one else can, has made convincing counterfeits harder to produce, but the counterfeiters have accepted the challenge. As long ago as 1997, four masked raiders burst into Thompson Lith, a Microsoft authorized replicator based in East Kilbride, Scotland, and made off with 100,000 CDs, many of which were copies of Microsoft Office, and 200,000 certificates of authenticity, or COAs as they are known in the trade.[2]

The COA is Microsoft's sophisticated hologram label with intricate printing that should tell us a product is real. 'We put more anti-counterfeiting technology into our COA than the British Royal Mint puts into its banknotes,' boasts Alex Hilton, Microsoft's UK anti-piracy director, surrounded in his London office by real and fake product, the fakes seized from software dealers and markets in the UK. The potential problem for the consumer: a fake COA may look different to a real one, but they both look equally likely to be real. Once Hilton has to pause, unsure which of his comparison discs is real and which a forgery. Both have fancy laser etching on the disc; both have the logo; both have the software. Only one is legitimate, and it turns out not to be the one with 'Genuine' stamped on it.

The orthodox way to deal with fake software is the same as for fake toothpaste: make a test purchase, confront the vendor, find the supplier, find the manufacturer and take them all on. In 2004, Microsoft in the UK broke the rules, by offering a free genuine replacement to users who sent in their counterfeit product if it was bought in good faith. 'We did it simply because we wanted to build up a lot of leads,' Hilton says. 'We wanted witness statements from those people. But before we did it, we had to ask ourselves, should Microsoft be allowing people to launder counterfeit products?'

Microsoft braced for the rush. It never came. Despite constant press coverage, 20 people sent in their product, and Microsoft found six that were convincing enough to justify a replacement. The other 14 were obvious copies, clearly fakes, sent in by people trying to get a free copy of Windows. Hilton concludes that, for all the effort that counterfeiters are putting into fancy labels and holograms, we know what we are getting when we buy counterfeit software – at least, all but six of us. Just like the Russian consumers, we know we are getting the fake, but Microsoft, the BSA, the police, the trading standards, the customs, the World Trade Organization, the Alliance Against Counterfeiting and Piracy, the Anti-Counterfeiting Group, the International Intellectual Property Institute, and a hundred other agencies have not convinced us we are doing anything wrong enough to pass up the opportunity. It seems Garret's really up against it.

The agencies may have the law on their side, but, in our lust for cheap product, when we who download illegally, buy counterfeits and pirate discs and help to distribute them we have taken sides and, understandably, are choosing not to look too closely at who we've lined up with. Digital piracy will continue to be a global crime bonanza.

Microsoft employees fondly relate that Bill Gates once said that his biggest competition was the counterfeiter. They are wrong. We cottoned on quickly that digital product can be free, or nearly free, if we want to go along with the sophisticated knockoff culture that exploits it. There is no copy protection or certificate of authenticity in the world that is strong enough to solve this problem alone. Unless software companies like Microsoft – and film companies and the music business – can convince us that their easily copied, easily distributed digital product does have the value they assign to it, it's not the counterfeiter that's the enemy; it's the cynicism of their own customers.

Lavinia Carey, chair of the Alliance Against Counterfeiting and Piracy, worries that if the cynicism wins there simply isn't a viable business model any more. 'The industry just has to work together,' she says. 'If we don't, we can all go home and make jam instead, because that's the choice we have.'

Notes

1. IDC/BSA survey, July 2004.
2. vnunet.com, 28 November 1997.

PART 4

Counterfeit killers

16 The capital of bogus parts

At 21.38 Eastern Standard Time on 20 December 1995, American Airlines flight 965 from Miami crashed into Mt St Jose, part of the Andes mountains 35 miles north of its destination airport in Cali, Colombia. It was the first time a Boeing 757 had been involved in an accident in 12 years of flying, 5.2 million landings and 11.5 million hours in the air.

When rescuers reached the scene of the crash, 155 passengers and all eight crew lay dead. Only four passengers survived. But the emergency services were not the only people interested in the crash site.

Within hours, an illegal salvage gang had stolen the aircraft's engine thrust reversers, its cockpit avionics system and enough spare parts to make a 14-page list. They flew the parts off the mountainside less than 24 hours later in the same helicopters used to ferry the aviation inspectors to the scene, cleaned and boxed them in Cali airport, and shipped them out.

Weeks later, the stolen parts were being hawked in Miami, where the gang was offering them for sale to the highest bidder. At the time, an anonymous local law enforcement source told the Associated Press that the thieves 'wanted to sell the whole lot, including the landing gear'.[1]

The scale of the theft forced American Airlines to release the full list of stolen parts, including their serial numbers. But the parts were never found. Like many parts at that time, they probably found their way to a parts dealership and from there were fitted to another of the 700-odd Boeing 757s in service at the time.

Bogus beware

No sensible airline would buy, and no mechanic would fit, a part knowing that it had recently been salvaged from a crashed aircraft, unless it wanted to entertain the possibility of disaster, death and a very large lawsuit. No parts broker would sell them as airworthy, because it's illegal to do so. Instead, the parts made their way into the system with forged documentation and fake serial numbers. It's a business that has been going on for the last 50 years. During that time, thousands of parts have been given false identities, patched up or simply sold 'as is', no questions asked, and installed on the sorts of aircraft that we might have flown in.

You don't hear a lot about it though. As one airline regulator told me, 'The industry doesn't want to talk about this. People who work in it are thinking, "Am I in aviation, or in the business of destroying it?"'

In the airline business, mechanics call these parts 'bogus' parts. They are counterfeits, because they are sold as something they are not – safety-tested, approved aircraft spares. The regime of testing for aircraft parts has a very good justification: if your car's clutch goes while you are driving to work, it's inconvenient but not a disaster. If an aircraft's tail breaks off or its engine turbine fails in mid-air, it can't just park and wait for the emergency services. Bogus parts are a potential death sentence for the travelling public.

It may surprise you to learn that, in the opinion of Matthew Andersson, chief executive of Aviation Development Holdings and a man with 30 years of experience in the airline business, 'Nearly every aircraft in the United States today may be flying with one or more bogus parts.'[2]

To air industry officials, bogus parts have a less emotive name. They are known as SUPs, or 'suspected unapproved parts'. This is a classic piece of obfuscation: a part is rarely 'suspected' of being unapproved; it either is or it isn't.

Not all bogus parts – SUPs – are counterfeits, and not all of them have something wrong with them. The name merely says that no one knows exactly where the part came from and how it got on to the aircraft. It could simply be a perfectly safe part whose paperwork has been lost in the system somewhere, the aircraft equivalent of a filing error. Yet an unapproved part could also be a straightforward counterfeit, made to look like the official part but built to a lower quality or made out of car parts or scrap, and sold to the repair station or airline with false documents. It could be a part that has reached its specified number of flying hours, but has been taken off one aircraft, had its documentation falsified and a new coat of paint, and sold on to a parts shop. It could be a salvaged part, like the items stripped from AA 965, again with falsified documentation. They all have three things in common: they are not what their documents claim them to be; they are potentially catastrophic; and if there's one on your aircraft you won't know it is there.

So it may disturb you to know that, at the time that AA 965 crashed, it was 'clear that bogus parts were out there in great numbers', according to the woman whose job it was to regulate the industry in the most sophisticated, largest and most lucrative market in the world.[3]

Mary Schiavo, the Inspector General of the US Department of Transportation between 1990 and 1996 – and a qualified pilot – was shocked when she took on her job that a complacent industry was doing little to weed out bogus parts. During her time in office, her inspectors found counterfeit helicopter blades, brakes, engines, fuel bladders, generators, cockpit warning lights, wheels and even entire wing and tail assemblies. 'We would confiscate parts made in basements, garages and weld shops,' she wrote later. 'They even showed up in the president's helicopters and the oxygen and fire-extinguishing systems of Air Force One and Two [the president's and vice-president's official aircraft].'

Schiavo, nicknamed 'Scary Mary' in the industry for her frequent safety warnings, made as many enemies as friends in the business. She accused the US Federal Aviation Administration of having a conflict of interest – while it was nominally in charge of safety, it also had a duty to help promote air travel. While she was using every opportunity to warn the world that the bogus parts problem was out of control, the FAA had a different attitude. As the FAA administrator David Hinson told a US government investigation in a notorious sound bite in May 1995: 'Do unapproved parts pose a significant safety problem for the flying public? The answer is no, they do not.'

Four year later, in yet another hearing, Michael Fanfalone, the president of the Professional Airways Systems Specialists (PASS) – an association of engineers – was saying exactly the opposite. 'Every day, inspectors discover parts they suspect of being "unapproved" during the course of surveillance and inspections. The current time lapse between the discovery of an SUP and the validation of an acknowledged unapproved part may enable hundreds of these parts to be installed in actual passenger-carrying operations. SUPs are a potential danger to everyone who flies.'

Blind and toothless?

So who is right? The truth is, we don't know. Some things we can say for sure. In the 1980s and 1990s, bogus parts were being put into the system by criminals, and they were causing aircraft to crash. As the Press Association report on AA 965 pointed out, one Colombian fake parts trafficker had told a Miami detective she switched to the trade from smuggling drugs, because it was so profitable. And when the Associated Press asked the FAA to check its database for accident incidents between May 1973 and April 1996 for crashes and accidents that had been directly attributable to fake parts, there were 174 of them, causing 17 deaths and 39 injuries. That's one every seven weeks.

Some of the incidents were nightmarish: on 19 June 1995, a ValuJet DC-9's engine exploded on take-off from Atlanta. Shrapnel smashed into the cabin and fire injured the passengers and crew. The fault: an SUP installed during a stopover in Turkey.

Also, the FAA's database looked at US-based data, and the US was not the only country affected by bogus parts. Six years previously, on 8 September 1989, a Convair 580 flying 22,000 feet above the North Sea between Oslo in Norway and Hamburg in Germany lost control when its tail section began vibrating violently, tore loose and plunged into the sea, killing 55 passengers. After investigators had salvaged 90 per cent of the plane from three and a half miles of sea, they found fake bolts and brackets were holding the plane together. The parts supplier was never found.

We also know that, while negative publicity has tightened regulations, we still probably fly in aircraft, as Andersson points out, that have bogus parts installed in them.

In a press conference in 2004, Boeing's manager for RFID Kenneth Porad admitted that its airline customers paid $100 million a year in Federal Aviation Administration fines and for the cost of replacing bogus parts that had been inadvertently fitted to its aircraft.[4] With each 747 having 6 million parts, SUPs may never be completely expunged from the system.

Instead, recent evidence suggests that the international regulator's watchdogs are, in the words of *Air Safety Week*, 'blind and toothless'.[5]

In September 2001, a team of FBI agents set down in Leonardo da Vinci airport in Rome. At the same time, another team were visiting Olbia Airport in Sardinia. Their brief was to investigate reports that three Italian parts brokers – New Tech Italia, New Tech Aerospace, and Panaviation – were supplying unapproved parts all over the world.

On 1 February 2002, the Italian Guardia di Finanza raided Panaviation warehouses and found crates of Airbus A300 parts, plus blank tags and data plates, plus parts with altered data plates. The plates and tags carry serial numbers that identify each part. When you change the numbers, you effectively give the part a new identity. Police also impounded six aircraft that Panaviation was cannibalizing for spare parts, and three containers of parts in Naples, which were about to be shipped to the US.[6]

On 4 February 2002, the FAA issued a worldwide alert: forms used to document the state of maintenance on some of the parts that it had sold had been forged. Investigators also found that parts that had been involved in accidents had been shipped to repair facilities to be certified. The facilities were not told that they were parts that had been taken off aircraft that had been involved in accidents. Non-airworthy parts had been shipped with documentation that claimed they had been overhauled, Captain Silvano Imparato, head of the safety department at the Italian regulator, the Ente Nazionale per l'Aviazione Civile (ENAC), explained later.

ENAC warned that as many as 1,000 aircraft might be affected by the bogus parts from these three companies.[7]

By 19 February, there were more revelations, this time in the European Parliament. 'The Italian and US authorities have revealed that American and Italian companies were marketing old, defective and recycled spare parts for aircraft,' said Alexandros Alavanos, a Greek member of the European Parliament. 'The problem reportedly affects 2 per cent of aircraft and it is estimated such unsuitable spares may be responsible for 10 per cent of recent aviation accidents.'

The investigation threw up more statistics that show that regulation has not cut bogus parts out of the market.

'Currently about 1 per cent of airline parts on the international market are suspect,' Alfredo Roma, the chairman of ENAC, told reporters on 10 April 2002.[8] 'The presence of unchecked parts could threaten the chain of safety.'

The $10,000 bolt

If bogus parts threaten our safety, it's not that no one in the industry is doing anything about it – but the sheer scale of the job makes the industry very hard to regulate. The response to worries over counterfeits in the last 10 years has been an avalanche of paper, says Juan Robbin, president of Skymart Sales Ltd in the industrial district of Miami close to the international airport where hundreds of parts brokers cluster.

Miami, Florida is the centre of the world's spare parts trade for aircraft: it combines a long history of flight and expertise in aviation with a convenient location where it is accessible from Europe, Africa and South America. It's no surprise that the spares from AA 965 were placed on the market in Miami.

It also combines legitimate companies like Skymart, with hundreds of less scrupulous brokers. Schiavo has called it 'the world's capital of bogus parts'. Miami's reputation bothers Robbin, whose firm has been in the business for decades without ever trading any suspect part; but he doesn't deny that other brokers are less scrupulous.

Robbin's warehouse is meticulously ordered. Literally every bolt that enters his warehouse has a paper trail behind it. To demonstrate, he shows me one of the bolts: a $14 item with sheets of paper to show where it came from, who has previously owned it, who inspected it and when it was approved. 'It's probably exactly the same bolt as you get for $4 on a boat. You are paying $10 for traceability,' he says. 'Unapproved parts used to be rampant here. Now it's tougher. Believe it or not, if you have a part you just overhauled and you can't find the paperwork, it needs to be completely overhauled again.'

There is a guaranteed market for spare parts because the aircraft we fly in are constantly being taken apart and rebuilt. For example, Boeing specifies four types of maintenance checks. The A check happens once a week. The B check takes place once every couple of months, and needs around 18 hours to complete. Every three years, the C check will involve a complete overhaul, and would normally require the interior to be completely ripped out and reinstalled. Finally, when the aircraft is around eight or nine years old, the D check is the most thorough possible: at that point, the entire plane is taken apart. 'Every item is taken off. You are literally remanufacturing the aircraft,' Robbin says.

Along the way, every part has a specified flying time before it has to be taken off and re-examined, and a lifetime after which it must be thrown away, regardless of its condition. The reasoning is that after a period of time the likelihood of failure goes up exponentially – and you don't want to run a part until it fails.

Ripping expired parts off a disused plane, giving them a lick of paint and attaching a new serial number (which Robbin shows me is attached via a plate with two small screws) and a forged set of identity forms is a cheap way to create an inventory of parts. It's not straightforward, as the documentation can be compared to a central database, and few airlines in the developed world will today take a part unless they are completely sure of its provenance.

But in the real world, not everyone is asking too many questions. 'Would you rather buy a used plane from BA or a third world country?' Robbin asks. In places where regulation is weak, he says, the process by which parts are bought and sold is more like the situation in Miami in the 1980s and early 1990s, which he describes as: 'Hey, that looks all right. I'll take it!'

The UN has a body called the International Civil Aviation Organization (ICAO), which sets safety standards for how airlines are run – for example, how qualified the inspection of parts is and how strong the regulation of the market is. The ICAO standards aren't enforced, as the ICAO doesn't have its own inspectors and, if it did, they would have no jurisdiction. For a clue as to how well ICAO standards are met, we can consult the FAA's International Aviation Safety Assessment. This has two categories of compliance: if you are in category 1, the FAA allows your airline to fly to the US. If you are in category 2, it means that, in the eyes of the FAA, you don't meet these standards. If you fly to the US, you can continue to do so, with additional security precautions. If you don't yet, you can't start until you have sorted out your problems.

Among the countries in category 2 are Argentina, Ecuador, Uruguay, Bulgaria and Greece. Few African countries pass: few have been assessed.

When Schiavo was investigating bogus parts for the US government, an audit of FAA-certified repair stations – based outside the United States – found 43 per cent of the parts they obtained from manufacturers lacked the documentation they needed. When the stations bought the parts from brokers, the statistics were even worse: 95 per cent were bogus. Overall, 'you had about a 50:50 chance of getting a genuine part', Schiavo said in 1999.[9]

Unapproved parts are still rife in the developing world, Robbin admits, even if the aircraft are refitted in Miami. 'What ends up happening is that after poor maintenance the plane goes to Africa, and in six months it's crashed.'

Robbin shows me a Boeing 757 air supply, yellow tag attached, documentation secured to it with a rubber band. It's not a valuable piece now, because there are plenty of 757 spares available – not least because a downturn in the fortunes of many airlines has resulted in literally hundreds of aircraft being parked in places like the Mojave Desert, waiting to be recertified or broken up for scrap. He remembers the time that AA 965 crashed, and explains why the parts were so valuable and why someone was willing to buy them and not ask questions. 'The 757 was a relatively new aircraft, and those parts were extremely expensive,' he says, explaining that in the early years of a new type of airliner some airlines even buy an entire spare aircraft (the going rate for a new commercial passenger aircraft is $100 million and up) to have a ready supply of available spares. 'When a new aircraft comes out, just after your warranty expires you're screwed. You might have to buy a bolt for $10,000,' he says.

Supplying bogus parts is big business, even in the knockoff economy, and it tempts some counterfeiters to take incredible risks. On 20 August 2004, Ralph Michael Cooper was sentenced in the US Federal District Court in Fort Lauderdale, Florida, to two and a half years in prison. Maybe it's something in the air in Florida: his crime was to sell counterfeit aircraft parts to the US air force, the army, the navy and NASA.

The US Department of Defense approved one manufacturer of engine seals for its Blackhawk helicopters, F-16 and F-14 jets, AWACS surveillance aircraft and Seahawk rescue helicopters. For 1,505 seals, the DoD was prepared to pay $54,902.50.

The problem for Cooper was that he didn't have 1,505 seals manufactured by Chicago Rawhide Co. He had the same number of counterfeit seals that he had bought from Taiwan for $1 each. He forged the labels, and hoped he wouldn't get caught. Presumably he hoped that the seals, which the US government described as 'a conscious or reckless risk of death or serious bodily injury', wouldn't be spotted. He hoped wrong.

Five miles away, you can stand next to a fence and see the less glamorous end of the airline parts business. Founded in 1927, Miami's Opa-Locka Airport was once Miami Municipal Airport, and the world's busiest: in 1967 over 650,000 flights either originated or landed there. It's hard to believe that now, as today's airport is home to a few executive jets, some cargo planes, several giant World War II hangars and a lot of rusting hulks.

On any day you can see what salvage means for aircraft parts at close quarters, because Opa-Locka is now a giant chop shop for obsolete aircraft, flown into the airport to be refitted as cheaply as possible before some disappear to other parts of the world. A large trailer is parked next to two 727s, which are being systematically gutted. The seats have been removed, as have the engines and the wings. Men with machine tools are setting about the cockpit. As each part comes down, it is placed in the trailer.

The parts are unlikely to be destined for the developed world, as the 727 is effectively obsolete. The last one was made in 1984, and many of the 1,700 manufactured date from the 1960s. Increased regulation on noise pollution and fuel consumption makes it uneconomic to fly and unwelcome at airports. Yet there are still many flying in other parts of the world, and 30-year-old aircraft need plenty of spare parts.

Close by, a sign tells me to keep out. But it's on a gate that has been unlocked and left open, so that it's easier for the fitters to walk in and out.

As you see the parts being driven away, it's easy to remember Robbin's advice on how to travel by air when you visit new countries: only fly on airlines that you've heard of before you got there.

Notes

1. Associated Press, 8 December 1996.
2. *Air Safety Week*, 9 February 2004.
3. Mary Schiavo with Sabra Chartrand (1997) *Flying Blind, Flying Safe*, Avon Books, New York.
4. *Information Week*, 14 June 2004.
5. *Air Safety Week*, 4 March 2002.
6. *Overhaul and Maintenance*, 1 March 2002.
7. NBC News, Florida, 6 February 2002.
8. Reuters, Air bodies seek end to cancerous parts trade, 10 April 2002.
9. *Insight on the News*, 27 September 1999.

17 Under the hood

The newspaper advertisement shows a car key shaped like a saw. 'Fake parts cut the life of your car,' it says in Arabic. 'Insist on Mercedes-Benz genuine parts.' The poster shows a chain breaking: 'One fake part ruins everything', it warns drivers. Along Shaikh Zayed Road, the giant hoarding bought by Al Futtaim motors implores Toyota drivers to say 'No to Counterfeit'. The Emirates Motor Company's advertising tells Dubai's Mercedes drivers that 'Counterfeit parts can kill. That's a fact. While human error is the cause of most road accidents, it would be a grave human error to use counterfeit parts in your Mercedes-Benz.'

In nearby Kuwait, Mohammed Naser Al-Sayer & Sons is warning us: 'Don't risk your life', with a picture of a giant mousetrap baited with counterfeit spares. At the Al-Sayer Group, every 5 Kuwaiti dinars ($17) that you spend on genuine spare parts gets you an entry into a prize draw.

Al Futtaim's campaign even reached the airwaves – one of Dubai's radio stations offered a competition for listeners to send in their reason not to buy fake auto parts, with every prize winner getting a 'Citizens Against Counterfeit' certificate.

If Miami is the capital of bogus aero parts, then Dubai can perhaps claim the title as capital of fake auto parts. In the United Arab Emirates, the manufacturers' estimate is that one in three workshops fits fake parts when you bring your car in for a service. In a city by the sea where the wind whips corrosive salt inland and where the temperature tops 32C for 200 days a year (and 45C regularly in the summer months), those workshops are continuously busy.

A perfect environment

'A vehicle here has to be serviced every 5,000 kilometres and, when it is serviced, that's when you change the oil filter, the spark plugs – the sort of products that we commonly see counterfeited,' says an investigator who asked not to be named, located in the Middle East region, working for a large US auto manufacturer. 'If they have their car serviced by an authorized dealer, they should have no worries. What I would worry about are the people who take their cars to an unauthorized dealer who is looking to cut costs, where they may get a counterfeit part.'

Dubai is the perfect environment for the problem to flourish: the port of Dubai is a common destination for goods shipped from the Far East. Car ownership is increasing rapidly as tourism creates a middle class. Oil is untaxed, and cheaper than water. And then, there's that climate.

'There are two ways that counterfeits get into the market here. The first is that they come into the country packaged in printed boxes, so the whole product is counterfeited. The other way is to manufacture the parts overseas, ship them in plain boxes and repackage them locally,' the investigator says. His employers put secret anti-counterfeit marks on its parts so that investigators can tell the fakes from the real parts. The counterfeits look that good.

That doesn't mean that there is no difference. The similarity is only skin deep, the investigator says. He has many times discovered fake oil filters that are not properly heat treated and might burst into flames, or bogus spark plugs that will see the car owner rolling to a stop somewhere in the desert.

Alyson Coady, the spokesperson for the Dubai-based Automotive Brands Protection Coalition (ABPC), says that 'The most common items are oil filters, brake pads, fan belts – but recently we had a big seizure here of windscreens. You might say that a counterfeit wheel cover is fine, but we are also talking about glass that isn't tempered, or a car bonnet that's made from metal that doesn't crumple properly in the crumple zone.'

It doesn't end there. As with every other branch of the knockoff business, there are some apocryphal stories of counterfeit auto parts that take your breath away. In Nigeria, there were the knockoff brake pads that were made from compressed grass, which – not surprisingly – tended to be better at starting a fire than stopping a car. Authentication News reports the gruesome tale of a bus that tipped over in 1987, killing seven children. Its brakes were made of sawdust.

GM, Toyota, Nissan, DaimlerChrysler, Honda and BMW are members of the ABPC, but the volume of investigative work to be done in the Middle East, and the fierce competition in the car business, means it rarely does investigations jointly. 'We did 400 raids in 2004 in Saudi Arabia, Kuwait and UAE. This year we have done fewer raids, but we are concentrating on larger raids, so we're finding more products,' the investigator says. He estimates that he and his colleagues will find and help the police seize around $4.5 million of auto parts in Dubai in 2005 – around 15 per cent of counterfeits that his employer estimates will reach the market.

Part of the problem with investigations in Dubai is the sophistication of the counterfeiters. 'A lot of the counterfeiters employ people, or are owned by people, who used to work for the big manufacturers. In some cases they have their own fleet of trucks. Some of the counterfeiting operations in the region are better set up than some of the auto manufacturers in the region,' he says. The other problem is that there are simply so many unauthorized dealerships to police. The investigator regularly works a single street in Jeddah, Saudi Arabia, where he estimates there are between 300 and 400 parts shops selling fake parts.

In April 2005, the Gulf's largest seizure of fake parts shows how well organized the problem has become. In a warehouse in Umm Al Quwain in Dubai, police found 36.7 million dirhams ($126 million) of auto spares. The loot included oil filters, air filters, brake pads, pistons and clutches.[1]

A workshop near you

If you're thinking that this is a problem for the Arab world, you're wrong. GM, whose products were copied by 10 per cent of the fakes the police found, found that many of the products were professionally boxed and stamped, ready for export.

The huge auto parts problem in the Middle East created the ABPC, whose remit is to increase public awareness. Coady wants it to be a template for the rest of the world. 'It is easier to work together to share information because of the scale of the problem,' she says. 'It's an uphill struggle for all of us.'

This currently looks unlikely. In Europe and the US, the manufacturers aren't talking to us about fake spares, perhaps taking the opinion that the potential for consumer panic and a loss of confidence in the auto business – or their brand – would outweigh the benefits of any public service. And, as they might point out, there is no proof to show that counterfeit parts are widespread killers.

There are three reasons that this could be true.

The first is that there may be few fake parts on the market. Dubai's problem shows that in some parts of the world this is not the case. In Europe and the US, one in three garages isn't fitting fakes or anything like that number – but no one is claiming the supply is clean. The problem, says John McCormack, a former vice-president of aftermarket sales for parts supplier Federal Mogul and now a consultant to the auto business in Europe, is that, before we find out how big the counterfeit business is, we'd have to be able to measure the legitimate trade. 'It's horrifying,' he says, 'but we don't even know the size of our own market. The counterfeit problem is big. We have no idea how big, but we all know it is affecting us. We're like the little Dutch boy, running around sticking our fingers in leaky dykes.'

The second is that the fakes may be of comparable quality and don't cause accidents. Some are – but the evidence of seized parts stretches credulity to imagine that they have not caused some accidents, or made some accidents more serious.

Which leaves the third explanation: that the industry or national governments are simply not counting. In 2003, the International Intellectual Property Institute tried to find the evidence of how fake parts contributed to accidents in the US. 'In 2000, 41,821 people were killed in the estimated 6,394,000 police reported motor vehicle traffic crashes. There are two data systems which track US auto accidents and injuries: the Fatality Analysis Reporting System (FARS) and the Crash Outcome Data Evaluation System (CODES). Neither codes for counterfeit parts,' the report concluded.[2]

Motor accidents – and the deaths that result – are so common that we're not measuring how much responsibility fake parts should take. Once fitted, a fake is almost impossible to spot. It would be impossible to test every part in every accident. And unlike bogus parts that are fitted to aircraft, we rarely know for certain the pedigree of any part, or how it reached the dealer. In the real world, the effect of fake parts can't be measured, because we don't even know they are there. 'I don't think any of us can be happy with our success in cutting the supply of counterfeits,' says McCormack, who is helping to establish the European Aftermarket Forum, a trade body for parts suppliers. Should car drivers be worried about the parts being fitted to their cars? 'Yes, they should.'

Brian Duggan, the Director of International Programs for the US-based Motor and Equipment Manufacturers Association (MEMA), says that it is almost impossible to track parts, legitimate or otherwise, that are fitted to cars, because so many people are doing it. 'There are thousands of companies out there in the business,' he says. 'There are maybe 10 manufacturers who sell cars in our market, but MEMA itself has 700 members.'

If the auto industry has a better idea of how big the counterfeiting problem is worldwide, it isn't telling. The figure commonly quoted is the US Federal Trade Commission's report in 1996, which spoke of $3 billion a year of losses to the US auto market and $12 billion a year worldwide: but this is about lost jobs and trade. There are no figures on numbers of parts, loss to consumers or injury or death. The FTC estimate is also a decade old. During that time, knockoffs in every other category have mushroomed, and auto business representatives admit that car parts are following that trend. 'I would not say this business is under control at all. In fact, in the last few years, the counterfeit problem is getting worse,' says Duggan. 'The companies that do this aren't in the auto part business. They are trying to make cash in the post 9/11 environment, and moving out of coke and heroin to a business where the liability is lower.'

In Europe, Lars Holmqvist, the CEO of Brussels-based Clepa, the European Association of Automotive Suppliers, points out that even in Europe's most regulated markets the two largest auto parts trade shows – one in France and one in Germany – are routinely preceded by a police raid on the exhibitors to clear illegal counterfeit parts off the stands in the exhibition halls. 'We know that 90 per cent of the organized supply chain is honest,' he says, but he echoes Duggan when he adds, 'but it is a problem that is getting worse. Counterfeiters generally sell to marginalized repair shops, so we have no idea about it at all, and we never will.'

Holmqvist sees one immediate solution might be for manufacturers to extend their warranties on new cars to between five and seven years, or even longer. That would encourage customers to visit repair shops approved by the manufacturers, for fear of compromising their warranty. The parts fitted would be, as far as it is possible to be certain, genuine.

But this would increase the financial pressures on the independent aftermarket business, which is also under pressure, and perhaps tempt them to buy cheaper parts – opening the door to counterfeiters. It would do little to affect the trade that behind the scenes is terrifying the auto business: cut-price backstreet repair shops that service older cars whose value is so low that the cost of servicing at an official dealership might be more than the cost of the car. 'Consumers should be concerned when they choose a garage. If they go to well-known workshops, 99 per cent are bona fide. If you go to one that's very cheap and find that instead of 50 euros to get your brakes fixed it costs you 25 euros, be careful,' says Holmqvist. He says that often those workshops get their cheapest stock when 'they are visited by a guy in a van who wants to sell them a part'. That part could literally be from anywhere.

It's a common warning: if something is too good to be true, it isn't true. In the auto business, we could call it the Holmqvist test. Unfortunately, the knockoff economy has already responded. The latest trick that auto part counterfeiters have employed has little to do with secret anti-counterfeit seals or sophisticated packaging. They are faking a pass on the Holmqvist test, and boosting their profits at the same time. Duggan says: 'One way we used to detect counterfeit parts was that they were too cheap. Anyone would know something is wrong. So to get round that problem, the counterfeiters simply raised their prices.'

Notes

1. *Gulf News*, 19 April 2005.
2. Michele Forzley (2003) *Counterfeiting Goods and the Public's Health and Safety*, July, IIPI.

18 Show us the dead bodies

In 2002, when he was 16, New Yorker Timothy Fagan had a liver transplant. Every week as he healed he would give himself injections of Epogen to boost his red blood cell count. Every week, after the injection, his muscles would cramp and he would be lame for several days. His parents assumed that it was a natural side effect of Epogen; his doctor fretted that he wasn't responding well to the treatment.

In reality, his body was responding the only way it knew how to the drug, because the Epogen he was shooting into his system was a counterfeit, containing a fraction of the active ingredients of the genuine drug. He hadn't bought the Epogen on a street corner: he had obtained the drug from a dispensing pharmacist owned by CVS, the giant drugstore and dispensing chain that has more than 5,400 stores across the US. CVS, like Fagan, had no idea that the drugs were not the real thing. Fagan discovered that his batch was fake only when his pharmacist told him they had received a warning about counterfeit Epogen issued by the US government, and found that his batch matched the labels on the counterfeits.

To this day, no one knows how his fake Epogen ended up in the dispensary, despite Fagan filing a lawsuit against the manufacturer, the distributor and CVS. 'Every time I take a pill, I still wonder, "Is this stuff counterfeit?"' he told the Associated Press in 2004.[1]

Redefining the problem

Counterfeiting valuable drugs has always been one of the most cynical but most profitable specializations in the knockoff business. In his novel *The Third Man*, Graham Greene's narrator describes from his experience the way that penicillin was counterfeited in post-war Vienna:

> Penicillin in Austria was supplied only to the military hospitals; no civilian doctor, not even a civilian hospital, could obtain it by legal means. As the racket started, it was relatively harmless. Penicillin would be stolen by military orderlies and sold to Austrian doctors for very high sums – a phial would fetch anything up to seventy pounds... Penicillin would not always be impossible to obtain legitimately; they wanted more money and quicker money while the going was good. They began to dilute the penicillin with coloured water, and in the case of penicillin dust, with sand.

The effects were horrifying: 'Men have lost their legs and arms that way – and their lives. But perhaps what horrified me most was visiting the children's hospital here. They had bought some of this penicillin for use against meningitis. A number of children simply died, and a number went off their heads. You can see them now in the mental ward.'

Fagan's case is still rare. Ashley How, the European director of the Pharmaceutical Security Institute – a not-for-profit membership organization for the pharmaceutical business – told me he doesn't like today's counterfeit medicine supply being described as 'a problem', as the word is too sensational and it scares the public unnecessarily. He prefers to describe it as 'an issue'.

The PSI isn't alone in downplaying the problem. 'Politicians ask us to show them the dead bodies,' says Richard Widup, the senior director of security for Purdue Pharma LP, headquartered in Stamford, Connecticut.

A lawyer representing companies that have suffered from counterfeiting hears something eerily similar: 'One guy in law enforcement said to me, unless there's a dead body, don't even pick up the phone to call me.'

But the world's market for counterfeit drugs is huge, and growing. Like Fagan, you might assume your symptoms are from the disease the drug is supposed to be treating, or you might never discover you took a counterfeit at all; thousands of patients worldwide are already in this position. According to the World Health Organization, around 10 per cent of the world's drugs are counterfeits. Most obviously, these are sold on the street markets and in the unregulated pharmacies of the developing world and created in the knockoff factories of China and India, but if you think that you could never see, or take, a counterfeit medicine in Europe or the US you're wrong. The World Health Organization made a survey on reports of counterfeiting in 2003, and found that 40 per cent of the reports came from the developed world. This is probably a distortion of the true picture, because reporting is better in the developed world. Western governments don't acknowledge a problem of anything like that scale. On 2 October 2003, the US Food and Drug Administration, the government body that polices drug quality, called a press conference on the subject, and commissioner Dr Mark McClellan stood up and reassured the public that less than 1 per cent of drugs supplied in the US were counterfeits.

On the other hand, the US annually spends 15 per cent of its GDP on drugs, a whopping $1.55 trillion, or $5,440 for every person in the US.[2] If McClellan is correct, patients in the US purchase and consume $15 billion of fake drugs every year, which if it's an 'issue' is certainly not a negligible one. So this raises the question, what's in the 1 per cent?

Widup, who previously investigated food and drug counterfeiting for the FDA, has a stock of pictures showing how counterfeit drugs are made. One shows a cave in China where dust mingles with piles of powder on the floor. The distinctive blue of the coloured powder gives the clue to what's in the plastic bags: thousands of fake Viagra tablets. There's a sheet of counterfeit labels there too.

In another picture, a grubby bedsit has been turned into a drug factory. 'The microwave oven isn't for heating their burrito at lunchtime. It was used to dry the tablets,' says Widup.

And while comparatively simple, big-selling tablets are the easiest targets for a counterfeiter, there's more profit in high-value life-saving drugs – for example, human growth hormone (HGH), used to counteract problems like AIDS-related wasting. On 18 May 2001, Serono Inc warned its customers that there was counterfeit Serostim in circulation.[3] Instead of 6 milligrams of active ingredient, the counterfeit contained 1 milligram.

Widup recalls an earlier HGH problem from his time at the FDA. 'In 2000, we found counterfeit HGH – but we only found it because a kid took it accidentally and reacted to the injection,' he says. 'Here's the tragedy: HGH is recombinant DNA. Your body adjusts to what you have been given. Now this kid can't take legitimate HGH in future, because his body was changed by the counterfeit.'

Tap water doesn't cure cancer

The story of counterfeit Procrit, a similar drug to the one that Fagan thought he was injecting, but used for cancer sufferers and patients with AIDS who are anaemic, shows how cynical and how profitable the business is. It retails for $500 a shot – but it's a clear liquid, so a recent batch of seized counterfeit vials in Florida had been filled with tap water. The vials were genuine, taken from bags filled with medical waste by dumpster divers.[4]

Robert Penezic, an assistant statewide prosecutor for the State of Florida, told a 2003 US congressional investigation into fake drugs[5] that 'we all know that significant precautions are taken in the preparation and manufacture of our prescription drugs. However, most of us are unaware of the current lack of controls on prescription drugs once they leave the custody of the manufacturer.'

He told the story of one of his investigations into counterfeit Procrit:

> A 2001 investigation discovered that South Florida criminals had counterfeited Procrit... The criminals re-labelled approximately 110,000 bottles of low strength Epogen to make the bottles appear to contain high strength Procrit, a drug 20 times the strength of the Epogen in the bottles. The criminals resold the re-labelled drugs into the wholesale market with forged pedigree papers, passing the drugs through four states. Investigators located 800 boxes of the counterfeit Procrit at a large Texas wholesaler, which had unknowingly purchased the counterfeit Procrit. In addition, investigators found some of the product in Kentucky. In all, investigators recovered less that 10 per cent of the counterfeit Procrit. It is estimated that the criminals in the chain may have made an illicit profit of approximately $46 million.

That means 90 per cent of the counterfeit medicine was sold. Almost 100,000 doses of fake Procrit were taken. You wouldn't be taking it unless you were critically ill – but we have no way to know if the drug hastened the death, or even helped kill, the people who took it. We can't show anyone the dead bodies, but it's safe to assume they exist.

'I am in the bad news business. People don't think about what I do unless there is a problem around. The reality is that the problem is bigger than many people are willing to discuss,' says John Theriault, Pfizer Inc's vice-president of global security. He joined the drug giant in 1996 after 26 years in the FBI, thinking that his main job was protecting Pfizer's secrets from industrial espionage. Now he has a much bigger problem on his hands:

> The fact is, the counterfeits are out there not only in the developing world but in the developed world too. In 2004 I was criticized by a wholesaler in London for daring to suggest that counterfeit drugs could enter the supply chain in the UK. Two weeks later, there they were. I have hundreds of packets of counterfeit pills in my office. The best ones, in 100 years you couldn't pick them as fakes.

The problem is often left to the drug companies to investigate, he says. 'In the real world, the federal and national authorities are coping with terrorism, and the local authorities are dealing with murder and mayhem. It's unfortunate, but we are not a priority.'

A good-looking tablet

It's a common game in the slide presentations given by the security officers of the big pharmaceutical companies: show two pills side by side, and have a show of hands to guess which one is a fake. One of the best counterfeits that Theriault has seen was some fake Ponstan tablets made in Colombia. Ponstan is a common anti-inflammatory drug used to treat arthritis and rheumatoid arthritis pain, but the fakes contained a potentially fatal poison. 'It was supposed to be Ponstan, but the primary ingredient in the tablet was boric acid, mixed with leaded yellow highway paint. The sheen was floor wax. Put it all together, it's a good-looking tablet,' he admits.

Pfizer has the unwanted honour of being the company subjected to the largest product recall in the history of the US.

In May 2003, customers began to complain that their Lipitor pills, a drug that earns Pfizer $8 billion every year as millions of people across the globe take it to reduce their cholesterol, tasted bitter.

The complaints sparked an investigation by the FDA,[6] which eventually resulted in a recall of 200,000 bottles of pills. The drugs were bought on the wholesale market by a company based in Nebraska called Med-Pro Inc.

Police finally traced the fraud to Julio Cesar Cruz, a Miami-based convicted drug dealer who had the drug manufactured in Costa Rica. In 2001, he had used a fake driver's licence and $1,000 to become a licensed drug wholesaler. If you live in Florida, or are thinking of holidaying there, you will be pleased to know that it has since tightened its regulations for wholesalers. But 'There are 1,500 drug wholesalers in Florida. Does a state like Florida need 1,500 wholesalers? No,' warns Theriault. 'The system is as strong as its weakest point. Trouble is, there are a lot of weak points. It blows a hole in the idea that we have a strong supply chain.'

Altogether, 17 people were arrested as part of a plot that had seen the Lipitor traded through a network of intermediaries, some honest and some not, before it got to Med-Pro from a seemingly impeccable source. The pills had actually been flown into the US 'in transit' so they could be heisted from a warehouse at Miami airport and introduced to the supply chain.[7]

Widup warns us not to underestimate the sophistication of the gang that put the Lipitor into circulation. 'They used drop cell-phones, companies that only existed on paper... It was truly an enterprising operation, and very profitable as well.'

Controlling the supply chain

And this, he says, is the fundamental problem that might let counterfeits into the supply chain for drugs anywhere in the developed world. It's not that we don't have a sophisticated supply chain: it's too clever for its own good. Across Europe and the US, a network of buyers and sellers are repackaging and reselling drugs for a profit in a way that makes it impossible for your pharmacist to know exactly where the drugs came from.

Thomas Zimmer, head of the corporate division of safety, quality and environmental protection at Boehringer Ingelheim, admits the system needs to be reformed. 'Are supply chains sufficiently controlled? A clear no. If you look at the distribution channel for drugs, it's like playing with spaghetti. It's not unusual for there to be 20 different transactions between the manufacturer and the public,' he says.

It's not just the supply of the drugs that isn't controlled. 'Is it allowed that anyone can legally print pharmaceutical packaging? It is. It doesn't make any sense. Compare this with the restrictions on who can print money. What happens to used machine tools that have been used to make drugs? They are sold second hand. It's an opportunistic business.'

There are many reasons why drugs pass through so many hands. One of the most obvious is that getting drugs from a manufacturer to thousands of hospitals and pharmacies is a complex job and not one that drug manufacturers can do well. They give the job to a network of distributors, as manufacturers in every other business will do, whether that business is selling tinned food, computers or furniture. Most of these transactions are straightforward and, in the US for example, 90 per cent of drug shipments go through three giant distributors who buy direct from the manufacturer and sell direct to the pharmacy.

The other 10 per cent is the source of the problem. They exist for a number of reasons: they may be specialists in one area or a particular region. Or they may be in the business to make a fast buck. There are opportunities to do this in the legitimate trade. An example is the trade in drugs that are close to expiry. If a distributor or a hospital has over-ordered, a smaller distributor might take the excess inventory off their hands at a discount. If they sell it on, it's perfectly legal and it cuts waste.

On the other hand, lax regulation has created Theriault's weak links. 'Not long ago, the Pharmaceutical Board had three investigators for the state of Florida,' says Jim Christian, global head of security for Novartis. 'They would follow people, see product being moved from the trunk of a car to the trunk of another car – it was a disaster.' Florida has since become one of a few US states to introduce tough regulations for its distributors.

The case of the counterfeit Lipitor shows that you don't need to be so obviously crooked to get your counterfeit drugs into the supply chain. The fear for Big Pharma's security officers is: what happens when the counterfeits look right and taste right? 'In many cases we're finding only the easy stuff. So that leads to the question, "How good are the really good guys?"' Theriault warns.

This isn't a US problem: in Europe, the supply chain for pharmaceuticals is even more tortuous. The potential for abuse is clearly there, warns Graham Satchwell, managing director of Proco Solutions.

A former Metropolitan Police detective superintendent, Satchwell was also director of corporate security for Europe, Middle East and Africa at London-based GlaxoSmithKline between 2001 and 2003, running investigations into drug counterfeiting. He echoes the worries of his peers that law enforcement doesn't take the initiative in investigating counterfeiting. 'Law enforcement does very little. It's a victimless crime, they say, so not a matter for the police,' he sighs.

The potential for counterfeiting in Europe is so great in Satchwell's view that in 2004 he wrote a book about it: *A Sick Business, Counterfeit Medicines and Organised Crime*[8] details his experience of the distribution network in Europe that makes it wide open to fraud. 'The UK and European citizen might currently be consuming counterfeit and other substandard medicines, and suffering as a result [but] we simply cannot know to what extent,' he warns.

The problem in Satchwell's view is the internal market in the EU. It's an extension of the internal markets for other goods, which allow them to be traded across frontiers – so a bottle of Coca-Cola can be traded by a wholesaler who picks it up cheaply in Greece, drives it across Europe and sells it at a higher price in France or the UK.

It might surprise you to learn that, in the EU, drugs are traded in exactly the same way. In the UK alone – where the high cost of drugs makes this 'parallel' trading financially attractive – the Social Market Foundation reports that 90 per cent of pharmacists source at least some drugs through parallel trade. There are 140,000,000 medicines parallel-traded every year in the EU, and around 20 per cent of prescription drugs have been parallel-traded at least once.

On one hand, this is entirely admirable, as national health services have access to a source of inexpensive drugs, independent pharmacies can increase their profit margins or offer cheaper prices, and excess stocks of drugs in one country can be put to good use in another. Parallel trade isn't counterfeiting: in fact, done properly, it can be a disincentive to counterfeiters, as more alternative stocks of low-price drugs become available.

The problem is how the trading is done today. Because a parallel-traded drug needs packaging and information for the country it will be going to, it also needs to be repackaged. This isn't done by the manufacturer. It's done by the companies that are trading the drugs; legally, the manufacturers can't stop this.

Julian Mount, European director of trade for Pfizer, sums it up:

> Parallel trade has spiralled out of control. You can no longer supply with any real guarantee of reliability to a pharmacy: I have no idea how to do a product recall on a parallel-traded medicine that has been through four countries, for example. There is no record of that movement, no record of how it was stored, no record of who it was traded to... We don't believe the current morass of medicines transferring across Europe is tenable.

The 1 per cent solution

Mount blames the way drugs are supplied – but does Big Pharma share in the blame for the explosion in the market for counterfeit pharmaceuticals? On one hand, it's the clear loser. If we all panic and stop taking drugs because we don't want to risk them being fake, the pharmaceutical giants go out of business.

On the other hand, while a potentially huge public health risk develops, many of the pharmaceutical manufacturers have been keen not to comment or take concerted anti-counterfeiting action. Their corporate culture, which prioritizes secrecy and caution, is ill suited to a campaign to educate consumers, and they simply are not used to acting together. Satchwell says, 'The sharing culture that anti-counterfeiting requires clashes with the need-to-know culture that pharmaceutical companies have.' He adds, 'In some organizations, the problem is owned by the lawyers, and there are many lawyers who think that the creation of legislation provides a solution to this problem. In the industry, we need to find common ground – and, when we find it, to share totally.'

'So often the pharma companies avoid the media because, if they speak to the media, it's the public's perception that only that one company has a counterfeit problem. So they think, better not buy their product. But we all have a problem,' says Christian.

The immediate solution to the problem of counterfeiting seems to be better, and more controlled, packaging. 'How many print shops do we use? Generally it's in the hundreds,' says Christian. 'In the EU, when you sell your product to someone, you have nothing to do with it. So you don't know where your packages are. It's not unusual any more to see real product in counterfeit packaging, and counterfeit product in real packaging.'

There are many packaging technologies that make packaging tricky to counterfeit: inks that shift colour, electronic tags in the foil pack and even a science fiction packaging technology from DuPont that introduces a strand of plant DNA on to the label, which matches a complementary strand in a detector pen (offering 10,000,000,000,000 different combinations), are realities today. A company called Schreiner ProSecure makes seals that only show information when they are cooled below 5 degrees centigrade. These are expensive to counterfeit.

They are also expensive for the pharmaceutical business. Like any commercial business, it can't guarantee a totally risk-free environment. Instead, the pharma companies have to evaluate the cost of improving security against the perceived risk; adding cost to drug packaging also makes drugs more expensive, which may mean that fewer can be prescribed, which means that more people are sick or die. It's a complex calculation.

In this case, it's the industry saying 'Show us the dead bodies.' A crime like counterfeiting, where the results may be hidden, isn't a good candidate for this type of analysis.

At Boehringer Ingelheim, Zimmer reminds his colleagues that, for the sake of a few cents, one of the Big Pharma companies may one day pay dearly if the law decides it has failed to act to protect us. 'What is a reasonable price? I would say one cent per pack. Some would say one, others would say two cents, others maybe five. But certainly not 10 cents,' he warns. 'But if we fail to act, the pharmaceutical business could one day soon be held responsible and found guilty when something happens. We are sued when we deliver something that is less than the community's standard. Perhaps some day, someone will sue the pharmaceutical business.'

Packaging is only a start to fixing this problem. Any security feature on the package will be lost when a medicine is parallel-traded and repacked across a border. And Fagan's suit against the manufacturer was tossed out because the judge ruled that the manufacturer could only place a security feature on the packaging – it couldn't reasonably ensure that packaging was completely tamper-proof.

Also, we tend not to look closely at what we buy, as we trust our pharmacists. Security hidden on the foil will be useful for pharmacies, but useless for consumers: for us, one pack looks like another, just as a counterfeit pill looks like the real thing. If the pharmaceutical companies spent millions on advertising to tell us what to look for on the label when we buy high-value drugs, it's also teaching the counterfeiters how to fake the label convincingly.

While it's easy to keep track of a drug in a truck or a stock room, the increasing automation of the supply chain makes it impractical to track while being picked or repacked. 'I used to run a Unichem distribution centre, and handled 1 million items a week. But 60 per cent of those were handled by an automatic picking machine, so it is almost impossible to know which product goes to which customer,' says Tony Garlick, now technical director of the British Association of Pharmaceutical Wholesalers.

Ultimately, the supply chain will only be fully secure when it is completely regulated: technologies like radio frequency ID (RFID) tags may one day mean that your drugs are electronically tagged and can be followed wherever they go. They will have a 'pedigree' – we know where they came from, where they have been and how they travelled, and pharmacists, hospitals and the public can make an informed choice. It's the electronic equivalent of the pile of documentation that travels with every aeroplane part – but, to set it up, every pharmacist, wholesaler and trader needs specialized equipment, and every manufacturer has to incorporate the tags, and someone has to pay for it all.

Larry Sasich, a pharmacist and research analyst at US-based watchdog Public Citizen, thinks that the industry's current fascination for technology like RFID deflects attention from the real failure: drug shipments could have had compulsory paper pedigrees years ago, but pharmaceutical companies and their wholesalers lobbied against them. This is 'a game played in Washington', he says. 'Do you know of any instances in which this kind of technology has shown results?'

There's a question over whether it suits drug wholesalers to have traceability of their products at all, because it provides an inconvenient impediment to their ability to cut a deal. 'A lot of wholesalers in the US have made lobbying efforts that have helped to stay the enactment of the pedigree laws,' Widup admits. 'They say they will only buy from you, but they will buy off the wire from anyone who offers the products.' This, you will recall, is how 100,000 bottles of fake Procrit got into the legitimate drug supply.

So a more practical first step has been the discipline that Pfizer, among others, has imposed on the supply of its drugs: today it insists that its wholesalers are all authorized; it sells only to authorized wholesalers, and tells pharmacies to buy only from authorized wholesalers. It amounts to self-regulation, but as long as the wholesalers and pharmacists do the right thing the chances of another huge batch of counterfeit Lipitor reaching the shelves would be reduced.

Yet there's a darker side to the marketing done by Big Pharma. How much of the trillions spent on drugs in the developed world is necessary?

Today, Lipitor is a 'blockbuster' – the elite group of drugs that pharmaceutical companies develop from which they derive most of their profits. When Big Pharma created the category of drugs Lipitor is part of, the public would have had no idea why they should need it. 'In the early 1990s, there were three or four companies looking at producing anti-cholesterol drugs,' Christian admits. 'All of a sudden, the first one got approved – but there was no market. No one knew what cholesterol was. So we had to build a market through advertising. Now every time you have a medical, your cholesterol is measured.' And if it is too high, you are prescribed a drug like Lipitor.

Nevertheless, Lipitor undoubtedly saves lives – but in the developed world we no longer see pharmaceuticals as simply a way to heal illness. We now actively seek out drugs to improve our quality of life, creating the market for what we casually name 'lifestyle' drugs. Today we are prepared to go to extraordinary lengths to obtain those drugs, even when we have very little idea where we are getting them from, and even when we have not been prescribed them. If you want to counterfeit Epogen or Procrit, you have to work out a way to sneak it into the supply chain. But when you counterfeit a drug like Viagra, if you let the public know you have it for sale then thousands of customers will come to you, no questions asked.

Of course, the counterfeiters know that already.

Notes

1. Associated Press, 11 April 2004.
2. *New York Times*, 9 January 2004.
3. Press release from Serono Inc, 18 May 2001.
4. *New York Times*, 3 October 2003.
5. Testimony to the Committee on Energy and Commerce, 24 June 2003.
6. FDA press release, 23 May 2003.
7. *Star-Ledger*, 14 December 2003.
8. Published by the Stockholm Network, ISBN 0954766326.

19 Men in white coats

There's a cement mixer, surrounded by bottles and powder. The room in Dubai is filthy. Probably the cement mixer dragged some of the filth in, because during the day it was being used to help plaster the walls of a building nearby. By night, it was moonlighting as a low-tech device for mixing batches of Viagra.

If you secretly ordered some Viagra from the internet recently and found it didn't deliver on its promise of sustained performance, your tablet might have been mostly cement and blue dye, like the ones made in this ad hoc factory in the United Arab Emirates.

The most common method of creating a fake tablet is to grind up some authentic tablets, add a bulking agent like lactose and remould them. At best, the effect is weak and short-lived, but perhaps Viagra fakers are depending on the fact that few men or their partners are going to want the full four-hour potential effect of the pill and will settle for five good minutes. Or perhaps they are depending on the power of the male imagination to produce a placebo effect.

You won't get any satisfaction if you complain to the website where you bought your Viagra because you have no real idea where it came from – or who supplied it.

A deal you can refuse

Email Systems, a company that measures spam emails on the internet, reports that in the first three months of 2005 two in five spam emails were offering drugs for sale. As the volume of spam is now almost 90 per cent of all email sent, that means one out of every three emails sent is offering you cut-price drugs over the net.

In September 2003, Dr Nic Wilson, a researcher at the University of London, announced to the British Pharmaceutical Conference in Manchester that she had been testing samples of internet-bought Viagra. She used a technique called near infrared (NIR) microscopy: it accurately measures the ingredients in each tablet. The result was that half of the pills were fakes. 'The user runs the risk of poor quality and possible toxicity, not to mention the fact that there is a high probability that the tablets have no clinical effect,' she told her audience, who probably looked around the room to see who was blushing – Brits being the largest consumers of Viagra in Europe.

It's comparatively easy to set up a Viagra factory, and some crooks have gone into the business in a big way: an example is 44-year-old Londoner Allen Valentine, convicted in November 2004 at Harrow Crown Court and sentenced to five and a half years in prison for supplying class C drugs. In effect, he was sentenced as if he had been supplying large amounts of cannabis.

His factory in Wembley was more than just a cement mixer: it could create 500,000 tablets a day.[1] On the side, he was also making steroids and anti-stress medication, and a great deal of cash: the day before his arrest in April 2004, he had offered cash for a £1.25 million house and bought a new jeep.

Valentine knew how much people wanted Viagra – he was previously a rep for Viagra's manufacturer, Pfizer.

The little blue pill is a common find for the drugs squads of Europe, the US and Asia. In January, £1 million of fake Viagra was found in an abandoned car outside Glasgow. 'It is quite common to recover one or two thousand fake Viagra pills. They are usually found along with Class A drugs like cocaine, heroin and ecstasy,' said Detective Sergeant Ken Simpson of Strathclyde Drugs Squad.[2]

This is no cottage industry: Richard Widup recalls a case from his time at the FDA: 'It was over the Christmas holidays 2002, in Southern California... There were 700,000 counterfeit Viagra manufactured over the holidays in a three-day period. It was done in a legitimate factory by the lower-level employees, who were offered a deal to do it that they just couldn't refuse.'

Then there was the case of Dr Frank Schwab, who imported white fluffy teddy bears to the US from China – each containing 6,000 fake Viagra tablets.[3] He was discovered after a Pfizer employee ordered some of the cut-price tablets from him and analysed them.

Viagra might be the most popular lifestyle drug on the net, but it is certainly not the only one, or the most dangerous.

Jan Peter van Suchtelen, the director of international pharmacy policy at NV Organon, says he went looking for one of his products using the Google search engine. 'In my opinion counterfeiting medicines is worse than drug trafficking, because people buying counterfeit medicines don't know they are getting something that's dangerous,' he says. 'I went to Google and typed in "Buy Deca Durabolin without prescription" and I got 27,600 hits.'

It helps that Deca Durabolin is an anabolic steroid – if you read the sports pages, you might be more familiar with the name of its constituent, nandrolone. Where some buyers are looking for more performance in bed, others are looking for more performance when they get out of it. 'The best overall steroid for results vs. side effects', promises PharmaEurope.com. Among the developed world's would-be Olympians, there's a lucrative market for steroids, no questions asked.

Deca Durabolin wasn't the only drug on van Suchtelen's list. 'A week or two ago I bought a product. It was made in the Netherlands for the South African market. It was bought in the UK and shipped from Vanuatu. It turned out to be original, but this product was a cold-store product. I have no idea how it was treated,' he says.

His product was real – but van Suchtelen was in a position to trace where it had come from, because he works for the manufacturer. When we buy online, we don't have that luxury.

'The problem is we don't know who is involved,' says Widup. 'The pharmacy can be based in Canada, the server's in Singapore, the money is laundered in Australia and the product is shipped from Spain,' he says.

Deca Durabolin, like Viagra, is a prescription drug in Europe and the US. Consumers who want to circumvent the rules – usually because they have no reason to be prescribed – find traders on the internet ready to take their business. 'If there's a white coat and a stethoscope, the site must be genuine,' says a British government investigator, disgusted at how easy it is for the websites he investigates to find gullible customers. European and US laws both stipulate that pharmacies must have full contact details on their websites, but for anyone who wants to cut corners it seems like a picture of a man in a white coat is assurance enough.

Drug tourism

This also makes a nonsense of local laws prohibiting the sale of more essential prescription drugs – as, understandably, local law enforcement doesn't track what happens to drugs once they are outside the country's borders; it also stymies the attempts by the drug companies to limit the supply of prescription drugs from outside national borders. In the US, it is legal to buy three months' supply of a prescribed drug from anywhere you want, and this has led to an unlikely senior citizen tourist trade, where busloads visit cheaper pharmacies in Canada or Mexico. More purchase from the internet because they are told to: 'I'd be very worried about buying anything over the net in the US, but some insurance companies are telling their customers to do exactly that,' says an exasperated senior executive from one of the large pharmaceutical companies, who asked not to be named. 'They have been purchasing from Canada for five or six years. Now they are telling them to go to Mexico.'

Food and Drug Administration research in US airports shows that between 86 and 88 per cent of the drugs packages arriving contain drugs that are not approved for sale in the US. Every year, 10 million of these parcels enter the country. The FDA has 100 inspectors assigned to looking at the problem. Fewer than one in 25 packages are opened.

So even if law enforcement was interested in catching counterfeiters, there's little chance of being caught if you are based outside the country to which you are sending the drugs, unless your local law enforcement authorities are sufficiently alarmed to track you down.

The gain for consumers: cheap prescription drugs, or maybe prescription drugs without a prescription. The risk: most online pharmacies carry small print that tells you the drug you receive might not be exactly the one you order.

Gabrial Levitt, a vice-president at New York-based PharmacyChecker.com LLC, runs a service that recommends licensed pharmacies online, which in his experience are no more likely to supply a counterfeit than a licensed pharmacy in the real world. 'If someone orders a product from a licensed pharmacy in Canada, or one licensed by the Royal Pharmaceutical Society in the UK for example, those products are regulated. If the customer knows he or she is purchasing from somewhere licensed, they are safe. It's a "buyer beware" environment,' he says.

Our desire to get something very cheap seems to override our common sense, he admits.

> Go to a website and there is no phone number, no address where it is located. That's dangerous. If it is not acting legitimately, it might still have something on the site that says it only sells safe drugs. But when there are no specifics, you don't know where the drugs are coming from. If you don't need a prescription to get prescription drugs, you can assume it is not a great place to get them.

Drug tourism in the US has taken on a more sinister aspect: instead of crossing the northern border to shop in regulated but relatively inexpensive Canadian pharmacies, increasingly consumers are crossing the border to the south to shop in largely unregulated – and even cheaper – Mexican pharmacies. Even the ones that are regulated offer a cornucopia of drugs without prescription. 'In Mexico, some pharmacies lure US citizens across the border with the promise of cheaper medicines,' says Widup. 'The guy behind the counter picks up a phone and calls a runner. The runner goes to a nearby location and picks up the pills. Those products often have no active ingredients. Basically, they are sugar pills.'

Not all Mexican pharmacies are clip joints, but Marvin Shepherd, director of the Center for Pharmacoeconomic Studies at the University of Texas at Austin, who has studied the trend, claims that Mexican pharmacies make $1 billion every year from US tourists – and that one in five drugs bought there are fake or substandard.[4]

Seniors are also being sent to prison for it – Raymond Lindell, 66, from Phoenix was arrested in May 2004 for buying 270 Valium pills in Nogales, and released in July. Dawn Wilson from San Diego got a five-year sentence in April 2003, and as of writing is in jail in Ensenada, Mexico.

If this seems heavy-handed, there is plenty of evidence that the production of lifestyle drugs is attracting the most dangerous counterfeiters you could imagine. In the UK, the National Criminal Intelligence Service warned in its 2003 threat assessment that 'Some smugglers of class A drugs will readily smuggle cannabis, amphetamine, or pharmaceuticals such as Viagra and its various copies.'

Some would go much further than this. On 2 August 2004, Lester Crawford, the acting commissioner of the FDA, told an audience in Washington, DC[5] that 'the prospect of any and all of the products we regulate being a vehicle for terrorism is a constant concern'. One week later he was telling the Associated Press in an interview that he was concerned that terrorists might place counterfeited drugs into Canadian pharmacies as an attack on the United States.

Is this going too far? The same article quoted a representative of the US Homeland Security Department admitting that: 'We do acknowledge that al-Qaeda and other terrorist groups have studied agroterrorism techniques [but] we have no specific information now about any al-Qaeda threats to our food or drug supply.' When internet purchasers are buying pills made in a cement mixer, it hardly seems necessary to scare the United States' drug tourists about terrorists lurking in Canadian pharmacies.

As Levitt points out, it's easy to confuse the legitimate online pharmacy trade with the spam-happy cowboys who supply counterfeits and the criminals who profit from it. Not all cheap drugs are counterfeits; not all pharmacies supplying them are illegal. Some allege that confusing the issue would suit Big Pharma very well, and large drug companies would secretly enjoy a warning that terrorists are poisoning us with imported painkillers. Drugs are more expensive in the developed world, because consumers can pay for them. Drugs bought in the West are responsible for most of the profits of Big Pharma – which is partly why there is such a boom in the production of 'lifestyle' drugs and consequently why we are prepared to look to the internet for those drugs, even if it's a 50:50 shot that we get a fake.

If we suddenly all start buying on the internet from Vanuatu, or even New Zealand, then those profits collapse. 'If America changes its tune on price controls, it would provide less incentive to shop in other countries,' says Levitt. 'This is the quintessential example of globalization giving a smack in the face to big companies. Companies make a lot of money from leaving markets segmented, and that weighs heavily on the Western consumer.'

Someone has to pay

At the International Intellectual Property Institute, Bruce Lehman, who as the US Assistant Secretary of Commerce from 1993 to 1998 helped raise awareness of the role of intellectual property as a development tool, defends high drug prices. Westerners can afford them, he says, and it's our responsibility to pay. 'Someone has to pay for the research. We wouldn't have wonderful antiretroviral drugs if someone didn't pay for the development. The reason we have those drugs is there's a market incentive for the pharmaceutical companies to develop them for rich people in rich countries.'

He says that, in the developed world, drug prices are fair. 'We need differential pricing. What's the alternative? The alternative is that as a pharmaceutical company you have no control over price and no control over your product. The pharmaceutical company gets sold off in a fire sale. I'm very gloomy about this.'

Whether you buy Lehman's argument that our high prices are the engine of development, or Levitt's that the internet allows us to strike back at the cynical pharmaceutical companies who are gouging us for profits, it doesn't affect the central point: if you're buying from an unregulated website, it's a toss of a coin whether what you get is real. And if it is fake, you're potentially killing yourself.

If you know the risks and still take the pill then it would, perhaps, be your own fault. That's because in the developed world we have choice. We can argue about the price of prescription drugs because we want to use our disposable income in other ways. In other parts of the world that we rarely see, there is no choice, and counterfeit drugs are a death sentence for millions every year.

Notes

1. BBC News, 19 November 2004.
2. *Scotland Sunday Mail*, 9 January 2005.
3. *Cincinnati Enquirer*, 20 September 2001.
4. *Los Angeles Times*, 8 August 2004.
5. Speech at the National Press Club.

20 Dora Akunyili must not die

In 1988, Dr Dora Akunyili watched her youngest sister Vivian die. Vivian was a diabetic, and she injected herself with poor-quality counterfeit insulin. At the time, no one could explain her death adequately: few people in Nigeria were aware of the dangers of the counterfeit drugs that had flooded the market.

Today, counterfeit drugs have several times nearly killed Dora Akunyili as well. Since 2001 she has been the director-general of NAFDAC, the National Agency for Food, Drugs Administration and Control, a job gifted her by President Olusegun Obasanjo thanks to a thorough knowledge of pharmaceuticals but, more importantly, a reputation for honesty and incorruptibility. It's her job to wage the war against counterfeit drug barons, and some of the counterfeiters are plainly of the opinion it's time to wage war on her. She has been shot, and on 7 March 2004 the secretariat office in Lagos caught fire – on two floors at once. Three days later her laboratory in Kaduna was burned down (an optimist, she claimed that it was 'a blessing in disguise' when it was replaced by an all-new, state-of-the-art drug testing facility). Her house has been broken into by six armed men – luckily, when she wasn't there. An anonymous caller told her husband that her family 'could be easily wiped out', and she finds fetish objects and bloodied feathers left symbolically in her office. The job, she admits, has been more difficult than she imagined, and if she makes it alive through to April 2006 she won't be doing another five years in the post. But you can't criticize her for that: to get her to the end of her posting, she lives with a 24-hour-a-day armed guard. Akunyili suffers all this because NAFDAC has made Nigeria the country that works harder than any other to rid itself of counterfeit drugs.

Along the way, Akunyili has become a hero to many ordinary Nigerians: slight, quietly spoken and dressed in a traditional Nigerian bold print dress and gele headscarf, she looks an unlikely choice to take on armed gangs.

The NAFDAC woman

'Dora Akunyili must not die' was the headline on the editorial page of the *Vanguard*, one of Nigeria's national newspapers, when it heard she had narrowly escaped death when a group of men raked her car with bullets. Akunyili was driving home to her village in Kano on 26 December 2003, when she was attacked. 'Gunmen fired at the vehicle I was travelling in,' she says. 'The back windscreen was shattered by bullets that pierced my headscarf and burnt my scalp. During the shooting, a commercial bus was riddled with bullets. The driver died instantly.'

The *Vanguard* knew who it blamed:

> Quite understandably, the hoodlums were suspected to be assassins sponsored by disgruntled fake, adulterated and expired drugs and food dealers whose activities have been the focus of Dora Akunyili's unrelenting crusade. We thank God that she escaped. *Vanguard* believes that the nation owes us a duty to ensure that Dora Akunyili lives and does not come to any harm... But for her efforts, the once flourishing fake and expired drugs and food business through which many Nigerians had met their untimely death will still be waxing strong... this woman is too precious to be allowed to be killed by enemies of the nation. Their devilish ploy must be halted.

Soon afterwards, the men the government suspected were the hoodlums in question were arrested: Chief Marcel Nnakwe, his son Nnamdi and five others. The Nnakwes ran a pharmacy business: a witness at their trial told the court that the sales assistants had told him 'because their master had informed them that by January 2004 the NAFDAC woman would be eliminated'.

The NAFDAC woman is currently very much with us: and the effects of four years of her ceaseless campaigning have been extraordinary. Far from accepting that counterfeits are an everyday part of life in Nigeria, Akunyili claims that a problem she considers is 'worse than malaria, because that can be prevented, worse than HIV, because that can be avoided, and worse than armed robbers, because they can only kill one man' is being beaten. 'We are winning already,' she says. 'Our progress is steady, but it is a fact.'

Akunyili has asked the World Health Organization to survey accurately how many counterfeits there are in Nigeria, but she expects the results to be well down on previous years. In 1990, Adeoye Lambo, a former WHO deputy director, reported that 54 per cent of drugs in one of Lagos's major pharmacies were fakes. By the following year, the figure had risen to 80 per cent. Even by 2001, a survey of 35 pharmacies in Lagos and Abuja found 48 per cent of the products were counterfeit.

When Akunyili took on the director-general's job, her solution was direct: no drugs could be sold legally unless NAFDAC had authorized them.

Authorized drugs are stamped with their 'NAFDAC number'. Radio and TV advertisements tell Nigerians not to take anything until they have checked the number and the expiry date. 'Everyone I meet is committed, because for them it is a war. There isn't anyone in Nigeria that has not suffered because of counterfeit drugs or known someone who has suffered,' she says. 'The level of awareness is unprecedented, so even someone who is illiterate in a village will call someone to say, "Come over and read this. Tell me if it has the number on it and an expiry date."' In a population where fewer than seven out of 10 adults can read, it's vital that the other three ask for help.

Of course, a number alone can't eliminate counterfeiting. There's the problem that, if you are going to go to the trouble of counterfeiting a drug, it's not much more effort to stamp a counterfeit number on the box when it reaches Nigeria. Akunyili accepts this, but points to the statistics that show a decline in unauthorized products: between 2002 and 2003, the number of products without a genuine NAFDAC number decreased by 67 per cent,[1] according to NAFDAC research. A year later, it had fallen by another 80 per cent. Two years previously, two out of three drugs on sale had been unregistered.

In 2001 and 2002, NAFDAC's progress was marked with fortnightly bonfires of between 10 and 20 trailers full of confiscated drugs. Today, the bonfires are smaller and less frequent, but they still go on. In a country the size of Germany, the UK and France combined, with a population of 129 million, there's plenty of demand for drugs: 3.6 million people are living with HIV or AIDS, life expectancy at birth is 46 years, and 60 per cent of the population lives below the poverty line. Malaria is endemic to the region.[2]

Cleaning up

Traditionally, as in much of Africa, drugs are sold by hawkers on the street and in markets. Walk through a Nigerian market and there is a bewildering variety of drugs that in the West are available on prescription only: antibiotics and antimalarials are especially popular. Some hawkers simply lay out a blanket on the ground.

It may be tradition, but NAFDAC is doing its best to stamp out this trade. In 2003, it closed Aba market, in the south-east of the country where the problem of counterfeits is at its worst, for six months. The owners of the market were allowed to reopen once they had apologized. Now, Akunyili says, the market polices itself, because honest traders don't want their livelihood taken away.

Peer pressure has also been used to clean up the country's buses. Nigeria's unique drug distribution network relied on its buses – hawkers would board a bus in the city and go down it selling drugs to the passengers as they headed home. 'We met the bus owners in 2001,' says Akunyili. 'We held workshops, pleaded with them, gave them lunch, anything to stop them letting the hawkers on board, and so that they wouldn't let them store drugs in their garages. Then after two months, we clamped down.' Today, if a NAFDAC inspector boards a bus and finds that the driver has allowed a hawker to sell drugs on it, he or she stops the bus and the passengers and driver are thrown off. If the bus owners don't like it, the stranded passengers are no happier.

The policy of informing the people is carried through with a rigour and energy that's inspiring, currently unique in the world and not what you might expect in a country famous in the West mostly for fraud, internet scams and corruption. Meetings of village leaders (one in the district of Kano attracted 10,000 people), poster and leaflet campaigns, spot checks on rural pharmacies, NAFDAC consumer safety clubs, regular updates naming the counterfeit drugs on the market and how to spot them, and billboards and prize-giving ceremonies in schools to pupils who successfully learn how to spot fakes are all having an effect on the consumer demand for fakes.

It helps that every village has a story of how a counterfeit drug became a killer: an antimalarial that had less than the right amount of active ingredient and not only provided no protection but built up an immunity to the drug, or a low-dose antibiotic that meant a sick child would be dead within a week of a preventable disease. Akunyili bridles at the blasé attitude of some politicians who confuse their opposition to the pricing methods of major pharmaceutical companies with approval for fakes. 'I was at a conference of the World Bank, and one of the delegates stood up and said that some counterfeits are OK, because they have the same amount of active ingredient,' she says. 'It makes me so mad to hear it.' The efficacy of a drug, she explains, also depends on factors like the quality of the ingredient, and the particle size: the sort of refinements that a back-street drug factory isn't going to consider. One of her inspectors had seized counterfeit ibuprofen a few weeks previously. It had the right amount of active ingredient for pain relief, but was amateurishly made: in one hour, only 3 per cent of the active ingredient would have dissolved into the bloodstream.

Ultimately, it's almost impossible to gauge the number of lives that changing consumer behaviour in Nigeria will save, because there is simply no reliable measure of the damage done by counterfeit drugs in the country. Partly, this is because there is little agreement on what is a counterfeit – for example, a drug made by an accredited manufacturer might be made of substandard ingredients. It's not a counterfeit, but it can be equally deadly. Mostly it is because, in a country where death from illness is not uncommon and much of the population has access only to the most rudimentary health care, it is sometimes impossible to assess what the real cause of death is. The antibiotics might have been counterfeits, or the patient was simply too ill to begin with. 'It's not exaggerating to say that if you give out sub-optimal doses you are just encouraging resistance to the drug,' says Nathan Ford, a spokesperson for Médecins sans Frontières.

'Thousands of people have probably died from not being immune to a disease when we thought they were.'

Occasionally though, the counterfeiters deliver a slaughter about which it is impossible to argue – like in neighbouring Niger in 1995, when a batch of counterfeit meningitis vaccine was, according to the World Health Organization's report, responsible for 2,500 avoidable deaths. The vaccine was actually made of tap water.

Children, who have less resistance to disease, are often worst affected. More than 100 children died in Nigeria in 1990 after taking cough syrup that was made of antifreeze.[3]

Public awareness of the dangers of counterfeit drugs is only half the solution. To change the problem radically, Nigeria's government needs to cut the supply too.

That's really two problems rolled up into one. The first is that for a long time Nigeria, as Africa's most populous country and with Lagos as a major port, was an easy dumping-ground for knockoffs. Today 98 per cent of its fake drugs are from India and China. The second is that the population of a country where the average gross income is $320 can't be picky about its drug purchasing habits; if there are no knockoffs, there need to be cheaply priced alternatives to replace them.

The key to the first problem is NAFDAC's authorization procedure: being accredited means, wherever you are in the world, yearly inspections by NAFDAC staff (thanks to President Obasanjo's patronage, Akunyili has 3,000 staff at her disposal internally, and dedicated inspectors in India and China). Drugs cannot be imported from neighbouring African states, but only through two airports and two seaports.

While the courts support the government hard line, punishments are – as will be no surprise by now – light for a wealthy businessperson. There have been around 30 convictions, and another 40 in the courts, but the standard penalty is three months in jail, or 500,000 nairas – around $3,000. Much more effective has been government action to close the shops and markets where they found the counterfeits. 'Close them for a month and they would gladly pay you $10,000,' Akunyili says.

Muddying the waters

The problem of availability will take longer to solve, and it is a problem that many believe the large pharmaceutical companies should be doing more to solve. 'We just want to ensure that the drugs are good quality,' says Ford at Medecins sans Frontières. 'There's a serious political problem here. The pharmaceutical industry is eager to muddy the waters between generics, counterfeits and substandard drugs. They are effectively saying that a branded drug is good and every other drug is bad.'

Big Pharma's spokespeople don't agree, but Médecins sans Frontières is not the only body making the accusation. For example, in Ghana in August 2002, the government Food and Drugs Board discovered a consignment of counterfeit antimalarial syrup, packaged as the GlaxoSmithKline product Halfan. The Board head, Emmanuel Agyarko, explains what happened:

> We called the agent of the multinational company and its attitude was, please don't put this out in the press. Because our attitude was, we were going to issue a public statement, and it creates panic to the extent that they would have to call their managers from overseas to come to our office to say, if you do this, you will damage our product.[4]

He met with the representative of GSK, who, in Agyarko's recollection of events, convinced him not to issue an alert, because it might convince customers not to buy the product. GSK's position was that the damage done to public health would outweigh the good done by alerting the public.

GSK denies that it had a specific meeting or that it put pressure on Agyarko – although that was clearly the impression that Agyarko took away from the conversation. It claims his impression was a misunderstanding.

Ford has no doubt about the attitude of the large pharmaceutical companies: 'The end product of what they do is to squash any product other than their own,' he says. 'There has to be a more informed debate on what we mean by a drug's "quality".'

His argument is that a strong generic drugs industry can make beneficial low-cost products for countries like Nigeria without resorting to counterfeiting – and at a comparable price. Using the knowledge that we have of the basic drugs that would alleviate the worst problems in the region, local companies can make drugs that might be of a marginally lower standard than the drugs we enjoy, but would be better than counterfeits and a lot better than nothing, and would not force Nigerians to choose between medicine and food for their families. Cheaply manufactured drugs can be good: there isn't one quality standard for all drugs worldwide – what matters is knowing that the drug inside the bottle or pack is what it claims to be on the outside.

'How do you determine "safe" and "effective"?' he says. 'That's a Western pharmaceutical company concept in collaboration with Western concerns. In a country where there is a lethal disease and we have a choice between a drug with US regulatory approval that costs a lot and a drug not approved in the West but that may help, a "bad" drug may be better than no drug at all.'

Nigeria's drug policy doesn't play favourites: whenever Akunyili finds a knockoff, she releases the information, even if there was only one example, because she says that she works for the people, not for pharmaceutical companies. On the other hand, she is encouraged that Big Pharma has never tried to pressure her to suppress a report. And she has the highest praise for the legitimate generic drugs that are coming from India, approved by her agent and given the precious NAFDAC number.

As long as counterfeiters are willing to exploit the poorest and least powerful members of society, we need more Dora Akunyilis. On the current evidence, they are outnumbered. In April 2004, in the eastern Chinese province of Anhui, almost 200 infants developed what locals called 'Big Head' disease. They were malnourished, because they had been fed with a counterfeit infant formula that had almost no nutritional value. Thirteen babies died. The Chinese government punished 97 government officials who had either colluded with the manufacturers or failed to stop the production of the powder in 54 factories.[5]

That cull is relatively minor in China's recent history. The *Shenzhen Evening News* – a government-controlled newspaper – reported that, in 2001, 192,000 people died in China because they took fake drugs.

I tell Akunyili about the Pharmaceutical Security Institute's wish for drug counterfeiting to be described as an 'issue' rather than a 'problem'.

'That makes me so angry,' she says. 'It's painful to me. This is how people feel when they are not affected. Sometimes when we burn the drugs and I see counterfeit insulin, it puts me into a depression. It brings back too many memories of my sister.'

Notes

1. NAFDAC research.
2. *CIA World Factbook 2005*, http://www.cia.gov/cia/publications/ factbook.
3. Dangerous fakes, *World Press Review*, January 1999.
4. BBC File on Four, 5 October 2004, http://news.bbc.co.uk/ nol/shared/bsp/hi/pdfs/fileon4_05102004_counterfeitdrugs.pdf.
5. BBC News, 8 November 2004.

Conclusion:
Whack a mole

'Respect for the system of intellectual property is falling apart. It could collapse completely in many parts of the world,' says Bruce Lehman at the International Intellectual Property Institute.

You might not find this terribly upsetting, but you should. If it falls apart, then the knockoff economy fills the void, and with it we get crime, unemployment, danger and death. Look around you; it's already happening. The knockoff economy is already so huge that it supports entire regions, even countries.

One lawyer who spends his entire working day chasing counterfeits on behalf of his clients claims that our attempts to stop counterfeiting are like playing 'whack a mole' – the fairground game where little moles pop their heads up and you frantically and pointlessly hit them with a tiny hammer, until there are so many moles you can't possibly hit them all.

Whacking fairground moles seems like a sober, ordered response compared with the way in which we are dealing with the menace of fakes. As consumers, we don't know whether we love them or hate them: we love them when we get a bargain, we hate them when we get ripped off, we are shocked when they affect our health and we don't seem to care when they kill babies on the far side of the world.

The companies that are getting ripped off are similarly confused: is their job to stop counterfeiting or just to make sure the knockoffs have someone else's brand name on? Should they be prosecuting the counterfeiters, wooing them or bribing them? Is money spent on fighting fakes an investment or a cost? Should they go it alone or cooperate with their rivals?

The forces of law are easily outflanked. They use regional or national forces to fight an international crime. Customs, police and lawyers throw cases to each other, no one taking the responsibility. Countries with inadequate laws, or no law at all, find themselves infested with knockoffs. Do they stamp them out or look the other way and collect duty?

Knockoffs are no one's priority, but everyone's problem. If we're going to stop playing whack a mole, and get a bigger hammer, we need to decide what we believe, and what sort of hammer we want.

Selfish capitalist pigs

First, we have to decide that intellectual property works. We have to stop imagining that economies based around knocking off other people's ideas will suddenly and spontaneously develop new innovations and create their own industries, unless there is a way that their innovations and ideas can be protected. This isn't going to be easy, if their experience is that anything can be ripped off.

It's also going to make today's global companies uncomfortable. When China develops its own brands, as Japan did 30 years ago, they will threaten many established Western companies, who might pine for the days when all the Chinese electronics and sportswear factories did was knock off their goods.

Governments must see the social benefit of being intolerant of knockoffs. A strong Indian generic drug business, based on companies that only a few years ago were counterfeiting Western drugs, can use its low costs, innovation and business nous to create the drugs that the developing world craves – if it is allowed to and if the laws on intellectual property are fairly enforced.

This fits the modern development agenda: over a generation, this can create sustainable businesses, where once there were people turning out cheap copies of Western goods. Knockoffs kill small enterprises more quickly than big ones: intellectual property doesn't protect just the mighty.

If that means that we are also supporting the right to profit for global megabrands that we find pointless or offensive, it's a price that may be worth paying. 'The beneficiaries are often selfish capitalist pigs. I don't [advocate intellectual property] because I care about them. I do it because I care about an economy where honest people can make a profit from using their brains,' says Lehman.

Second, governments and law enforcement need to create an international response to an international problem, or we simply chase counterfeiters to where the law tolerates them. We effectively give the criminals in the most lawless societies a place to do business while the local authorities look the other way, and then react with shock and horror when we feel the effect in the rest of the world. Without a system of cooperation between law enforcement agencies inside countries and across borders, without greater standardization of laws and penalties, and without lowering barriers and tariffs that discourage legitimate trade, what do we really expect will happen?

It's not going to be pleasant for some companies who don't want to think about the effects of counterfeiting. Waiting until knockoffs in a 'problem' country go away before investing in it just means the knockoffs will never go away. Instead they will probably seep back out into the rest of the world. Investment has to mean more than opening an office: asking a first world price from people with third world wages is unrealistic and insulting. And companies that react in hours to competitors, but take years to react to counterfeiters or pirates, need to accept that in some countries – and for some types of customer – fakes are their biggest competition.

Third, companies should be honest with us, if they expect us to respect their property. Every time a company hides the truth about dangerous counterfeits of its products, we are being hoodwinked by both the counterfeiter and the counterfeited. The same goes for government and law enforcement: every time the budget for enforcing the law is trimmed and every time that counterfeiters are let off with an insignificant fine, it reinforces the message that fakes are not worth caring about.

Most important though, we have to wake up to the consequences of our own actions when we knowingly buy knockoffs. We think knockoffs are just a bit of fun. We're wrong. As long as we blame the big brands, the police, the counterfeiters, the television and anyone except ourselves, we're part of the problem. Just because we can get away with it doesn't make it right

One day a car mechanic, an airline executive or a pharmacist might fancy getting away with it too – in a way that might maim or kill you. It's not so amusing when that happens.

Here's a newspaper report for *Discount Store News*: 'Warning that organized crime families are beginning to muscle in on the trademark-counterfeiting racket,' it says. 'A newly released Congressional report calls for "direct and forceful action" by the Federal Government to halt the distribution of bogus goods… product counterfeiting is a "rapidly growing problem which seriously threatens the health and safety of consumers".' Oh, hang on, that's dated 14 May 1984. More than 20 years on, we're still waiting for the 'direct and forceful action'.

Knockoffs are corrosive. There are no good counterfeits. Fakes destroy honest companies and kill innocent people. When you buy them, you're helping it to happen.

Appendix:
Further reading
and contacts

Surprisingly, for a problem of this magnitude, there's very little accessible literature on the subject of counterfeiting. Many of the books in this field are written by, and for, lawyers, and concentrate on the details of intellectual property law – a subject that is as impenetrable to us as it is important to them.

Two books that are accessible to a general reader are:

David M Hopkins, Lewis T Kontnik and Mark T Turnage (2003) *Counterfeiting Exposed: Protecting your Brand and Customers*, John Wiley & Sons, Inc.
ISBN 0 4712 6990 5

This book is written for businesspeople who want to do something about their counterfeiting problem. It has a wealth of practical advice and some interesting anecdotes from three experts in the field.

Graham Satchwell (2004) *A Sick Business*, Stockholm Network.
ISBN 0 9547 6632 6

This is a fascinating and readable insight into the trade in counterfeit pharmaceuticals written by someone who learned everything he knows about the problem first hand.

Otherwise, the best resources are the pamphlets, booklets and other publications – too numerous to list – produced by many of the organizations below. Many are available for downloading from the internet, while others can be acquired by post on request. As most of these organizations have a remit to raise public awareness they are, in the main, approachable and responsive.

A word of caution: as most of these organizations are dedicated to the fight against counterfeiting and piracy, it goes without saying that they have an editorial bias. Sometimes that extends to portraying the owners of brands that have been knocked off (who, after all, provide the funding for many of these organizations) as responsible and accountable, which doesn't always follow. For example, the fact that counterfeiters use sweatshop labour doesn't mean that multinationals never do; you can believe that counterfeit cigarettes are more dangerous than genuine ones without believing in a person's right to light up in a restaurant.

British organizations

Alliance Against Counterfeiting and Piracy
167 Great Portland Street
London W1N 5FD
United Kingdom

Website: www.aacp.org.uk

Anti-Counterfeiting Group
PO Box 578
High Wycombe
Buckinghamshire HP11 1YD
United Kingdom

Website: www.a-cg.com

The British Phonographic Industry Limited (BPI)
Riverside Building
County Hall
Westminster Bridge Road
London SE1 7JA
United Kingdom

Website: www.bpi.co.uk

Business Software Alliance (UK)
79 Knightsbridge
London SW1X 7RB
United Kingdom

Website: www.bsa.org

Counterfeiting Intelligence Bureau (CIB)
Maritime House
1 Linton Road
Barking
Essex IG11 8HG
United Kingdom

Website: www.icc-ccs.org

Federation Against Copyright Theft (FACT)
7 Victory Business Centre
Worton Road
Isleworth
Middlesex TW7 6DB
United Kingdom

Website: www.fact-uk.org

Federation Against Software Theft (FAST)
Clivemont House
54 Clivemont Road
Maidenhead
Berkshire SL6 7BZ
United Kingdom

Website: www.fast.org.uk

Medicines and Healthcare Products Regulatory Agency
Market Towers
1 Nine Elms Lane
London SW8 5NQ
United Kingdom

Website: www.mhra.gov.uk

The Tobacco Manufacturers' Association
5th Floor
Burwood House
14–16 Caxton Street
London SW1H 0ZB
United Kingdom

Website: www.the-tma.org.uk

The Trading Standards Institute
First Floor
1 Sylvan Court
Sylvan Way
Southfields Business Park
Basildon SS15 6TH
United Kingdom

Website: www.tsi.org.uk

International organizations

Business Software Alliance (World)
1150 18th Street NW
Suite 700
Washington DC 20036
USA

Website: www.bsa.org

Coalition for Intellectual Property Rights
The PBN Company
3 Uspensky Perulok, Building 4
Moscow 127006
Russia

Website: www.cipro.org

European Brands Association
9 Avenue des Gaulois
B-1040 Brussels
Belgium

Website: www.aim.be

Indicam
Via Serbelloni 5
20122 Milan
Italy

Website: www.indicam.it

The International AntiCounterfeiting Coalition
1725 K Street NW
Suite 1101
Washington DC 20006
USA

Website: www.iacc.org

International Federation of Pharmaceutical Manufacturers and Associations (IFPMA)
15 Ch. Louis-Dunant
PO Box 195
1211 Geneva 20
Switzerland

Website: www.ifpma.org

The International Federation of Phonographic Industries (IFPI)
54–62 Regent Street
London W1B 5RE
United Kingdom

Website: www.ifpi.org

International Intellectual Property Institute
906 Pennsylvania Avenue SE
Washington DC 20003
USA

Website: www.iipi.org

International Labour Organization (ILO)
4 route des Morillons
1211 Geneva 22
Switzerland

Website: www.ilo.org

International Pharmaceutical Federation
Andries Bickerweg 5
PO Box 84200
2508 AE The Hague
The Netherlands

Website: www.fip.nl

International Trademark Association (INTA)
1133 Avenue of the Americas
New York
NY 10036
USA

Website: www.inta.org

Interpol
200 quai Charles de Gaulle
69006 Lyon
France

Website: www.interpol.int

Motion Picture Association of America (MPAA)
Motion Picture Association (MPA)
15503 Ventura Boulevard
Encino
CA 91436
USA

Website: www.mpaa.org

Motor Equipment and Manufacturers Association (MEMA)
10 Laboratory Drive
PO Box 13966
Research Triangle Park
NC 27709–3966
USA

Website: www.mema.com

Nigerian National Agency for Food and Drug Administration (NAFDAC)
Plot 2032
Olusegun Obasanjo Way
Wuse Zone 7
Abuja
Nigeria

Website: www.nafdacnigeria.org

Pharmaceutical Security Institute
8100 Boone Boulevard
Suite 220
Vienna
VA 22182
USA

Website: www.psi-inc.org

Quality Brands Protection Committee
Beijing Representative Office
2005 China World Tower 2
1 Jianguomenwai Avenue
Beijing 10004
PR China

Website: www.qbpc.org.cn

Recording Industry Association of America, Inc (RIAA)
1330 Connecticut Avenue NW
Suite 300
Washington DC 20036
USA

Website: www.riaa.org

SNB-REACT
Amstelveenseweg 864
1081 JM Amsterdam
The Netherlands

Website: www.snbreact.org

Union des Fabricants/Global Anticounterfeiting Group
16 rue de la Faisanderie
75116 Paris
France

Website: www.unifab.com

World Customs Organization
Rue du Marche 30
B-1210 Brussels
Belgium

Website: www.wcoomd.org

World Health Organization (WHO)
Avenue Appia 20
1211 Geneva 27
Switzerland

Website: www.who.int

World Intellectual Property Organization (WIPO)
34 Chemin des Colombettes
1211 Geneva 20
Switzerland

Website: www.wipo.org

World Trade Organization (WTO)
154 Rue Lausanne
1211 Geneva 21
Switzerland

Website: www.wto.org

Index

Abacus Security   32, 39
  Oberfeldt, A   32–35, 38,
    40–41
Abraham & Co   125
  Sabair, O   125
Abro Industries   61–62
  Baranay, P   61–62
  stolen brand name   61–62
AC Nielsen   20
Adidas   57
AIDS   189, 190
Air Safety Week   173
aircraft   169–78
  accidents   169, 171, 173
  American Airlines   169
  bogus parts   169–73
  categories of compliance
    (FAA)   175–76
  certified repair stations (FAA)
    176
  engine parts   2
  Ente Nazionale per
    l'Aviazione Civile
    (ENAC)   173
  fines (FAA)   173

International Aviation Safety
    Assessment, FAA
    175–76
  investigations and raids
    173
  market for spare parts   175
  salvage: Miami Opa-Locka
    Airport   177
  suspected unapproved parts
    (SUPs)   170–72
  testing regime   170
  worldwide alert (2002)   173
  see also Boeing
aircraft spare parts industries
    174–77
  Robbin, J (Skymart Sales Ltd)
    174–76
Airways Systems Specialists,
    Professional (PASS)   171
  Fanfalone, M   171–72
alcohol knockoffs   21–22, 76
  dangers of   21–22
  Johnny Walker   21, 76
  methyl and industrial alcohol
    21

Alliance Against Counterfeiting
and Piracy (AACP) 112,
164, 165
Carey, L 112, 114, 165
al-Qaeda 141, 143, 206
see also terrorism
Amazon 89, 146
anti-counterfeiting agency:
Pyramid International 68,
71–72
Warwick, R 68–72
Anti-Counterfeiting Group
164
automobile parts 8, 16, 179–85
accidents and fake parts
182–83
brake pads 2, 181
Dubai and fake parts 179–82
European Aftermarket Forum
183
McCormack, J 182–83
raids and seizures 181, 184
warranties, extension of 184
Automotive Brands Protection
Coalition (ABPC) 180–81,
182
Automotive Suppliers,
European Association of
184
Holmqvist, L 184
Aviation Development Holdings
170
Andersson, M 170, 172

bags 2, 20, 39, 55, 60, 68–70,
87
Chanel 9, 60
Fendi 68
Gucci 60, 69

Hermès/Hermès Birkin
43–47, 50, 81
Kate Spade 33, 51–52
Louis Vuitton 33, 60
no-label 'blanks' 34
see also purse parties
Barchiesi, B 36, 37
Barranikova, O 104–05, 159,
161
Barzano & Zanardo 72
baseball caps 20
batteries
Duracell 24
mobile phone 23, 26
Verizon Wireless 23
Becker & Poliakoff 27
Quinter, P 27
Beijing 1–2, 19, 60, 62, 84, 85,
102
Silk Alley market 55–57,
59–60, 63
and the 2008 Olympics 64
see also China
Big Pharma 82, 196, 198, 206,
215
Bilon, B 131–32
Birkin, Jane 44
Bloomberg, Mayor 39
Boehringer Ingelheim, 193,
196
Zimmer, T 193, 196
Boeing 159, 172–73, 176
maintenance checks 175
Porad, K 172–73
Bollywood films 128, 131
see also films
bombs and explosives 137,
142
see also Northern Ireland

BP and counterfeit petrol
     stations   79
brand bandits *see* brands
brand equity   51
brand owners   20
     Abro: stolen brand name
          61–62
brands   14–15, 19–29
     alcohol knockoffs   21–25
     cigarettes   22–23
     economics of counterfeiting
          20–21
     global   17
     shift-working: extra shifts   26
     stolen brand names   61–62
     superbrands   25
Brazil   22, 121
bribery   105
British Film Council   130
British Phonographic Industry
     Limited (BPI)   130–31,
     136
Brokate, B   88–89, 90–91
Buhecha, J A   131
Bulgaria   125
Burberry sunglasses   57
Business Software Alliance
     (BSA)   12, 15, 160, 162–63
     Garret the Ferret   162–63
     Mayster, D   163
buyer–seller meeting-places
     87–94
     global marketplace   88–89
          see also main entry
     Holmes Detective Agency/Rob
          Holmes   87–88, 92–94
     internet trading
          platforms/bulletin boards
          92–93

trust and safety   89–92
see also eBay *and* internet

Canon   63, 73
car boot sales   129–30, 131
carcinogens   22
cars   14–15
see also automobile parts
CDs   17, 73, 74, 77, 83, 110,
     114, 117–23, CDs 138–39,
     160
     disc copying/copying plants
          119–20, 131–32, 134–35,
          138, 142
     drop in sales   112–13
     see also DVDs *and* digital
          content piracy
Chanel No 5   76
cheese   8–9
     Laughing Cow   9, 17
chewing gum   20–21
child labour   17–18
children: involvement in
     counterfeiting   73
China   3, 4, 19, 20, 25, 50, 52,
     55–65, 80, 81, 101, 103,
     156, 214, 220
     Alibaba.com   4, 59
     anti-counterfeiting law   55,
          62
     Big Head disease and infant
          deaths   216
     Birkin bags   47
     chewing gum   20–21
     condoms   23
     contracts and consensus
          management principles
          58
     copying expertise   59

court case: Horace Chang
61
deaths from fake drugs (2001)
216
and Disney   101–02
economy, effect of crackdown
on   64–65
economy and exports   57–58
exports   57
gangs   93
income of citizens   57
intellectual property laws   64
law enforcement   61–62,
63–64
legitimate products   18
police raids   63
size of counterfeiting business
58
and World Trade
Organization   3, 4, 62
see also Beijing
China Small Commodities City
59
China United Intellectual
property Protection Centre
(CUIPPC)   59, 63
Fan Liming   63, 65
Li Guorong   63, 64, 65
Chinatown (New York)   38–41
illegal immigrants   40
see also wholesale warehouses
Chopra, Y   112
cigarette lighters (Bic)   22–23,
25
cigarettes   22–23
dangerous content of   22
Clinton, President   120
counterfeit memoirs   19
clothes   68

Coady, A   180
Coca-Cola   11, 23, 59, 63, 194
computer games
Gran Turismo   4 146
Half-Life   2 146, 148
condoms   23
Consumer Credit Counseling,
American   16
consumer society and choice
14
consumer(s)
activism   27
behaviour   113, 213
indifference   18
and responsibility   15–18,
113, 143–44, 221–22
copy protection   150
copyright   10–11
infringement conspiracy
153
material   146
websites: infringements and
immunity   89, 90–91
corruption   84
see also customs/customs
officers
counterfeiting
definitions of   13
economics of   20–21
effect of crackdown on
Chinese economy
64–65
as theft   11–12
see also China
Counterfeiting Intelligence
Bureau (CIB)   21–22, 28
crime/criminals *see* ordinary
criminals *and* organized
crime

customs/customs officers   79–85
   containers/shipments,
      targeting   81
   counterfeit medicines   82
   French   84
   German   120
   inside information   81
   routes and documentation
      82–83
   training agents   82
   tricks   83
   underwater objects   83–84

debt, UK and US levels of   16
definitions of counterfeiting   13
digital content piracy   110–12,
   114
   anti-piracy squads and levies
      112
   optical disc plants   111
   pirated films   110–11
Disney   100–02, 103–04, 138
   incentives for counterfeiters/
      government   101–02
   intellectual property/
      copyright   101
   Sonny Bono Copyright Term
      Extension Act   101
   South-East Asian subsidiary
      100
   theme parks   102
Dora Akunyili   209–17
   attacks on   209–10
   attitude of pharmaceutical
      industries   215–17
   campaigning   211
   NAFDAC numbers on drugs
      211
   see also drugs *and* Nigeria

DrinkOrDie (DOD)   150–52
   see also The Scene
   Grimes, D   152
   informants   151
   members of   151–52
   Sankus, J   152
drugs   2, 3, 15, 16, 33, 82, 172,
   201–17
   amphetamines   206
   buying by e-mail/internet
      202–04
   cannabis   206
   Class A   202
   Deca Durabolin   203–04
   differential pricing   207
   global buying and selling
      204–07
      prison sentences for seniors
         205–06
      senior citizen tourist trade
         204
   insulin   209
   lifestyle drugs   206
   local law enforcement
      204–05
   Mexican pharmacies
      205
   near infrared (NIR)
      microscopy   202
   prescription drugs   203–04,
      206
   steroids   203
   and terrorism   206
   see also medicines *and* Viagra
Dubai   179–82, 201
   and automobile parts
      179–82
   and drugs   201
Duggan, B   183–84

DVDs   57, 60, 74, 75, 114, 119, 122, 150
   pirates and security 122–23
   ripping software   150
   see also videos and DVDs

eBay   88–92, 94, 146
   Brett Healy: intellectual property counsel   91
   Garreth Griffith   89–90, 91–92
   Verified Rights Owner Programme (VeRO)   90, 91, 94
Envisional   147
ethics   17, 52
European   67–78
   crossing borders   77
   dark side, the   73
   making crime pay   70–72
   trade barriers reduction   68, 77
   see also Italy *and* Poland
European Commission   67
   Counterfeiting and Piracy, DG Taxud: Christophe Zimmermann   81
   Directive 2004/48/EC: intellectual property rights   67
European Parliament   173
European Union   71, 73
   counterfeit products in   77
   internal market   194

fair trade   17–18
Federation Against Copyright Theft (FACT)   140

films   110–11, 147
   Harry Potter and the Prisoner of Azkaban   145
   Snow White and the Seven Dwarfs   160
   The Hulk   148, 150
flowers   27–28
Food, Drugs Administration and Control, National Agency for (NAFDAC)   209–14
Food and Drugs Administration (USA)   189, 192, 202, 204, 206
   Crawford, L   206
   Widup, R   202–03
Fortune   500 11
France
   anti-counterfeiting laws   9
   see also Union des Fabricants 7–10

Garda (Republic of Ireland police)   138
Gates, B   164
Gateway Inc   152
Ghana Food and Drugs Board   215
Gibney, Anthony & Flaherty LLP   35, 88–89
Gillette Company   24–25, 26, 27
   Kitts, J   24–25
Gioconda, J   46–47, 48, 50–52, 82
Giorgio Armani   8
GlaxoSmithKline   194, 215
   Halfan   215
global counterfeit economy   2

global information networks
110
global market, exploitation of
25
global marketplace: internet
sites 88–89
copyright infringements and
immunity 89
global police sting: Operation
Buccaneer 150–52
see also The Scene
globalization 18, 25, 73, 207
Grant, I 121–22
Gucci 17, 56, 57, 60
guilt-free knockoffs 17

Haberman, M 12–13, 15
handbags *see* bags
Harry Potter novels: Chinese
knockoffs 19
Hermès 8, 17, 44, 46–47, 50,
82
see also bags *and* purse parties
Hinson, D 171
Holmes Detective Agency 93
Holmes, R 87–88, 92–94
Hong Kong 83, 87, 124, 125
Disneyland 102
human rights compliant
factories 52

Indian Chambers of Commerce,
Federation of 111
intellectual property (IP) 8,
10–11, 26, 28, 46, 68, 105,
132–33, 219–21
Chinese laws 64
copyright 10–11, 89, 90–91
court cases 64

EC Directive 67
flowers 28
law specialist 77
laws 13–14, 220
patents 10–11
theft 12
Intellectual Property Rights,
Coalition for 104, 159
International Federation of the
Phonographic Industry
(IFPI) 111, 112, 117, 118,
120, 121, 139
Commercial Piracy Report
121
International Intellectual
Property Institute 113,
164, 207, 219
fake automobile parts and
accidents, report on
182–83
Lehman, B 113–14, 207,
219
International Labour
Organization 17–18
internet 4
auction sites/bulletin boards
88, 89
e-commerce 3
games developers 113
illegal file sharing 112–13
music downloads 113
online counterfeiters 92–93
peer-to-peer networks/
technology 148
stolen content on 146–54
and The Scene 146
see also eBay; Scene, The
Interpol 140–41
Noble, N 140–43

testimony to US House of
Representatives   142
Italy   68–70
anti-counterfeiting agency:
Pyramid International
68–69
Camorra, the   70–71
Ente Nazionale per
l'Aviazione Civile
(ENAC)   173–74
Guardia di Finanza   173
Indicam   70–71
law and counterfeiting   69
penalties and court cases   72
and quality counterfeits   47,
71
social pressures   71

Jefferson, T   13

Keats McFarland & Wilson
LLP/Anthony Keats   91
Kessler, M   27
Kessler International   27
Kirkland & Ellis LLP   46, 82
Klein, N   26
knockoff economy   1–4
Kodak   59, 63
criminal prosecution   63
Kolsun B   51–52
KPMG   26
Kroger Co supermarkets   24
kudos   2–4

Lazewski, M   76
Lea & Perrins   8
legal problems/law enforcement
60–62, 63–64
Leinster, R   140, 143–44

Levi's   56
Loyalist Volunteer Force (LVF)
140

MacDonald-Brown, C   77
mafia crime   70
see also organized crime
market traders   128–36
and children as stallholders
133
in Ireland   137–38
payment to market security
staff   129
underpolicing   134
see also ordinary criminals and
trading standards service
Martin, D   130–36
Masetti, A   72
Maslow, A   48, 52
hierarchy of needs   48
Matz, S   21–22, 28
Mayster, D   11–12
McClellan, Dr M   189
McDonald, H   35, 37
medicines   82, 187–99
controlling the supply chain
192–95
Epogen   187, 190, 198
EU internal market   194
Fagan, T   187–88, 190, 197
human growth hormone
(HGH)   189–90
Lipitor   192, 194, 198
packaging   195–99
Schreiner ProSecure   196
technology   196–97
parallel trading   194–95
penicillin   188
Ponstan   191

Procrit 190–91, 198
Serono Inc and Serostim
  189
tap water, use of 190–91
Viagra 189, 199, 201
see also drugs *and* packaging
Médecins sans Frontières 213,
  215
  Ford, N 213–14, 215–16
Med-Pro 192
Microsoft 14, 27, 59, 63, 113,
  163–65
  COA hologram label 163–64
  Hilton, A 163–64
  raids on 163
  software 163
Microsoft Russia 155–62
  Alpatov, S 158
  amnesty 156–57
  Danilov, E 156–57
  Dergunova, O 155,
    157–58
  percentage of pirated
    software 155
  software 160, 161, 162
  see also Russia
Mitnick, K 149–50
mobile phones 23, 26
  see also batteries
money laundering 97, 105
Mont Blanc pens 56, 57
Motion Picture Association of
  America 122
movies *see* films
music
  business and prices 114
  downloading files 113
  value of market 121
  Whitney Houston 117

National Criminal Intelligence
  Service 206
National Hi-Tech Crime Unit
  91
New Balance 60–61
  court case: Horace Chang
    61
  Larsen, J 60–61
New York Times Magazine: The
  Ethicist column 48
Newell, G 146
Nigeria 209–17
  avoidable deaths 214
  buses, drugs on 212
  consumer behaviour 213
  HIV and AIDS 212
  informing the people
    212–13
  malaria 212
  markets 212
  National Agency for Food,
    Drugs Administration
    and Control (NAFDAC)
    209–14
    campaigns and consumer
      safety clubs 212–13
  Obasanjo, President
    Olusegun 209, 214
  punishments 214
  Vanguard 210
  see also Dora Akunyili *and*
    drugs
Nike 14, 26, 27, 57, 60, 76,
  158
No Logo 26
North Face Gore-Tex jackets
  (North Fakes) 57
Northern Ireland 137–41, 143
  bomb plot 137

Irish National Liberation Army (INLA)   140
Irish Republican Army (IRA)   140
Organized Crime Task Force (OCTF)   138
paramilitaries   137, 138–39, 142
Police Service (PSNI)   137, 139
Sunday markets   137, 140
terrorism and piracy 138–41
see also terrorism
Novartis   193
Christian, J   193, 198
NV Organon   203
van Suchtelen, J P   203

O'Leary, M   143, 151, 153–54
Olympics (2008)   64
see also Beijing *and* China
optical disc processing plants 121
ordinary criminals   127–36
global cottage industry 130–32
market traders and snide 128–30
trading standards service 127–29, 132–36
see also main entry
see also market traders
organized crime   3, 17, 28, 68, 71–72, 105, 123–26
intimidation   124
outsourced manufacturing 26–27

parallel trading   194–95
patents   10–11
infringements by larger companies   12–14
Penezic, R   190
people, trafficking in   85
Pfizer Inc   191–92, 195, 198, 202, 203
Mount, J   195
Theriault, J   191, 193–94
Pharmaceutical Conference, British (2003)   202
Pharmaceutical Security Institute   188, 217
How, A   188
Pharmaceutical Wholesalers, British Association of   197
Garlick, T   197
PharmacyChecker.com LLC 205
Levitt, G   205, 206–07
PharmaEurope.com   203
Philips   63
pills *see* drugs
Pogoda, D   24, 60
Poland   73–77
bootlegs   75
Centralne Biuro ŚZledcze agency   75
governments   74, 76
guide/language tutorial   75
as point of entry   77
and the Russians   74–75
Siciarek, M   76
software   74–75
Stadium (Russian) Market 73–77
Taszczuk & Wspolnicy   76
turnover   75

possession v personal use   33
Powers, A (Powers and
    Associates)   48–50
Proco Solutions   194
    Satchwell, G   194, 195
Procter & Gamble   24, 25
    dangers to impaired immune
        systems   24
Public Citizen (US watchdog)
    197
    Sasich, L   197
Puma   57
Purdue Pharma LP   188
    Widup, R   188–90
purse parties   43–52
    Hermès Birkin bag   43–47
    hotel sales   50
    involvement of middle classes
        50–52
    party bags   48–50
    and private investigators
        48–49
    punishment for suppliers
        49
    see also bags

Rabenold, R   55, 102–03
    Vaudra Ltd   102–03
radio frequency ID (RFID)
    172, 197
raids, police/government   63,
    74, 76, 98–99, 128–29,
    133–34, 136, 142, 150–53,
    160, 163, 173,   181, 184
    Midtown, New York   35–38
Ralph Lauren   8, 56
Ray-Ban sunglasses   57
Redd Solicitors (London)   77
Reebok   57

research
    into debt levels (Datamonitor)
        16
    Email Systems   202
    Food and Drugs
        Administration (FDA)
        204
    Forrester Research   113
    Gallup Organization   17
    Select Committee on Trade
        and Industry   17
    University of Leicester   25
responsibility and consumers
    15–18, 113
Reuters News Agency   90
Russia   40, 60, 75, 87, 95–105,
    122, 125
    anti-counterfeiting methods
        95–96, 160
    CD ROMs   157, 160
    corruption   97–100
    criminal gangs/organized
        crime   93, 96–97, 100,
        104, 105, 123
    customs officers   97–98
    Federal Financial Task Force
        97
    fifth place in global piracy
        table   156
    Gorbushka Market   159–61
    laws   95
    legalization of software   156,
        158
    Matveyev, A   161
    money laundering   97, 105
    motivation to reduce
        counterfeiting   102–05
    penalties   97
    pirate discs   122

police raids 98–99, 142, 160
shipping and routes 98
violence 100, 104
see also Microsoft Russia *and*
        Poland

Samsung 63
Scene, The 146–51
    copyright material 146
    Courier Weektop Scorecard
        149
    couriers 148–49
    dumps 148
    Fastlane couriers 153
    films/movies 146
    Griffiths, H R (Bandido) 152
    Martin, G 152–53
    peer-to-peer technology:
        Kazaa 148
    raids on 152–53
    release groups 147
    Sandro, B 147, 154
    'The Races' 149, 159
    topservers 147–48
    Warez 153
    see also computer games;
        DrinkorDie (DOD); films
        and software
Schiavo, M 171, 171, 176
Schmitt zur Hohe & Ferrante
        Intellectual Property 59
    Schmitt zur Hohe, E 59
Schwab, Dr F 203
self-reporting economy 26–27
Sex and the City 43–44, 50
shampoo 24, 25, 76
*Sick Business: Counterfeit
        Medicines and Organised
        Crime, A* 194

Silk Alley market 55–57,
        59–60, 63
    see also Beijing
social engineering 150
Social Market Foundation 194
software 74, 110, 113
    CheckPoint 152
    DVD-ripping 150
    piracy 12
    Surplus Computers 150
    see also digital content piracy
Speid, G 127–29, 132, 134
Sproule, A 139–40, 142, 143
stab vests 127, 133
Stewart, Martha 45–46
Stroguine, V 123–24
sweatshop economy 25–26
sweatshops 17–18

Tanov, A 123–24
Tariq, M 127–28, 131, 132,
        135
teabags: Brooke Bond and
        Lipton's 24
terrorism 3, 17, 39, 138
    and CDs 137–44
    and drugs 206
    in Middle East 141
    Osama Bin Laden 141
    and piracy 140–41
    see also Northern Ireland
The Gap 26, 27
The Scene *see* Scene, The
theft *see* counterfeiting as theft
Third Man, The 188
Tiffany jewellery 90
trademarks 16
    fraud 70
    infringement 90–91

trading standards service
127–36
limited powers of 133
raids on markets/factories
128–29, 133–34, 136
use of stab vests 127, 133
Trainer, T 62, 112, 113

Ukraine 156, 160
disc copying plants 120
Ulster Defence Association
(UDA) 140
Ulster Volunteer Force (UVF)
Union des Fabricants 7–10, 73
M Guillou 9–10
Museum of Counterfeiting
8–10
wine stopper 7–8
United Arab Emirates
see Dubai
United States of America
Congress investigation into
fake drugs (2003) 190
counterfeiting laws (New
York) 39
Customs 50, 151
Defense, Department of
177
Digital Millennium Copyright
Act 89
District Court, Chicago 153
District Court for Central
District of California 23
Family Entertainment and
Copyright Bill (2005)
145
Federal Aviation
Administration 171,
172, 173

Federal Bureau of
Investigation (FBI)
143, 146, 151, 152, 173
Federal Trade Commission
183
Food and Drugs
Administration (FDA)
189, 192, 202, 204, 206
Homeland Security
Department 206
House Committee on
International Relations,
testimony to 140–41
House of Representatives,
testimony to 122–23
intellectual property laws
13
International
AntiCounterfeiting
Commission (IACC) 60,
62, 112, 113
International
AntiCounterfeiting
Coalition 24
International Civil Aviation
Organization (ICAO)
175
Justice, Department of 143,
151
Motor and Equipment
Manufacturers
Assocation (MEMA)
183
New York Police Department
(NYPD) 35–36, 39
New York State Real Property
Actions and Proceedings
Law (Bawdy House Act)
35–36

Office of Information and
Public Affairs: mobile
phone warning   23
patent laws   10
Recording Industry
Association   36
Transportation, Department
of   171
see also Business Software
Alliance

Valenti, J   122
Valentine, A   202
Valve   146
Versace coats   70
Viagra   189, 201–03, 206
factories   202–03
via the internet   201, 203
see also drugs *and* medicines
videos and DVDs   109–15
digital content piracy   110–12
see also main entry
illegal file sharing   112–13
Lion King   138
regional protection   109
see also internet
Vietnam/Hanoi   113–14, 156
violence   100, 104, 112

Warsaw Uprising   74
watches   1, 20, 55, 56–57, 76
Rolex   1, 15, 17, 56, 57, 69,
88

wholesale warehouses
31–41
cash sales   33
Chinatown: Canal Street
38–41
padlocked buildings   37
police raids   35–38
task force   36–37
veteran/disabled stallholders
34–35
Wilson, Dr N   202
wine: an early knockoff   7–8
World Customs Organization
(WCO)   2, 3, 79, 84
Danet, M   79–85
fight against counterfeiting
80–85
see also customs/customs
officers
World Health Organization
(WHO)   189, 214
survey on counterfeit drugs in
Nigeria   211
World Intellectual Property
Organization   11, 156
World Trade Organization
(WTO)   3, 25, 62, 105,
156, 158, 164
anti-counterfeiting rules   3
Wrigley Chewing Gum Co
20–21, 25

Yves Saint Laurent   63